E X T R E M E
LO-CARB
CUISINE

250 FABULOUS
RECIPES WITH
VIRTUALLY NO
CARBOHYDRATES

By
Sharron Long

ADAMS MEDIA
Avon, Massachusetts

Published by
Adams Media, an F+W Publications Company
57 Littlefield Street, Avon, MA 02322. U.S.A.
www.adamsmedia.com

Portions of this book were previously published by Humility Publications as
Low Carb Cooking at Sharron's Place, ©2002 Humility Publications.

ISBN: 1-59337-007-5

Printed in United States of America.

J I H G F E D C B A

Library of Congress Cataloging-in-Publication Data
Long, Sharron.
Extreme lo-carb cuisine / by Sharron Long.
p.   cm.
ISBN 1-59337-007-5
1. Low-carbohydrate diet--Recipes. I. Title.

RM237.73.L66 2004
641.56383--dc22

2003019088

Interior illustrations courtesy of © Digital Vision.

This book is available at quantity discounts for bulk purchases.
For information, call 1-800-872-5627.

Table of
Contents

Dedication / viii

Thank You! / ix

Introduction / x

Appetizers

Appetizers (continued)

Salads

Breakfasts

Main Courses

Main Courses (continued)

Main Courses (continued)

Veggies and Sides

Dressings and Sauces

Desserts

Desserts (continued)

Dedication

Dear Heavenly Father,
I ask that you bless this humble work of mine.

That you would use it to bless and
encourage those who read it.

That it would be of great benefit to them.

"Do everything for the glory of God,
even your eating and drinking."
–I Corinthians 10:31 (Living Bible)

Thank You!

$\mathcal{I}$ just wanted to say "thank you" to all the various folks who have helped me along the way!

Thanks to the folks at Adams Media for taking an interest in my self-published book! Thanks to Danielle Chiotti for helping me through this transition. She's got a great attitude!

I need to thank Leo Pena who was the one who urged me to do a cookbook. Without his insistence, I never would have taken the leap of faith.

I want to profusely thank Andrea Mondello, the owner of *www.Low CarbEating.com*, who has provided unlimited encouragement and support!

Special thanks to Steve May at Wisdom Herbs (*www.wisdomherbs.com*), and to Mike Small, his assistant, for their incredible support.

I need to thank my sister, Susan Franklin, who provided many recipes for this book and helped test and develop several others. Whenever I have a question about cooking techniques, I know whom to call!

A super big hug for Lori Rainey, who also provided several recipes as well as tested more recipes than anyone could ever believe! Thanks also to Margaret Fries and the others who contributed recipes for this book!

Thanks to Kelly Austin for helping me with the nutritionals!

A big "Thank you!" to my family, who endured my endless recipe development and kept my courage up with their positive feedback.

Special thanks to all the folks who have tested recipes for me: Carolyne Radon, Connie Pritchett, Roger Ebner, Stephanie Gabinet-Bethoulle, Vicki Dewald, Penny Quinn, Kim Debus, Jennifer Paske, DJ Rosales, Kelly Clark, Connie Rutledge, Brenda Czaya, Terese Smythe, Dan McKee, and countless others from the *www.LowCarbEating.com* community who have tried recipes for me. Also, a general thanks to the *www.LowCarbEating.com* community for providing me great feedback and support during the times that haven't been so easy. Thank you for being such a great bunch of folks!

Of course, I need to thank the Lord for enabling me to accomplish this task. My life is nothing without Him.

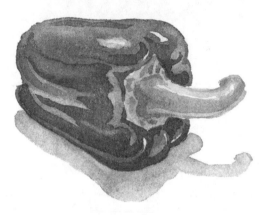

Introduction

hank you for picking up this copy of *Extreme Lo-Carb Cuisine*! It has been my goal to provide "Real food for real families." That is my purpose in writing these recipes. I am a simple homeschooling mommy with three kids and a husband. The food you see described within these pages is the food that I fix for my family! I try to always use readily available ingredients and keep things simple and to the point. Not only have these recipes been created by a real mom with a real family, but they have been tested by real families as well! Nearly all of the recipes contained within these pages have been tested by real folks using real food. I trust you will enjoy the recipes and get many good years of service out of this humble work of mine.

You may be curious about how I came to write a low-carb cookbook. It all started in January 2001, when I had a blood pressure spike of 172/92 in a doctor's office. He insisted that I start on a low-carb, high-protein diet immediately. Within ten days, my blood pressure had dropped to 100/70 and has stayed there since! Along the way, I received treatment for and recovered from a serious candida infection. Because I had to change the way I ate, it only stood to reason that I would also change the way my family eats. The recipes contained in this book are the result of that change. While you read through this book, you will find various tips, techniques, and tidbits of information that I hope will prove useful as you walk your journey of low-carb eating. I wish you all the best!

Blessings,
Sharron Long

Appetizers

BEEF SALAMI

Makes about 10 servings

Portable snacks are often a problem when low-carbing. It is quite easy to go to the store and pick up one of those "low-carb meal replacement bars." Too easy! The moral of the story: Be sensible, and eat real food! Note: This may be made using pork, turkey, venison, or combinations thereof. It isn't as dense as storebought salami, but is still very yummy!

½ cup water
1 packet ranch salad dressing mix
½ teaspoon Sweet & Slender
½ teaspoon chipotle pepper granules, roasted
¼ teaspoon lemon pepper
1 pound lean ground beef

1. In a large mixing bowl, combine the water and seasonings. Add the beef and mix it very well.
2. Place an 18" sheet of foil on the work surface and place the meat on the foil. Form the meat into approximately a 12"-long log. Wrap the meat tightly in the foil, folding the center and ends down tightly. Refrigerate the meat for 24 hours.
3. When ready to cook the meat, prick the underside of the foil (not the folded side) with a fork about 1" apart down the length of the foil. Fill the bottom of a broiler pan with water. Place the meat, still wrapped in the foil, on the broiler rack, pricked side down, and bake it at 325°F for about 1½ to 2 hours. The meat should feel solid to the touch when done.
4. Remove the foil and drain the salami on a cooling rack placed over paper towels. Wrap it in plastic wrap and store it in the refrigerator for up to 10 days or in the freezer for up to a month. The flavor improves with age.

NUTRITIONAL INFORMATION PER SERVING:
Carbohydrates: 2 • Effective Carb Count: 2 grams
Protein: 8 grams • Fat: 9 grams • Calories: 129

REDUCED-FAT VARIATION:
Use lean ground beef or venison combined with ground chicken or turkey.
Carbohydrates: 2 • Effective Carb Count: 2 grams
Protein: 9 grams • Fat: 6 grams • Calories: 102

A modern comparison of chili peppers is "the Official Chile Pepper Heat Scale," with a rating of 0 to 10. Bell peppers rate a zero because they contain no capsaicin. Jalapeño and chipotle peppers score a 5, serranos score a 6, cayenne peppers score an 8, and chiltecpin and Thai hot peppers score a 9. This is useful if you are going to substitute cayenne for the chipotle. Cayenne is nearly twice as hot!

BLUEBERRY
CREAM CHEESE SPREAD
Makes 4 servings

This is *sooo* yummy! Spread on low-carb crackers or celery sticks or use as a frosting on low-carb cakes, cookies, or muffins.

³/₄ cup cream cheese
1 tablespoon blueberries (about 8 medium to large berries)
¹/₈ teaspoon cinnamon
¹/₈ teaspoon ginger
¹/₄ teaspoon vanilla
¹/₄ teaspoon Sweet & Slender
¹/₄ teaspoon SteviaPlus
¹/₁₆ teaspoon lemon or orange zest–(that is ¹/₂ of ¹/₈ teaspoon!)

Place all of the ingredients into a small mixing bowl. Using an electric mixer, begin mixing the ingredients on lowest speed, gradually increasing the speed to high. Mix for a total of about 1½ minutes.

NUTRITIONAL INFORMATION PER SERVING:
Carbohydrates: 2 grams • Effective Carb Count: 1 gram
Protein: 3 grams • Fat: 15 grams • Calories: 154

REDUCED-FAT VARIATION:
Use low-fat cream cheese.
Carbohydrates: 1 gram • Effective Carb Count: 0 grams
Protein: 2 grams • Fat: 5 grams • Calories: 58

You don't think you could grow herbs? Keeping potted herbs is very convenient and even an apartment dweller could grow cooking herbs if he or she gets a little bit of sun in a window! You can do it from seed, but the easiest way is just to go to your local hardware store's garden center and choose the ones you want. Sure, you may be spending a bit more, but none of these plants is that expensive! The most expensive ones still cost less than $3.00.

CHEESE CRACKERS

Makes about 20 crackers

Even low-carb kids love Cheese Crackers!

½ cup almonds, ground
¼ cup soy protein (not soy flour!)
¼ cup Parmesan cheese
¼ teaspoon SteviaPlus or ½ packet sucralose
1 tablespoon butter or lard
¼ cup Almond Milk (page 240), cream, or water
Seasoning salt

1. Using a food processor with a chopping blade, or by hand, combine the ground almonds, soy protein, Parmesan cheese, SteviaPlus, and butter. Pulse until well mixed. With the motor still running, pour in the Almond Milk and process until the mixture is thoroughly combined. Remove the dough from the bowl and wrap it in a sheet of plastic wrap. Set it aside for 10 minutes.
2. Sprinkle some soy protein onto a piece of waxed paper or other clean surface and place the dough on top. Roll with a rolling pin until thin, about ⅛". Be careful not to roll the dough so thin that it falls apart!
3. Cut the rolled dough into squares, triangles, or whatever shapes suit your imagination, about 2½" across. Use a spatula to move the crackers to an ungreased baking sheet. Sprinkle the crackers with seasoning salt. Bake at 325°F for 10 to 20 minutes (keep an eye on them!) or until they are lightly browned on top. For easy cleanup, simply roll up the waxed paper and discard!

NUTRITIONAL INFORMATION PER SERVING:
Carbohydrates: 1 gram • Effective Carb Count: 0 grams
Protein: 2 grams • Fat: 4 grams • Calories: 41

If planting herbs makes you nervous, here are some tips: Place some broken bits of clay pots, bricks, and so forth into the bottom of an appropriate pot. They provide drainage for any excess moisture. For a very large pot, like a 10-gallon bucket, you can fill it about ¼ full with bits and pieces of bricks and wood. For a smaller pot, just a couple of inches of the drainage material will do. Pile in the potting soil to within a few inches of the top. Make a well in the soil, pour in lots of water mixed with some liquid fertilizer, remove the plant from the store's container, plunk it in, and keep it moist. Water it every day for the first week or so, then just don't let it get dried out. I can't tell you how many dishes have gone from being just good to spectacular by adding just a pinch of fresh herbs. Growing your own herbs is worth it, even if you live in the city or in an apartment. Just keep them like you would any houseplant.

CHEESE CRISPS

Serves 4

This is a simple, versatile recipe. To get a tortillalike effect, the crisps can be made out of 2 or 3 ounces of cheese placed closely together and cooked until they are semifirm. Before they get hard, they can be molded into taco shells. Leave them flat and they are tostada shells. Make them small and they are chips! You can even make a very large one, drape it over an upside-down bowl while it is still hot, and you've got a taco salad shell! A side benefit for folks reducing their fat intake is that nearly all of the fat cooks out!

4 ounces cheese, sliced
(Cheddar, Monterey jack, Co-Jack, etc.)

Place the cheese on a large skillet or griddle at least 1½" apart and cook it over medium heat until the bottom becomes golden brown, about 4 minutes. Turn the crisps and cook them until they are browned on both sides. Remove them from the heat and allow them to cool slightly on paper towels.

NUTRITIONAL INFORMATION PER SERVING:
Carbohydrates: trace • Effective Carb Count: trace
Protein: 7 grams • Fat: 9 grams (*Note:* Most of the fat cooks out!
There is no way to account for this in the calculations, though.)
Calories: 114 (Actually less because of the fat's cooking out.)

CHEESE STICKS

Serves 8

Mozzarella sticks are a staple of burger joints all across the country and are loved by kids and grownups alike. This is my low-carb version of that favorite treat! Dip in Creamy Ranch Salad Dressing (page 244) or the pizza sauce from Sue's Pizza Sans Bread (page 147), if desired.

1 cup pork rinds, ground
2 1/2 tablespoons soy protein (not soy flour!)
1/4 teaspoon lemon pepper (optional, a good "grown-up" variation!)
1 teaspoon Italian seasonings (optional)
1 egg
1 tablespoon water
1/4 cup lard
8 ounces mozzarella string cheese, cut into 16 pieces

1. Combine the pork rinds, soy protein, lemon pepper, and Italian seasonings in a shallow dish. In another shallow dish, combine the egg and water.
2. Heat the lard in a medium-sized frying pan over medium heat until it is melted.
3. Meanwhile, dip the cheese sticks first into the egg/water mixture, then into the pork rind mixture. Fry them, turning often, over medium heat until they are golden brown. Serve warm.

NUTRITIONAL INFORMATION PER SERVING:
Carbohydrates: 1 gram • Effective Carb Count: 0 grams
Protein: 9 grams • Fat: 14 grams • Calories: 158

CINNAMONY-SWEET CRACKERS

Makes about 20 crackers

Remember cinnamon graham crackers? This low-carb variation reminds me of that childhood treat.

³/₄ cup almonds, ground
¹/₄ cup soy protein (not soy flour!)
¹/₂ teaspoon SteviaPlus
1 packet sucralose
1 tablespoon butter or lard
¹/₄ cup Almond Milk (page 240), cream, or water

Topping:

¹/₄ teaspoon SteviaPlus
1 packet sucralose
¹/₂ teaspoon cinnamon

1. Using a food processor with a chopping blade, or by hand, combine the ground almonds, soy protein, SteviaPlus, sucralose, and butter. Pulse until well mixed. With the motor still running, pour in the Almond Milk and process until the mixture is thoroughly combined. Remove the dough from the bowl and wrap it in a sheet of plastic wrap. Set it aside for 10 minutes.
2. Sprinkle some soy protein onto a piece of waxed paper or other clean surface and place the dough on top. Roll with a rolling pin until thin, about ¹/₈". Be careful not to roll the dough so thin that it falls apart!
3. Cut the rolled dough into squares, triangles, or whatever shapes suit your imagination, about 2¹/₂" across. Use a spatula to move the crackers to an ungreased baking sheet.
4. In a small bowl, combine the topping ingredients. Sprinkle the crackers with the topping. Bake at 325°F for 10 to 20 minutes (keep an eye on them!) or until they are lightly browned on top. For easy cleanup, simply roll up the waxed paper and discard!

NUTRITIONAL INFORMATION PER SERVING:
Carbohydrates: 1 gram • Effective Carb Count: 0 grams
Protein: 2 grams • Fat: 4 grams • Calories: 47

CLAM CAKES

Serves 4

Clam cakes are a sure way to please any seafood lover. Besides making a great appetizer, they are good served alongside a salad for lunch. *Note:* Salad-sized shrimp or chopped crabmeat may be substituted for the clams.

½ pound fresh clams, chopped
(or equivalent canned clams, without sugar, drained)
1 egg
1 tablespoon water
⅔ cup pork rinds, ground
½ teaspoon lemon juice
1 tablespoon parsley flakes
½ teaspoon garlic salt
Dash lemon pepper (less than ⅛ teaspoon)
Lard
Lemon juice for serving

1. In a mixing bowl, combine thoroughly the clams, egg, water, pork rinds, lemon juice, parsley, garlic salt, and lemon pepper. Allow the mixture to rest for 3 to 5 minutes.
2. Put about 3 tablespoons of lard into the bottom of a large skillet. Heat over medium heat until hot. Form the clam mixture into 1½" patties and fry them on each side in hot oil until they are deep golden brown, about 7 minutes total. Serve hot with lemon juice drizzled on top.

NUTRITIONAL INFORMATION PER SERVING:
Carbohydrates: 1 gram • Effective Carb Count: 0 grams
Protein: 6 grams • Fat: 5 grams • Calories: 76

CLAM DIP

Makes 16 servings

Oh, how I used to love clam dip! Then I looked at the list of ingredients. Yuck! This is a simple way to make it, and it is every bit as yummy.

1 16-ounce container of sour cream
1 packet Ranch-style dip mix
1 6.5-ounce can of minced clams, drained, juices reserved

In a mixing bowl, combine the sour cream and the Ranch dip mix. Add the drained clams and 1½ teaspoons of the reserved juices. Stir the dip well and enjoy with your favorite veggies!

NUTRITIONAL INFORMATION PER SERVING:
Carbohydrates: 3 grams • Effective Carb Count: 3 grams
Protein: 2 grams • Fat: 6 grams • Calories: 74

REDUCED-FAT VARIATION:
Use low-fat sour cream.
Carbohydrates: 2 grams • Effective Carb Count: 2 grams
Protein: 2 grams • Fat: 1 gram • Calories: 23

Lemons and limes are an essential element of any kitchen. Fresh juice is always preferable, though bottled lemon juice is an acceptable substitute for large quantities or in a pinch. Next time you're at the grocery store, pick up a bag of lemons and limes to be juiced at home to add to your favorite fish, poultry, or vegetable dishes. Lemons and limes can be stored whole, refrigerated, for several weeks. If you prefer, you can juice them all at once and freeze the juice in ice cube trays for convenient "instant" fresh juice.

CRACKERS

Makes about 20 crackers

While using sliced cucumbers and zucchini is an easy and tasty way to make a "cracker" base for most spreadable salads, certain things, like meatloaf, really need something with more substance! Use these crackers for bases for meatloaf, Beef Salami (page 2), and other party treats.

3/4 cup almonds, ground
1/4 cup soy protein (not soy flour!)
1/2 teaspoon salt
1/4 teaspoon SteviaPlus or 1/2 packet sucralose
1 tablespoon butter or lard
1/4 cup Almond Milk (page 240), cream, or water
Seasoning salt

1. Using a food processor with a chopping blade, or by hand, combine the ground almonds, soy protein, salt, SteviaPlus, and butter. Pulse until well mixed. With the motor still running, pour in the Almond Milk and process until the mixture is thoroughly combined.
2. Remove the dough from the bowl and wrap it in a sheet of plastic wrap. Set it aside for 10 minutes.
3. Sprinkle some soy protein onto a piece of waxed paper or other clean surface and place the dough on top. Roll with a rolling pin until thin, about 1/8". Be careful not to roll the dough so thin that it falls apart!
4. Cut the rolled dough into squares, triangles, or whatever shapes suit your imagination, about 2½" across. Use a spatula to move the crackers to an ungreased baking sheet. Sprinkle the crackers with seasoning salt. Bake at 325°F for 10 to 20 minutes (keep an eye on them!) or until they are lightly browned on top. For easy cleanup, simply roll up the waxed paper and discard!

NUTRITIONAL INFORMATION PER SERVING:
Carbohydrates: 1 gram • Effective Carb Count: 0 grams
Protein: 2 grams • Fat: 4 grams • Calories: 46

CRANBERRY SMOOTHIE

Serves 4

This smoothie makes a great all-in-one breakfast! If you can't locate cranberries, blueberries make a wonderful variation. Also, 1 tablespoon of sugar-free almond-flavored syrup makes a great substitute for either one of the sweeteners listed.

2 eggs
1 quart whole milk yogurt
1 1/2 teaspoons SteviaPlus
1 1/2 teaspoons Sweet & Slender
1/2 cup cranberries, fresh or frozen
1 1/2 teaspoons cinnamon
1 1/2 teaspoons almond extract
1/2 teaspoon orange zest

1. If you are concerned about the safety of your eggs, coddle them. To coddle eggs: Fill a small saucepan with enough water to cover the eggs. Bring the water to boiling; then gently place the whole eggs into the boiling water for 20 seconds. Remove the eggs from the boiling water and immerse them in ice-cold water to stop them from cooking any further.
2. Place all of the ingredients into a blender container. Begin blending on low speed, turning it up to high speed. Blend the smoothie for about 30 to 45 seconds, or until it is well combined. Pour into tall glasses.

NUTRITIONAL INFORMATION PER SERVING:
Carbohydrates: 7 grams • Effective Carb Count: 6 grams
Protein: 11 grams • Fat: 10 grams • Calories: 201

REDUCED-FAT VARIATION:
Use skim milk yogurt.
Carbohydrates: 7 grams • Effective Carb Count: 6 grams
Protein: 17 grams • Fat: 3 grams • Calories: 180

A note about yogurt: Studies have been done on yogurt and other cultured milk products like buttermilk and kefir (see *www.LowCarbLuxury.com/yogurt.html*) that have shown that these products actually have very little actual carbohydrates left in them. The bacteria (healthful acidophilus and others!) actually consume most of the sugars in the milk, leaving a true carb count for such products of 4 carbs per cup. That is the value I have used for calculating the nutritional information throughout this book.

CREAMY SEAFOOD DIP

Makes 16 servings

A wonderful variation to this delightful dip is to add 2 mashed avocados for Creamy Avocado Seafood Dip!

2 cups sour cream
1/2 cup celery, chopped
1/2 cup salad shrimp, cooked
1 packet Ranch dip mix
1/8 teaspoon chipotle pepper granules, roasted, or hot chili oil
1/8 teaspoon lemon pepper

Combine all of the ingredients in a small mixing bowl. Stir them well to combine. Refrigerate about 20 minutes before serving. Use within 3 days.

NUTRITIONAL INFORMATION PER SERVING:
Carbohydrates: 2 grams • Effective Carb Count: 2 grams
Protein: 2 grams • Fat: 6 grams • Calories: 71

REDUCED-FAT VARIATION:
Use low-fat sour cream.
Carbohydrates: 2 grams • Effective Carb Count: 2 grams
Protein: 1 gram • Fat: 1 gram • Calories: 20

Certain spices and seasonings are pantry basics: seasoning salt, lemon pepper, garlic salt, mustard powder, ground ginger, dried onions, dried parsley, dried Italian seasonings, dried chives, ground ginger, cinnamon, vanilla, and almond extract. Still more are: rosemary, lemon thyme (if it is available in your area), mint, fresh chives, fresh garlic, and onions. When you're choosing a seasoning salt, try to find one that contains little or no sugar. For the industrious chef, some of these pantry basics can be made right at home, but all can be found at the local grocery store.

DEVILED EGGS

Serves 12

What says "picnic" or "potluck" more than deviled eggs? To keep the eggs from sliding during transportation or storage, simply place a paper towel in the serving dish, and place the eggs on top. This also absorbs excess moisture, helping to maintain freshness.

12 eggs
½ cup Blender Mayonnaise (page 241) or
commercially prepared mayonnaise
⅛ teaspoon dry mustard powder
2 teaspoons onion flakes
10 drops (about ⅛ teaspoon) hot chili oil or a tiny pinch of cayenne
½ teaspoon seasoning salt
About 1 tablespoon parsley, chopped, for garnish

1. Place the eggs into a saucepan. Put a pinch of salt in the water to keep the eggs from cracking. Add enough water to cover the eggs, and bring it to a full boil. Reduce the heat, and simmer for 10 minutes. Drain the water and refill the pot with cold water to cool the eggs.
2. Remove the shells from the eggs and slice the eggs in half, lengthwise. Put the yolks into a small mixing bowl, and set the egg whites aside. Add the Blender Mayonnaise, mustard powder, onion flakes, hot chili oil, and seasoning salt to the yolks. Mix on medium speed with an electric mixer, or mix by hand, until the yolk mixture is smooth and creamy, about 2 minutes.
3. Place the egg white halves on a serving plate. Fill the holes with the yolk mixture, using either a piping tube or a teaspoon. Sprinkle a tiny amount of parsley over all when completed for a pretty finish.

NUTRITIONAL INFORMATION PER SERVING:
Carbohydrates: 1 gram • Effective Carb Count: 1 gram
Protein: 6 grams • Fat: 12 grams • Calories: 133

REDUCED-FAT VARIATION:
Use low-fat mayonnaise.
Carbohydrates: 2 grams • Effective Carb Count: 2 grams
Protein: 6 grams • Fat: 6 grams • Calories: 90

Egg Drop Soup

Serves 4

Now you can enjoy this Chinese restaurant treat in your own home. This is great served as an appetizer before Barbecue Pork (page 95).

4 cups chicken or turkey Rich Stock (page 254)
or commercially prepared broth
1 large egg
1/3 cup peas, frozen
1/4 cup finely chopped jicama or water chestnuts
1 teaspoon arrowroot powder mixed into 1/4 cup water
Salt to taste

1. Place the stock into a medium-sized saucepan over medium heat, and heat it just to the boiling point. While the stock is heating, beat the egg in a small dish and set aside.
2. When the stock is hot, add the peas and jicama. Simmer 2 minutes. Add the arrowroot/water mixture and stir until the stock becomes clear again. Season with salt as desired.
3. Pour the egg, in a small stream, into the simmering stock. Use a large circular motion when pouring the egg in. Do it slowly over the entire surface area of the pan, but only in one direction. Also, stir only in one direction. This will keep the "egg flowers" from becoming "egg shreds." It takes a little bit of finesse, but it is worth it! Serve immediately.

Nutritional information per serving:
Carbohydrates: 5 grams • Effective Carb Count: 4 grams
Protein: 7 grams • Fat: 3 grams • Calories: 75

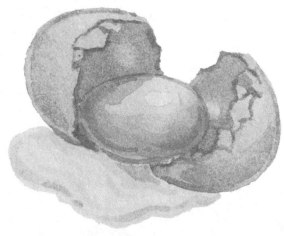

EGG ROLLS

Makes 24

This is one of my family favorites, and I'm so pleased to pass the low-carb version on to you. This recipe is very involved, but it is so worth it if you love egg rolls as my family does!! Serve these Egg Rolls hot with "Honey" Mustard Dipping Sauce (page 251); Fiery Hot Mustard (page 246); or Sweet and Sour Sauce, Low-Carbed (page 257) and sesame seeds.

⅓ cup lard, approximately
6 cups cabbage, shredded
2 large carrots, shredded (optional)
½ zucchini, shredded (optional)
1 small onion, grated (optional)
4 cloves garlic, minced
1 large broccoli stem, peeled and shredded
Other optional veggies include:
Bean sprouts, water chestnuts, peas, mushrooms, etc.
½ pound meat, cooked (chicken, turkey, pork, beef, or shrimp)
Seasoning salt
Lemon pepper
Sesame oil
Hot chili oil
Bragg's Liquid Aminos or soy sauce
Mountain Bread
1 tablespoon cornstarch mixed into 2 tablespoons water
Cooking oil spray

Equipment needed:

Wok or other large skillet
Large spatula
Large strainer and large bowl (durable plastic, preferred)
¼ cup measuring cup
Very small bowl and a small spoon
Large cutting board or baking sheet
Kitchen towel, slightly dampened
Dinner plate or another cutting board
Kitchen scissors and tongs
Paper towels

Recipe continues on page 16 ➤

➤ Recipe continued from page 15

1. Place about ⅓ cup of lard into the wok. Heat the lard and add the cabbage, carrots, zucchini, onion, garlic, broccoli, and meat. Cook on high, stirring constantly until the veggies are tender. Season the mixture liberally with seasoning salt, lemon pepper, and sesame oil. Add a few drops of hot chili oil and the liquid aminos. I've learned the hard way that you HAVE to taste this to get the seasonings just right! If it isn't perfect in the pan, it won't be perfect in the Egg Rolls.
2. Place a large strainer over a large mixing bowl and carefully place the cooked mixture into the strainer and allow it to cool. If I am really organized and together, I'll get this done early in the day, or even the day before I'm making the egg rolls. Unfortunately, I am rarely that on the ball! At this step, I am often found sticking the whole thing into my deep chest freezer and stirring it every 15 minutes to hasten cooling. The mixture has to be completely cooled to fill the wraps. If it isn't, it will melt the wraps, and that is not a pretty sight!
3. To use the Mountain Bread wraps, trim them to 6½" squares. Set aside the excess bits for later use in Mountain Bread Crisps (page 28). Thoroughly wet the Mountain Bread under slowly running water. Allow it to rest for a minute or so before filling. This allows the bread to soften and become pliable enough for rolling.
4. Place on the workspace in front of you: The cutting board, cooled filling, damp towel, small bowl and spoon, dinner plate, scissors, and Mountain Bread. The dinner plate should be directly in front of you.
5. Mix the cornstarch/water in the small bowl with the spoon. Place a wrapper diagonally on the plate. Measure ¼ cup filling and place it in a "log roll" crossways slightly below the center of the wrapper. Fold up the bottom ⅓ of the wrapper. Using the back of the spoon, spread a small amount of the cornstarch/water mixture around the edges of the wrapper wherever it will be touching other parts of the wrapper. This is the glue. Fold over the sides, so that it looks like a little pouch. Seal the new edges. Using gentle pressure, roll it up like a burrito. Make sure it is very well sealed.
6. Place the completed Egg Rolls uncovered on a baking sheet. When all Egg Rolls are completed to this point, they may be placed on baking sheets and individually frozen for later use.
7. Arrange Egg Rolls evenly on baking sheets. Carefully spray all of the surface areas of the Egg Rolls with cooking oil spray. Bake at 375°F for about 15 minutes, until they are golden brown.

NUTRITIONAL INFORMATION PER SERVING:
Carbohydrates: 9 grams • Effective Carb Count: 6 grams
Protein: 3 grams • Fat: 4 grams • Calories: 84

REDUCED-FAT VARIATION:
Use cooking oil spray to cook the meat and veggies instead of the lard.
Carbohydrates: 9 grams • Effective Carb Count: 6 grams
Protein: 3 grams • Fat: 1 gram • Calories: 58

EXTRA SPECIAL EGG NOG

Makes 1 1/2 quarts, or 12 1/2-cup servings

A wonderful treat for cold winter days. I often serve this after dinner instead of a regular dessert when we have company.

6 large eggs
2 cups cream (heavy whipping type if available)
thinned with 2 cups water (4 cups total liquid)
1/2 teaspoon SteviaPlus
8 packets sucralose
1/4 teaspoon salt
2 teaspoons vanilla

Garnishes:

Chocolate curls (low-carb, of course!)
Ground nutmeg and/or cinnamon

1. Since the eggs won't be cooked, coddle them: Fill a small saucepan about half full. Bring the water to boiling; then gently place the whole eggs into the boiling water for 20 seconds. Remove the eggs from the water and immerse them in ice-cold water to stop them from cooking any further.
2. Separate the eggs. Beat the egg whites with an electric mixer on medium-high speed until stiff peaks form. Set the yolks aside.
3. In a nonaluminum saucepan, heat all of the thinned cream over medium heat for about 5 minutes, until it is beginning to steam. Do *not* allow the cream to boil! Pour the cream into a large nonaluminum bowl.
4. In another bowl, beat together the egg yolks, SteviaPlus, sucralose, salt, and vanilla. Slowly pour the egg yolk mixture into the cream, whisking constantly with a wire whisk while pouring. Fold in the egg whites, combining well. Serve immediately. Garnish as desired in individual cups.

NUTRITIONAL INFORMATION PER SERVING:
Carbohydrates: 2 grams • Effective Carb Count: 2 grams
Protein: 4 grams • Fat: 12 grams • Calories: 132

REDUCED-FAT VARIATION:
Use fat-free half-and-half (or evaporated skim milk) instead of the cream.
Carbohydrates: 4 grams • Effective Carb Count: 4 grams
Protein: 3 grams • Fat: 2 grams • Calories: 61

FRIENDSHIP TEA, LOW-CARBED

Makes approximately 44 servings

A very dear friend's mother used to serve the high-carb version of this tea on chilly winter mornings. Now, that tradition can continue! Thank you Lori Rainey for sharing a bit of your childhood with us!

4 envelopes unsweetened orange drink mix (2 quart-size packets)
1 envelope unsweetened lemonade drink mix (2 quart-size packets)
40 packets sucralose
2 teaspoons SteviaPlus
½ cup unsweetened instant tea mix
2 teaspoons cinnamon
1 teaspoon ground cloves

1. Mix all ingredients together and store covered in an airtight container.
2. To use: Add 1 teaspoon of the tea mix to a cup of boiling water. Stir it well and enjoy!

NUTRITIONAL INFORMATION PER SERVING:
Carbohydrates: trace • Effective Carb Count: trace
Protein: trace • Fat: trace • Calories: trace

GROWN-UPS' GUACAMOLE

Makes 2 large or 4 small servings

This authentic Mexican sauce is called Grown-Ups' Guacamole because most adults prefer this style. For a kid-friendly version, check out Kids' Guacamole (page 25). Serve this terrific sauce with salads, tacos, Mountain Bread Crisps (page 28), etc.

1 ripe avocado
½ small tomato, finely chopped,
seeds removed
2 tablespoons sweet onion, freshly chopped
¼ teaspoon lemon juice
⅛ teaspoon garlic salt
⅛ teaspoon lemon pepper

Mash the avocado well in a small bowl. Add the remaining ingredients, mixing well.

NUTRITIONAL INFORMATION PER SERVING:
Carbohydrates: 5 grams • Effective Carb Count: 3 grams
Protein: 1 gram • Fat: 8 grams • Calories: 86

If you like spicy or Mexican-style cooking, then there are several essential ingredients you'll want to keep in your pantry. Keep your closet stocked with tomato sauce, canned tomatoes (without sugar, of course!), chili powder, chilies or jalapeño peppers, and cumin. Ground cumin is the quintessential Mexican spice. It is what gives Mexican-style dishes that special richness. Low-carb tortillas are nice to have, if they are available in your area, or you can make High-Protein Wraps (page 225). Roasted chipotle pepper granules and hot chili oil are also useful ingredients to spice up any meal.

HOT CRAB DIP

Serves 12

This creamy dip is perfect for parties or for a fun midweek snack. For a little extra kick, garnish with chopped scallion.

1 8-ounce package cream cheese, softened
1 cup Blender Mayonnaise (page 241) or
commercially prepared mayonnaise
1 tablespoon lemon juice (fresh is always best!)
½ teaspoon garlic powder
½ tablespoon Old Bay seasoning
1 teaspoon Worcestershire sauce
¾ teaspoon dry mustard powder
1 pound crabmeat
1 ½ cups Cheddar cheese, grated, divided

1. In a mixing bowl, combine all of the ingredients, reserving half of the Cheddar cheese.
2. Spread the crab mixture evenly into an 8" baking dish. Top with the reserved cheddar cheese. Bake the crab dip for 15 to 20 minutes at 350°F, or until it is bubbly around the edges. Enjoy hot with celery sticks or pork rinds.

NUTRITIONAL INFORMATION PER SERVING:
Carbohydrates: 1 gram • Effective Carb Count: 1 gram
Protein: 13 grams • Fat: 27 grams • Calories: 293

REDUCED-FAT VARIATION:
Use low-fat cream cheese and low-fat Cheddar.
Carbohydrates: 4 grams • Effective Carb Count: 4 grams
Protein: 13 grams • Fat: 10 grams • Calories: 159

HOT SPINACH DIP

Makes 9 servings

This popular appetizer is very simple to make and will liven up any meal. It's so tasty you may even want to skip the main course!

Dip ingredients:

1 8-ounce package cream cheese, softened
2 tablespoons half-and-half, cream, or Almond Milk (page 240)
1/2 cup sour cream
1/4 cup shredded cheese (Co-Jack, Monterey jack, Colby, or a blend)
2/3 cup chopped spinach (fresh or frozen)
2 tablespoons minced onion, dried
1/4 teaspoon garlic granules
1/4 teaspoon seasoning salt
1/8 teaspoon lemon pepper
4 drops hot chili oil

Topping ingredients:

1 tablespoon melted butter
1/2 cup pecan pieces
1/4 teaspoon seasoning salt

1. In a mixing bowl with an electric mixer, combine the dip ingredients. Spread the cheese mixture into an 8" baking dish.
2. Drizzle the butter over the cheese mixture; then sprinkle the nuts and seasoning salt over all. Bake the dip at 350°F for about 20 minutes or until the edges puff slightly and it is heated through. Serve hot with veggies or pork rinds.

NUTRITIONAL INFORMATION PER SERVING:
Carbohydrates: 3 grams • Effective Carb Count: 2 grams
Protein: 4 grams • Fat: 19 grams • Calories: 191

REDUCED-FAT VARIATION:
Use low-fat cream cheese, fat-free half-and-half, low-fat
sour cream, and low-fat cheese. Omit the butter.
Carbohydrates: 4 grams • Effective Carb Count: 3 grams
Protein: 4 grams • Fat: 10 grams • Calories: 122

TIP FOR WASHING FRUITS AND VEGGIES: You don't need the pricey "fruit and vegetable washes" that have been popping up in grocery stores to be sure your food is pesticide- and residue-free. Try this simple, safe alternative instead: place 1 tablespoon distilled white vinegar into 1 gallon clean water. Simply immerse your fruits and vegetables in this wash and you will get the same results at a fraction of the cost!

Hot Texas Pecan Dip

Makes 9 servings

This traditional southern recipe comes from deep in the heart of Texas and is perfect for the low-carb way of life!

Dip ingredients:

1 8-ounce package cream cheese, softened
2 tablespoons half-and-half, cream, or Almond Milk (page 240)
2 ounces cooked roast beef, finely chopped (lunch meat acceptable)
¼ cup green pepper, minced (optional)
1 tablespoon minced onion, dried (or 2 tablespoons fresh onion, minced)
½ cup sour cream
¼ teaspoon garlic granules
¼ teaspoon seasoning salt
⅛ teaspoon lemon pepper
½ tablespoon parsley flakes

Topping ingredients:

1 tablespoon butter, melted
½ cup pecan pieces
¼ teaspoon seasoning salt

1. In a mixing bowl with an electric mixer, combine the dip ingredients. Spread the cheese mixture into an 8" baking dish.
2. Drizzle the butter over the cheese mixture; then sprinkle the nuts and seasoning salt over all. Bake the dip at 350°F for about 20 minutes or until the edges puff slightly and it is heated through. Serve hot with veggies or pork rinds.

Nutritional information per serving:
Carbohydrates: 3 grams • Effective Carb Count: 2 grams
Protein: 4 grams • Fat: 20 grams • Calories: 200

Reduced-Fat Variation:
Use low-fat cream cheese, fat-free half-and-half, and
low-fat sour cream. Omit the butter.
Carbohydrates: 4 grams • Effective Carb Count: 3 grams
Protein: 4 grams • Fat: 12 grams • Calories: 138

KEFIR SMOOTHIE

Makes about 6 1-cup servings

Kefir? What in the world is a kefir? If candida is an issue for you, kefir may be helpful in your healing process. This wonderful yogurt-type food can be a part of your regular diet. Kefir is a buttermilk/yogurt product that has a strong, pleasant flavor and is loaded with friendly bacteria. It is available in health food stores or, if you know someone who has kefir "grains," you may get starter from them and have an infinite supply of this super food! This recipe increases in volume by about 30 percent.

General amounts:

4 cups (1 quart) kefir
½ cup berries, see below
½ teaspoon cinnamon
½ teaspoon ginger
¼ to ½ teaspoon orange zest (optional)
Sweetener varies, see below
Almond or vanilla extract, see below

Variations (use the basic recipe, above, plus the following):

Cranberry:	*Use 1 teaspoon SteviaPlus, 1 teaspoon Sweet & Slender, and ½ teaspoon almond extract.*
Blueberry:	*Use ¾ teaspoon SteviaPlus, ¾ teaspoon Sweet & Slender, and ½ teaspoon almond extract.*
Strawberry:	*Use ¾ teaspoon SteviaPlus, ¾ teaspoon Sweet & Slender, and ½ teaspoon vanilla extract.*
Strawberry/blueberry:	*Use ¾ teaspoon SteviaPlus, ¾ teaspoon Sweet & Slender, and ½ teaspoon vanilla extract.*

Place all of the ingredients into a blender container. Begin blending on lowest speed, until the seasonings begin to mix in, then turn the blender up to high and whip for approximately 1 minute.

NUTRITIONAL INFORMATION PER SERVING:
Carbohydrates: 4 grams • Effective Carb Count: 4 grams
Protein: 6 grams • Fat: 5 grams • Calories: 109

REDUCED-FAT VARIATION:
Use fat-free kefir.
Carbohydrates: 4 grams • Effective Carb Count: 4 grams
Protein: 9 grams • Fat: trace • Calories: 99

KETTLE CORN

Serves 8

This recipe is useful for those who are at or near their goal weight. Yum-yum!
Watch the serving sizes. It is very easy to go overboard.

4 tablespoons lard, melted
½ cup unpopped popcorn kernels
½ teaspoon SteviaPlus
½ teaspoon Sweet & SlenderSea salt

1. Melt the lard over medium-low heat in a medium-large pot with a lid. Pour
   the popcorn and sweeteners into the pot, shaking the pot to mix the sweeteners in thoroughly with the oil, and cover the pot.
2. Over a medium heat, begin to pop the popcorn. Shake the pot frequently to
   ensure that the popcorn kernels and oil do not burn.
3. Once the popping has slowed, remove the pot from the heat. Pour the popcorn at once into a large bowl and season to taste with sea salt.

NUTRITIONAL INFORMATION PER SERVING:
Carbohydrates: 13 grams • Effective Carb Count: 10 grams
Protein: 2 grams • Fat: 6 grams • Calories: 114

PANTRY-STOCKING TIP: It's always a good idea to have fresh veggies on hand, and
certain veggie staples keep very well. Prewashed, bagged spinach leaves keep much
longer than fresh bunch spinach. Rutabagas, celery, and radishes are also perfect
pantry companions. Radishes are great for a quick veggie snack on the run. Just wash
and trim them and store in an airtight container, and you've got a fresh snack that will
keep for about a week.

KIDS' GUACAMOLE

Makes 4 small or 2 large servings

This is called Kids' Guacamole because this is the guacamole for which my kids beg! This recipe is simple and makes the perfect after-school treat. Serve with Mountain Bread Crisps (page 28), tacos, etc.

1 ripe avocado
¼ cup sour cream
¼ teaspoon lemon juice
¼ teaspoon seasoning salt

In a small bowl, mash the avocado. Add the remaining ingredients and mix well.

NUTRITIONAL INFORMATION PER SERVING:
Carbohydrates: 4 grams • Effective Carb Count: 3 grams
Protein: 1 gram • Fat: 11 grams • Calories: 112

REDUCED-FAT VARIATION:
Use low-fat sour cream.
Carbohydrates: 4 grams • Effective Carb Count: 3 grams
Protein: 1 gram • Fat: 8 grams • Calories: 86

Here are some tips for choosing the perfect avocado. A ripe avocado (if it is a dark-skinned one) is just about black. It yields to gentle pressure but is not mushy. It is rather like a peach in that respect. If you purchase several unripe avocados all at once, just place them in a brown paper bag and stick them in a cool dark place to ripen for a few days. They will ripen evenly and will usually not get all mushy like they do when they are ripened on the counter.

LEMONADE

Makes 4 1-cup servings

This perennial summer favorite doesn't have to be a sweet memory. This simple low-carb version is sure to please on those hot afternoons!

6 tablespoons lemon juice, fresh
1 1/2 teaspoons Sweet & Slender
1 1/2 teaspoons SteviaPlus
4 cups ice water

Combine the lemon juice and sweeteners in a pitcher, mixing well. Pour the ice water over the top and mix it well. Serve cold.

NUTRITIONAL INFORMATION PER SERVING:
Carbohydrates: 3 grams • Effective Carb Count: 3 grams
Protein: trace • Fat: 0 grams • Calories: 12

It is generally recommended that those under candida treatment avoid vinegar, cheese, all dairy, peanuts, pistachios, mushrooms, soy sauce, sugar, white flour, and any other food that is high in carbohydrate content. Anything containing yeast or that can be turned into sugar in the body, like fruit, as well as anything fermented are the normal recommendations of foods to avoid. Sounds like a lot of food, doesn't it? It is! But, there are a lot of other wonderful foods out there just waiting to be discovered–all it takes is a little creativity!

MINI CHEESE BALLS

Makes 16 appetizers

My kids came up with the original idea for these tasty tidbits. They are much easier to eat than a traditional cheese ball!

1 8-ounce package cream cheese, softened
½ cup Cheddar cheese, shredded (or Colby or Co-Jack)
¼ cup Swiss cheese, shredded
1 tablespoon Parmesan cheese
¹⁄₁₆ teaspoon chipotle pepper granules, roasted, or hot chili oil
¼ teaspoon garlic granules
¼ teaspoon seasoning salt
¼ cup almonds, ground (approximately)

1. Combine all of the ingredients, except the ground almonds, in a mixing bowl and mix on medium-low speed until the mixture is smooth.
2. Roll the cheese mixture into 1" balls and then roll the balls in the ground almonds. Place them on a serving dish and chill them until they are ready to be served.

NUTRITIONAL INFORMATION PER SERVING:
Carbohydrates: 1 gram • Effective Carb Count: 1 gram
Protein: 3 grams • Fat: 8 grams • Calories: 85

REDUCED-FAT VARIATION:
Use low-fat cream cheese and reduced-fat Cheddar and Swiss cheeses.
Carbohydrates: 1 gram • Effective Carb Count: 1 gram
Protein: 3 grams • Fat: 5 grams • Calories: 61

℃ NUTS AND NUT BUTTERS: Almonds, both raw and blanched, are great to keep on hand. Aside from making a great portable snack, you can also use them to make almond flour or almond butter. For almond flour, just fill your food processor with whatever amount you desire and chop away! Be careful, if it is processed too long, the oils will separate out and it will turn to almond butter. When making almond butter, process until the mixture forms a ball. *Note:* You don't have to limit yourself to almonds—experiment with your favorite nuts to see which you like best!

MOUNTAIN BREAD CRISPS

Serves 2

These may be used as a stand-alone appetizer or as a cracker or chip base for spreading dips, egg salad, etc. Store leftover crisps in a bread bag tied loosely. They keep well for several days.

1 piece Mountain Bread
Lard
1 teaspoon cinnamon mixed with ½ teaspoon
SteviaPlus or 2 packets sucralose or seasoning salt

1. Cut the Mountain Bread into 1½" × 2" rectangles. Melt about ½" lard in a large skillet over medium heat.
2. When the oil is hot, fry the Mountain Bread pieces on each side until golden brown, about 1 minute total. They will sizzle at first, then stop. When they stop sizzling, they are ready to be removed from the oil. Otherwise they become overdone very quickly.
3. For a sweet treat, sprinkle the crisps with the cinnamon mixture. For savory crisps, season liberally with seasoning salt.

NUTRITIONAL INFORMATION PER SERVING:
Carbohydrates: 5 grams • Effective Carb Count: 3 grams
Protein: 1 gram • Fat: 4 grams • Calories: 62

REDUCED-FAT VARIATION:
Spray the Mountain Bread pieces with cooking oil spray
and bake at 375°F until they are golden.
Carbohydrates: 5 grams • Effective Carb Count: 3 grams
Protein: 1 gram • Fat: trace • Calories: 24

QUICK AND EASY HOT COCOA

Makes 16 servings

Sit down, put up your feet, and relax with a bit of comfort! This low-carb version is just as delicious as the high-carb thing and is a perfect winter treat.

Dry mix ingredients:

1 cup cocoa powder
4 teaspoons SteviaPlus
16 packets sucralose
¼ teaspoon sea salt
¼ teaspoon cinnamon

To serve:

¾ cup boiling water, approximately
¼ cup half-and-half, cream, or Almond Milk (page 240)

1. Place all of the dry mix ingredients into a bowl and stir them well. Place them into a covered container and label it as "Hot Cocoa Mix." Store it in a cool, dark place.
2. To serve: Place 1 tablespoon of the dry mix into the bottom of a mug. Slowly, while stirring, pour in about half of the hot water. Stir it well to disperse any lumps. Pour the half-and-half into the mug; then finish filling it with the water.

NUTRITIONAL INFORMATION PER SERVING (MIX ONLY):
Carbohydrates: 3 grams • Effective Carb Count: 1 gram
Protein: 1 gram • Fat: 1 gram • Calories: 12

RANCH ALMONDS

Makes 12 servings

This is a great snack. You can try a variety of salad dressing mixes with your nuts, just watch out for sugar in the mixes! If you want to use Ranch Almonds as a salad topper, use slivered or sliced almonds.

3 cups almonds, raw
2 tablespoons olive oil
1 packet Ranch-style salad dressing mix

1. Place the almonds and olive oil into a bowl. Stir them well to coat evenly with the oil. Pour the salad dressing mix over the nuts and stir them well to coat evenly.
2. Place the nuts on a baking sheet and bake at 350°F for about 7 to 10 minutes. Cool before serving.

NUTRITIONAL INFORMATION PER SERVING:
Carbohydrates: 9 grams • Effective Carb Count: 5 grams
Protein: 7 grams • Fat: 21 grams • Calories: 236

What does lemon thyme taste like? It has a wonderful lemony smell and taste combined with something like a mild mint—quite distinctive from traditional thyme. Lemon thyme is a great herb to use to flavor a special dish or to add an extra layer of flavor to your favorite meal. Try lemon thyme on roasted chicken, meats, or vegetables for a new and exciting flavor.

ROASTED PECANS

Makes 4 servings

This is another great on-the-run snack. It is also an integral component of Pumpkin Granola (page 76) and Peanut Butter Chicken Salad (page 208).

1 tablespoon butter
1 cup pecan pieces, broken
¼ teaspoon SteviaPlus
¼ teaspoon cinnamon
¼ teaspoon vanilla
2 packets sucralose

1. Soften the butter in the microwave for 15 seconds. Place the pecans into a mixing bowl. Pour the butter over the pecans and stir them well to coat. Stir the remaining ingredients into the pecans, coating them evenly.
2. Place the coated nuts onto a baking sheet and bake at 325°F for 10 minutes. Cool the nuts thoroughly before eating.

NUTRITIONAL INFORMATION PER SERVING:
Carbohydrates: 5 grams • Effective Carb Count: 3 grams
Protein: 2 grams • Fat: 21 grams • Calories: 207

ROASTED PUMPKIN SEEDS

Serves 2

Ooo! These are good! Save the seeds from Baked Winter Squash (page 216) after you've baked it. Rinse them, allow them to dry, and then follow this recipe for really fresh pumpkin seeds!

1 tablespoon cooking oil
½ teaspoon fresh, snipped rosemary (or ¼ teaspoon dried)
¼ teaspoon fresh, snipped lemon thyme (or ⅛ teaspoon dried thyme leaves)
⅛ teaspoon lemon pepper
⅛ teaspoon garlic granules
3 drops hot chili oil or a tiny pinch of cayenne
⅓ cup pumpkin seeds, raw, shelled (or any raw, shelled nut would work)
Seasoning salt, to taste

1. In a small frying pan, place the cooking oil, rosemary, lemon thyme, lemon pepper, garlic, and chili oil.
2. If you like your food hot and spicy, up to ½ teaspoon hot chili oil may be added at this time. Be aware that the heat of this spice intensifies as it cooks, so allow for this in your seasoning.
3. Warm the oil and spices over medium heat until the herbs begin to smell, about 1½ minutes. Add the pumpkin seeds, stirring frequently until they lose their green hue and begin to turn very pale tan, about 1½ minutes. Do *not* overcook them! If they become brown, all that will be left will be a hollow crispy "shell" of a seed!
4. Season with seasoning salt and enjoy!

NUTRITIONAL INFORMATION PER SERVING:
Carbohydrates: trace • Effective Carb Count: 0 grams
Protein: trace • Fat: 7 grams • Calories: 65

REDUCED-FAT VARIATION:
Use 1 teaspoon oil.
Carbohydrates: trace • Effective Carb Count: 0 grams
Protein: trace • Fat: 3 grams • Calories: 25

RUTABAGA CHIPS

Makes 2 servings

Rutabagas are excellent sources of calcium, potassium, and vitamin A. They are also reported to be very helpful in the healing process of candida infections. This recipe also works very well with Jerusalem artichokes, which have the same beneficial properties.

One rutabaga, medium sized
Lard for frying
Seasoning salt

1. You have to have a food processor with a slicer for this one because rutabagas are *so* hard! Thinly slice the rutabaga into about 1½" to 2" slices.
2. Heat a 3- to 5-quart saucepan half filled with water to a full, rolling boil. Carefully place the sliced rutabagas into the water and return to boiling. Boil the rutabaga slices for 5 minutes or until they begin to become slightly translucent. Pour them into a colander and pour cold running water over them. This stops the cooking process and allows them to cool completely.
3. In the same pot, with the water removed and the pot dried, or in a large deep fryer or wok, heat about 3" of lard. Heat the lard until it is very hot (375°F) and cook the slices about 6 minutes, turning occasionally until they are slightly dark. These chips get cooked slightly past what is "perfect color" for potato chips. They need the extra color because they start out darker. Drain them on paper towels and season with seasoning salt. They crisp up as they cool.

NUTRITIONAL INFORMATION PER SERVING:
Carbohydrates: 6 grams • Effective Carb Count: 4 grams
Protein: 1 gram • Fat: 5 grams • Calories: 65

Sharron's Beef Jerky

Makes about 36 servings

This is the perfect candida-friendly snack. Since traditional beef jerky always uses soy sauce, this recipe is a great variation and can be modified easily according to taste.

3 1/2 to 4 pounds beef steak or roast
4 tablespoons lime juice, fresh
1/2 teaspoon garlic granules (or 1 clove garlic, minced)
1 1/2 teaspoons lemon pepper
1 tablespoon seasoning salt
1 tablespoon minced onion, dried, or 1/4 cup fresh, minced
1 teaspoon ginger
1/2 teaspoon dry mustard powder
1 teaspoon hot chili oil or a pinch of cayenne
1/8 to 1/4 teaspoon SteviaPlus (or 1/2 to 2 packets sucralose) depending upon taste
1 1/2 cups beef Rich Stock (page 254) or commercially prepared stock

1. Make thin slices of beef by slicing it at an angle across the grain of the meat. Some prefer to partially freeze the meat before slicing, but I find that slicing at an angle with a very sharp knife does just fine. Set the beef aside.
2. Place the remaining ingredients into a large nonmetal bowl with a lid, stirring well to combine. Add the beef, mixing thoroughly.
3. Allow the meat to marinate refrigerated at least overnight, turning and shaking the container occasionally to stir it. If the meat is very fresh, it can be marinated up to 3 days. The flavors will intensify the longer it remains in the marinade.
4. When you are ready to dry the meat, lay it out on the drying racks of a food dehydrator. Discard the marinade. Dry the meat for about 4 to 6 hours. Alternatively, it may be dried on baking sheets in an oven set on the lowest setting for about 4 hours.
5. To test the jerky for doneness: The meat should no longer be mushy. It should be firm, but not crisp. Turn the dehydrator off when you believe it is getting close to being done and allow the meat to cool. It will continue to firm up as it cools. The jerky should be able to bend and show fibers when it is bent. That is how you will know when it is done. After this step, I usually have a few pieces that need a little more dehydration. I remove the pieces that are done drying and turn the machine back on for about 1/2 hour with the remaining pieces still in it. Then I turn it off and allow it to cool back down again. That usually finishes the job. Store the jerky in a plastic bag in the refrigerator.

Nutritional information per serving:
Carbohydrates: trace • Effective Carb Count: 0 grams
Protein: 11 grams • Fat: 4 grams • Calories: 81

SMOKED SALMON DIP

Makes 12 servings

Smoked Salmon Dip is the perfect appetizer when you have special company coming for dinner. This recipe is a delightful way to use Smoked Salmon (page 184), no matter what the occasion!

1 cup smoked salmon
2 cups sour cream
1 tablespoon minced onion, dried
1 ½ teaspoons dill weed
½ teaspoon orange zest
¼ teaspoon seasoning salt

Combine all of the ingredients in a small bowl and mix them thoroughly. Chill for at least 30 minutes before serving. Serve with veggies or pork rinds.

NUTRITIONAL INFORMATION PER SERVING:
Carbohydrates: 2 grams • Effective Carb Count: 2 grams
Protein: 3 grams • Fat: 9 grams • Calories: 97

REDUCED-FAT VARIATION:
Use low-fat sour cream.
Carbohydrates: 2 grams • Effective Carb Count: 2 grams
Protein: 3 grams • Fat: 1 gram • Calories: 28

Do-it-yourself dried orange or lemon rind: Grated orange rind or lemon rind is useful to have and is a snap to make with a food processor. Just put the leftover peel, without the membranes, in the food processor with the chopping blade in place. Chop the peel until it is finely ground. Lay the chopped peel out on a baking sheet in an oven set at the lowest temperature for about 2 hours or until it looks well dried (a deep golden brown) but not scorched. It can also be left out to air-dry in some low-use area for a couple of days. No worries about overdrying that way! Store in an air-tight container.

SPINACH DIP

Makes 12 servings

Serve it with your favorite sliced meats and veggies. Cucumber and jicama slices are particularly nice! Also, if you start with chilled ingredients, the chilling time can be omitted or reduced if you are in a hurry!

½ cup Blender Mayonnaise (page 241) or
commercially prepared mayonnaise
¾ cup sour cream
½ cup jicama, finely chopped
½ cup spinach, finely chopped (about 8 large leaves)
1 teaspoon chives, chopped (fresh would be great!)
1 teaspoon parsley flakes (fresh would be great!)
1 ½ teaspoons minced onion, dried
¼ teaspoon lemon pepper
½ teaspoon seasoning salt

In a medium-sized bowl, combine all of the ingredients and mix them thoroughly. Chill the dip for about ½ hour.

NUTRITIONAL INFORMATION PER SERVING:
Carbohydrates: 1 gram • Effective Carb Count: 1 gram
Protein: 1 gram • Fat: 11 grams • Calories: 100

REDUCED-FAT VARIATION:
Use reduced-fat sour cream and mayonnaise.
Carbohydrates: 3 grams • Effective Carb Count: 3 grams
Protein: trace • Fat: 2 grams • Calories: 31

SWEET AND SPICY ALMONDS

Serves 2

These almonds are a snap to make. They are a perfect salad topper and a fun snack that kids will love!

½ tablespoon butter
¼ teaspoon cinnamon
⅛ teaspoon SteviaPlus
1 packet sucralose
⅓ cup almonds, blanched
¼ teaspoon orange zest
¼ teaspoon almond extract

1. Place the butter, cinnamon, SteviaPlus, and sucralose in a small frying pan. Warm over medium heat about 1 minute.
2. Add the almonds and heat them through, stirring frequently until the seasonings begin to really smell good and the almonds begin to get faintly darker than their normal white color, about 3 minutes. Remove the pan from the heat.
3. Add the orange zest and almond extract, combining thoroughly. Pour the nuts into a serving dish and serve warm.

NUTRITIONAL INFORMATION PER SERVING:
Carbohydrates: 5 grams • Effective Carb Count: 2 grams
Protein: 5 grams • Fat: 15 grams • Calories: 167

Why butter and lard for cooking instead of cooking oils? I learned on *www.WestonAPrice.org* that the sources of fats in our diet can be vitally important to our health. In a nutshell, natural fats, such as butter and lard, do not require "rearranging" by our bodies for processing. The man-made liquid oils are also know as "trans fats" and are linked to cancer and many other health troubles. By making the switch to the natural fats of older generations, many have experienced a great increase in quality of life. My quality of life actually improved a lot once I switched from cooking with oil to using lard as my primary cooking fat. My allergy symptoms, low thyroid symptoms, and fibromyalgia symptoms all improved greatly!

Zucchini "Bread" Patties

Makes 6 servings

These tasty Zucchini "Bread" Patties taste just as good as they smell, and they're simple to make. They make a great afternoon treat for the kids or a nice sweet appetizer at a gathering of friends and family!

½ pound zucchini
1 egg
½ teaspoon vanilla
¾ cup pork rinds, crushed
½ teaspoon cinnamon
¼ teaspoon nutmeg
⅛ teaspoon orange (or lemon) zest
½ teaspoon SteviaPlus
2 packets sucralose
¼ cup pecan halves
Butter for cooking

1. Using a food processor with a shredding disk, or by hand, finely shred the zucchini. Place the shredded zucchini into a mixing bowl. Add the egg and vanilla, and mix well.
2. In a separate bowl, combine the pork rinds, cinnamon, nutmeg, orange zest, SteviaPlus, and sucralose. Mix well and add it to the zucchini mixture. Stir in the pecan halves and allow the batter to rest 3 to 5 minutes.
3. In a skillet, melt 1 tablespoon butter over medium heat. Form the batter into 1½" to 2" patties, being sure to tuck at least 1 pecan piece into the center of each patty. Fry them until golden on each side, about 4 minutes total. For each subsequent batch, add more butter to the pan as needed. Serve warm.

Nutritional information per serving:
Carbohydrates: 2 grams • Effective Carb Count: 1 gram
Protein: 2 grams • Fat: 6 grams • Calories: 71

Zucchini Cakes

Serves 4

This is a simple low-carb appetizer that will even please a die-hard zucchini hater! These cakes are a really nice complement to a simple meal of soup and salad.

½ pound zucchini
1 green onion
1 egg
¾ cup pork rinds, ground
⅛ teaspoon lemon pepper
¼ teaspoon garlic salt
⅛ teaspoon dill weed
1 tablespoon butter
¼ cup lard

1. Using a food processor with a grating disk, or by hand, shred the zucchini. Using the chopping blade, or by hand, mince the onion. Place the zucchini and onion into a mixing bowl and add the egg, pork rinds, lemon pepper, garlic salt, and dill weed.
2. Melt the butter and lard in a large skillet over medium heat. Shape the zucchini mixture into 1½" patties and carefully place into the hot oil. Fry the patties until they are golden brown on each side, about 8 minutes total. Serve hot with sauces of choice.

Nutritional information per serving:
Carbohydrates: 2 grams • Effective Carb Count: 1 gram
Protein: 3 grams • Fat: 18 grams • Calories: 175

ZUCCHINI PUFFS

Makes about 28 puffs

Do you love Tater Tots? Now you can enjoy this fantastic low-carb variation of that drive-in treat!

½ cup soy protein powder (not soy flour!)
1 teaspoon baking powder
½ teaspoon seasoning salt
1 teaspoon parsley flakes
¹⁄₁₆ teaspoon chipotle pepper granules,
roasted (or a few grains of cayenne)
¼ teaspoon onion powder
¼ teaspoon garlic powder
1 cup zucchini, shredded, including juices
1 egg
Lard or other cooking oil

1. In a mixing bowl, combine all of the dry ingredients and mix them well. Add the zucchini and egg to the dry ingredients, beating well to incorporate them fully into the batter. Allow the batter to rest for about 5 minutes.
2. Heat about 1" of lard in a frying pan over medium heat. Carefully drop the batter into the hot oil by teaspoonfuls. I like to use another spoon to push the batter off the scooping spoon to drop the dough into the hot oil. I'm much less likely to burn myself that way!
3. Cook the Puffs until they are golden brown, about 2 minutes total, turning them over halfway through the cooking time. Remove them from the oil and drain them on paper towels. Be careful–they will be very hot on the inside!

NUTRITIONAL INFORMATION PER SERVING:
Carbohydrates: 2 grams • Effective Carb Count: 0 grams
Protein: 18 grams • Fat: 11 grams • Calories: 181

Salads

BROCCOLI SLAW

Makes 8 servings

Broccoli slaw is available in the bagged salad section of most good produce departments. Next time you go shopping, pick up a bag and enjoy this crunchy, delicious alternative to coleslaw!

½ cup sour cream
2 tablespoons half-and-half
2 teaspoons minced onion, dried
½ teaspoon dill weed
½ teaspoon orange zest
½ teaspoon lemon pepper
½ teaspoon seasoning salt
¼ teaspoon SteviaPlus
2 packets sucralose
1 tablespoon lime juice, fresh
6 cups broccoli slaw

Combine all of the ingredients except the broccoli slaw. Mix them well. Add the broccoli slaw and stir well to coat.

NUTRITIONAL INFORMATION PER SERVING:
Carbohydrates: 11 grams • Effective Carb Count: 6 grams
Protein: 1 gram • Fat: 3 grams • Calories: 92

REDUCED-FAT VARIATION:
Use low-fat sour cream and skim milk.
Carbohydrates: 11 grams • Effective Carb Count: 6 grams
Protein: trace • Fat: trace • Calories: 63

It's easy to make a very basic broccoli slaw, too! Simply cut the stems off of several large stalks of broccoli. Using a grater or the shredding disk of a food processor, grate the stems. That is it–you've got freshly prepared broccoli slaw!

Greek Salad

Serves 6

Add some Easy Lemon Pepper Chicken (page 201) or your favorite grilled fish to this and turn this simple salad into a succulent meal!

Dressing:

6 tablespoons olive oil
4 tablespoons lime juice, fresh, and/or red wine vinegar
1 1/2 teaspoons oregano
1/8 teaspoon seasoning salt
1/8 teaspoon lemon pepper

Salad:

1 head romaine lettuce, rinsed, dried, and chopped
1 red onion, thinly sliced, or equivalent green onions, cut up
1 6-ounce can black olives, pitted and sliced
1 red bell pepper, chopped
2 large tomatoes, chopped
1 cucumber, sliced
1 cup feta cheese, crumbled

1. In a small bowl, combine the dressing ingredients. Set them aside.
2. In a large salad bowl, combine the remaining salad ingredients. Drizzle the dressing over the salad and toss the salad well.

Nutritional information per serving:
Carbohydrates: 12 grams • Effective Carb Count: 8 grams
Protein: 7 grams • Fat: 19 grams • Calories: 239

Reduced-Fat Variation:
Use 2 tablespoons olive oil.
Carbohydrates: 12 grams • Effective Carb Count: 8 grams
Protein: 7 grams • Fat: 10 grams • Calories: 159

Marinated Asparagus Salad with Almonds

Serves 6

Bring this recipe to your next get-together or potluck. This salad is quite elegant and delicious–don't expect any leftovers!

Dressing:
2 tablespoons lemon juice, fresh
3 tablespoons olive oil
½ teaspoon seasoning salt
¼ teaspoon lemon pepper
2 small sprigs lemon thyme, minced (or ½ teaspoon dried thyme leaves)
⅛ teaspoon celery seed
1/16 teaspoon dill weed (that is ½ of ⅛ teaspoon!)
¼ teaspoon Sweet & Slender

Salad ingredients:
1 ½ pounds asparagus
¼ cup almonds, sliced thinly
2 strawberries (optional)
2 mint sprigs (optional)

1. Combine the dressing ingredients in a small bowl and set the dressing aside.
2. Wash and break tough ends from the asparagus. Place the asparagus in a pan with ½" water. Cover and bring to a boil. Boil the asparagus for 8 minutes, or until crisp-tender. Immediately remove the pot from the heat and drain it. Cover the asparagus in cold water to keep it from continuing to cook.
3. After it is cooled, cut it into 2" lengths and place the pieces into a shallow serving dish, like a pie pan or quiche plate. Pour the dressing over the top of the asparagus and stir it gently. At this point the salad may be covered and marinated overnight.
4. Just before serving, sprinkle the almonds around the outside edge of the dish. Slice the strawberries and arrange them like a flower in the middle of the dish. Tuck the mint sprigs into the strawberry flower.

Nutritional information per serving:
Carbohydrates: 4 grams • Effective Carb Count: 2 grams
Protein: 2 grams • Fat: 8 grams • Calories: 86

Reduced-Fat Variation:
Use 1 ½ tablespoons olive oil.
Carbohydrates: 4 grams • Effective Carb Count: 2 grams
Protein: 2 grams • Fat: 5 grams • Calories: 64

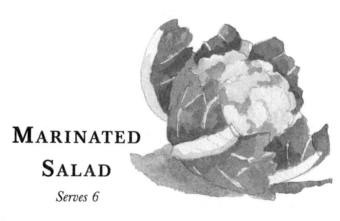

MARINATED
SALAD

Serves 6

There is a beautiful retreat center in the heart of the Willamette Valley in Oregon that serves a salad similar to this. That was the inspiration for this recipe. Enjoy!

2 cups cauliflower florets, cut into bite-sized pieces
2 cups broccoli florets, cut into bite-sized pieces
1 carrot, cut into bite-sized pieces (optional)
1 cup pitted black olives

Dressing:

2 tablespoons fresh lemon juice
3 tablespoons olive oil
½ teaspoon seasoning salt
¼ teaspoon lemon pepper
2 small sprigs lemon thyme, minced (or ½ teaspoon dried thyme leaves)
⅛ teaspoon celery seed
1/16 teaspoon dried dill weed (that is ½ of ⅛ teaspoon!)
¼ teaspoon Sweet & Slender

Combine the cauliflower, broccoli, carrot, and olives in a serving dish. Sprinkle all of the remaining ingredients over the vegetables and toss well. The salad may be served immediately or covered and allowed to marinate in the refrigerator overnight. Either way, it is yummy!

NUTRITIONAL INFORMATION PER SERVING:
Carbohydrates: 5 grams • Effective Carb Count: 3 grams
Protein: 1 grams • Fat: 7 grams • Calories: 83

REDUCED FAT VARIATION:
Use 1½ tablespoons olive oil and follow all remaining instructions as given.
Carbohydrates: 5 grams • Effective Carb Count: 3 grams
Protein: 1 gram • Fat: 4 grams • Calories: 60

MOCK POTATO SALAD

Serves 6

Many folks love potato salad, but once they embark on the low-carb way of life, it is out of their eating plan. Now you can enjoy "potato" salad without the negative side effects. Even folks who don't like ordinary potato salad enjoy this one!

1 pound cauliflower, cut into ½" dice (fresh or frozen)
1 tablespoon minced onion, dried, or ¼ cup fresh onion, minced
1 large stalk celery, chopped
3 strips bacon, cooked and crumbled
2 hard-cooked eggs, chopped
¼ cup ranch dip—made with sour cream from a packet, Creamy Ranch Salad
Dressing (page 244), or Creamy Roasted Garlic Salad Dressing (page 245)
½ teaspoon seasoning salt
¼ teaspoon lemon pepper
¼ cup sliced olives (optional)
½ tablespoon parsley flakes

1. Pour about 1" of water into a medium-sized saucepan with a lid and add the cauliflower. Cook it covered over medium heat until it is done, about 5 to 8 minutes. It should still be slightly firm when done. Immediately run cold water over the cauliflower to stop it from cooking any further. Make sure it is completely cooled, drain it, then set it aside.
2. Place the drained cauliflower and the remaining ingredients, except the parsley, into a serving bowl. Stir them well to combine. Garnish the salad with the parsley flakes. Serve chilled.

NUTRITIONAL INFORMATION PER SERVING:
Carbohydrates: 8 grams • Effective Carb Count: 6 grams
Protein: 5 grams • Fat: 5 grams • Calories: 97

REDUCED-FAT VARIATION:
Use low-fat sour cream in the dressing
and turkey bacon instead of those listed.
Carbohydrates: 8 grams • Effective Carb Count: 6 grams
Protein: 5 grams • Fat: 3 grams • Calories: 79

SESAME SLAW

Serves 4

This is a fun, low-carb variation of a popular coleslaw that ordinarily uses ramen noodles. Serve with Barbecue Pork (page 95).

1 tablespoon lemon juice, fresh
2 tablespoons olive oil
1 teaspoon sesame oil
Pinch SteviaPlus or sucralose (ever so much less than ⅛ teaspoon!)
1 teaspoon chives, snipped (optional)
2 sprigs lemon thyme, chopped (optional)
½ teaspoon seasoning salt
¼ teaspoon lemon pepper
2 cups cabbage, shredded
1 tablespoon sesame seeds

Combine the lemon juice, olive oil, sesame oil, SteviaPlus, chives, lemon thyme, seasoning salt, and lemon pepper in a medium-sized bowl, and mix well. Add the shredded cabbage and sesame seeds. Toss well.

NUTRITIONAL INFORMATION PER SERVING:
Carbohydrates: 3 grams • Effective Carb Count: 2 grams
Protein: 1 gram • Fat: 9 grams • Calories: 93

REDUCED-FAT VARIATION:
Use 2 teaspoons olive oil.
Carbohydrates: 3 grams • Effective Carb Count: 2 grams
Protein: 1 gram • Fat: 5 grams • Calories: 53

SHARRON'S LAYERED SALAD

Serves 12

This is a low-carb version of that traditional potluck favorite. Enjoy it at your next get-together! Instead of the shrimp, cooked chicken or crab may be used.

Dressing:
1 cup yogurt, whole milk, or sour cream (see instructions)
1 cup Blender Mayonnaise (page 241)
½ teaspoon SteviaPlus
¼ teaspoon Sweet & Slender

Salad ingredients:
4 to 5 cups romaine lettuce, chopped
1 cucumber, peeled and chopped into ½" to ¾" chunks
2 cups red cabbage, shredded
½ pound snow peas
2 cups salad shrimp, cooked
4 ounces Monterey jack cheese, shredded
1 12-ounce package bacon, cooked and cut up
1 tablespoon parsley flakes

1. In a small bowl, combine all of the dressing ingredients and mix well. Set dressing aside. If you want a thick dressing that stays in one layer at the top of the salad, use sour cream. If you want a dressing that is more pourable and will soak through the salad for a more even coating, use yogurt.
2. In a 9" × 13" × 2" pan, place the lettuce in an even layer. Place the chopped cucumber in an even layer on top of the lettuce. Spread the shredded cabbage atop the cucumber.
3. Blanch the snow peas: Fill a medium-sized saucepan with water and bring to a boil. Put the snow peas into the pan and cook them for 2 minutes. Drain them in a colander and pour cold running water over them until they are completely cooled. When the snow peas are cooled, cut them into 1" to 1½" lengths and place them over the cabbage in the salad dish.
4. Rinse the shrimp and drain them well. Place the shrimp over the snow peas; then spread the dressing evenly over the shrimp. Sprinkle the cheese, then the bacon, and finally the parsley over the top of the salad. Allow the salad to rest at least 20 minutes up to overnight before serving.

NUTRITIONAL INFORMATION PER SERVING:
Carbohydrates: 3 grams • Effective Carb Count: 2 grams
Protein: 10 grams • Fat: 23 grams • Calories: 245

REDUCED-FAT VARIATION:
Use low-fat yogurt or sour cream, reduced-fat mayonnaise, reduced-fat cheese and turkey bacon.
Carbohydrates: 6 grams • Effective Carb Count: 5 grams
Protein: 10 grams • Fat: 8 grams • Calories: 137

SPINACH SALAD
WITH LEMON DRESSING

Makes 4 servings

This is such an easy, tasty dressing–the lemon and oil complement each other perfectly. To make this salad into a single main-dish serving, add 1 cup chopped cooked meat to the salad and use as many of the additional ingredients as possible. It makes a very satisfying lunch!

3 cups spinach, fresh, washed and stemmed
8 black olives, sliced
1 tablespoon lemon juice, fresh
1 1/2 tablespoons olive oil
1/4 teaspoon seasoning salt
1/8 teaspoon lemon pepper

Optional additional ingredients:

1/2 tablespoon chives, fresh, snipped
2 tablespoons parsley, fresh, snipped
1/4 cup Parmesan cheese, freshly grated
3 slices bacon, cooked and crumbled
2 radishes, thinly sliced
1 green onion, sliced
1 hard-boiled egg, sliced
2 tablespoons sunflower seeds

Combine the spinach, olives, lemon juice, olive oil, seasoning salt, and lemon pepper in a serving bowl. Add any additional ingredients desired. Mix well. Garnish with hard-boiled egg and sunflower seeds.

NUTRITIONAL INFORMATION PER SERVING (INCLUDING ALL OPTIONS):
Carbohydrates: 3 grams • Effective Carb Count: 2 grams
Protein: 6 grams • Fat: 14 grams • Calories: 162

REDUCED-FAT VARIATION:
For the optional ingredients, use turkey bacon and reduced-fat cheese.
Carbohydrates: 3 grams • Effective Carb Count: 2 grams
Protein: 6 grams • Fat: 12 grams • Calories: 144

SUMMER CUCUMBER SALAD

Makes 4 servings

Enjoy the summer's bountiful supply in this recipe. It is delightful served immediately, but the flavors blend and enhance each other as it marinates.

3 8" cucumbers, peeled and sliced
1 cup jicama, sweet red pepper, or both, cut into 1/2" sections (optional)
3/4 cup sweet onion, cut into 1/2" sections
4 to 6 mint leaves, fresh, chopped (about 1 teaspoon)
3/4 teaspoon lemon thyme, fresh, chopped
1/4 cup lemon juice, fresh
1/4 cup water
1/2 cup olive oil
1/2 teaspoon Sweet & Slender
1/2 teaspoon seasoning salt
1/8 teaspoon lemon pepper
1/8 teaspoon celery seed (optional)

1. Combine all of the ingredients in a tightly covered container. If you don't
   have any fresh mint leaves, an unused mint tea bag will work. Just be sure it
   is just mint—not mint plus other things! Simply open it up and measure the
   amount of mint you need. If you don't have any fresh lemon thyme, dried
   thyme leaves are a suitable substitute.
2. Shake well and refrigerate overnight. Allow to come to room temperature
   approximately 15 minutes before serving.

NUTRITIONAL INFORMATION PER SERVING:
Carbohydrates: 11 grams • Effective Carb Count: 8 grams
Protein: 2 grams • Fat: 27 grams • Calories: 287

REDUCED-FAT VARIATION:
Use 2 tablespoons olive oil.
Carbohydrates: 11 grams • Effective Carb Count: 3 grams
Protein: 2 grams • Fat: 7 grams • Calories: 108

YUMMY COLESLAW

Serves 6, with enough dressing left over for 1 more salad

The shrimp is a great addition to this recipe. Serve along with Barbecue Pork (page 95) for a fun cookout treat.

½ small head of cabbage

Optional additions to salad:

*1 ½ teaspoons each snipped fresh garden herbs
like lemon thyme, parsley, chives
⅛ teaspoon dill weed
3 ounces salad shrimp, cooked*

Dressing:

*½ cup Blender Mayonnaise (page 241) or
commercially prepared mayonnaise
¼ cup Almond Milk (page 240) or cream
2 tablespoons lemon juice, fresh
½ teaspoon SteviaPlus
1 packet sucralose
¼ teaspoon celery seed
½ teaspoon seasoning salt
⅛ teaspoon lemon pepper*

1. In a food processor with a slicing blade, or by hand, shred the cabbage. Place the shredded cabbage into a large bowl, adding any of the optional ingredients you desire. Set it aside.
2. In a separate container, combine all of the ingredients for the dressing. Add half of the dressing to the salad fixings, and stir well. Store the extra dressing in a covered container in the refrigerator for up to 2 weeks.

NUTRITIONAL INFORMATION PER SERVING (INCLUDING ALL OPTIONS):
Carbohydrates: 5 grams • Effective Carb Count: 3 grams
Protein: 4 grams • Fat: 8 grams • Calories: 101

REDUCED-FAT VARIATION:
Use reduced-fat mayonnaise and canned skim milk.
Carbohydrates: 7 grams • Effective Carb Count: 5 grams
Protein: 5 grams • Fat: 2 grams • Calories: 62

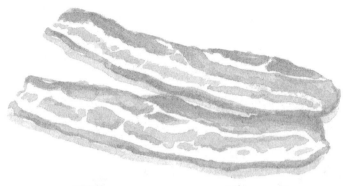

Breakfasts

1946 Pork Sausage

Makes 16 servings

This is my sister's favorite sausage recipe. When she got married in 1969, she was given a set of cookbooks that were printed in 1946. This simple, "old time" sausage recipe came from those cookbooks. If you like things hot, use up to 1 ½ teaspoons cayenne to spice things up.

4 pounds ground pork
1 teaspoon cayenne pepper
1 teaspoon sea salt
1 ½ teaspoons lemon pepper
2 teaspoons ground sage

Combine all ingredients in a mixing bowl. Mix well. Form into patties or crumble and cook in a frying pan until well done.

Nutritional information per serving:
Carbohydrates: trace • Effective Carb Count: 0 grams
Protein: 19 grams • Fat: 24 grams • Calories: 300

Reduced-Fat Variation:
Use lean ground beef, chicken, or turkey instead of the pork.
(Lean ground turkey calculated below.)
Carbohydrates: trace • Effective Carb Count: 0 grams
Protein: 23 grams • Fat: 8 grams • Calories: 163

The staples of the low-carb way of eating are quite different from those of many other popular ways of eating. One of the most basic elements is butter. Be sure to use real, creamy butter, not margarine or some imitation butter-flavored spread, because those contain dangerous trans fats, which are linked to cancer. Even if you are following The Zone's reduced-fat plan, butter is a far healthier alternative than the imitations available. Some grocers even carry real butter in a "light" version.

BACON CAULI HASH

Serves 6

A great thing to do with leftover Bacon Cauli Jumble (page 94)! This is a very hearty breakfast, very suitable for brunch or lunch.

4 cups Bacon Cauli Jumble
1 tablespoon lard
¼ teaspoon seasoning salt
4 eggs
½ cup cheese, shredded (Colby, Monterey jack, Cheddar, or blend)
Low-carb tortillas or High-Protein Wraps (page 225), optional

1. Cook the Jumble in the lard over medium heat in a large frying pan for 15 minutes or until browned, turning about halfway through.
2. In a small bowl, whisk together the seasoning salt and eggs. Pour the eggs over the hash in the pan and cook until almost set. Top the eggs with the cheese, but *do not stir* the cheese in. Immediately place the hash into a serving dish.

NUTRITIONAL INFORMATION PER SERVING:
Carbohydrates: 1 gram • Effective Carb Count: 0 grams
Protein: 18 grams • Fat: 20 grams • Calories: 262

REDUCED-FAT VARIATION:
Use the Reduced-Fat Variation for the Bacon Cauli Jumble and cook it using cooking spray instead of the suggested method. Use low-fat cheese.
Carbohydrates: 1 gram • Effective Carb Count: 0 grams
Protein: 18 grams • Fat: 15 grams • Calories: 221

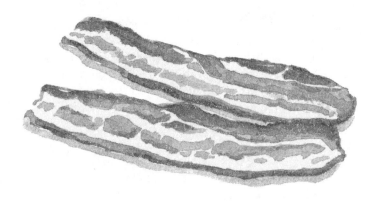

BEST BACON

Makes about 12 servings

I'm sure you're wondering why I am putting cooking instructions for bacon in this cookbook when the directions are right on the package. For picture-perfect bacon every time, follow these easy steps.

1 pound bacon, cured without sugar and nitrates, if available

1. Lay bacon out evenly on a large baking sheet. Be sure edges don't overlap. All of the bacon may not fit on the baking sheet at first. The bacon will shrink as it cooks, leaving excess room. The additional slices may be added in at that time.
2. Place baking sheet in 350°F oven for approximately 30 minutes. Remove when the fatty portion is translucent; it should no longer be white. It won't appear brown the way panfried bacon does, but the meat will be a deep red color. If it is overcooked, it will crumble when cooled. If it is perfect, it will be tender and juicy. It will also lay out flat, rather than being curly and lumpy. Place on a serving plate lined with paper towels to drain.

NUTRITIONAL INFORMATION PER SERVING:
Carbohydrates: trace • Effective Carb Count: trace
Protein: 11 grams • Fat: 19 grams • Calories: 218

REDUCED-FAT VARIATION:
Use turkey bacon.
Carbohydrates: 1 gram • Effective Carb Count: 1 gram
Protein: 6 grams • Fat: 7 grams • Calories: 92

Save the bacon grease in a jar with a lid, and you'll get some "free" cooking oil out of it! If you are using a glass container, just be sure to place a metal object, such as a table knife or a spoon into the jar before you pour the hot grease into it. Pour the grease in so it touches the metal object first. Otherwise, the glass will explode from contact with the heat. Use bacon grease in any recipe that requires just a little cooking fat for browning the food.

BREAKFAST BURRITOS

Serves 4

A quick and easy way to eat breakfast on the run! Extras can be wrapped in plastic wrap and frozen for later use. Just warm them in the oven or microwave and you're set to go.

4 commercially prepared low-carb tortillas or
High-Protein Wraps (page 225)
4 slices (4 ounces) Monterey jack cheese
4 slices bacon, cooked
4 eggs
Seasoning salt
Butter or lard for frying

Optional:

Commercially prepared salsa
Sour cream
Chives

1. Quickly pass the commercial tortillas through running water and allow them to rest for approximately 3 minutes. (Don't pass the High-Protein Wraps under the water.) Heat a large skillet over medium heat and place tortillas into skillet one at a time, warming on each side about 30 to 45 seconds. Remove to plates. Place the cheese and bacon down the center of each tortilla.
2. Meanwhile, combine the eggs and seasoning salt to taste in a small bowl, mixing them thoroughly. Melt the butter in a medium skillet over medium heat. Pour the eggs into the skillet and allow them to cook without stirring until the bottom becomes opaque and solid enough to flip, about 1½ minutes. Turn the eggs over and cook them until they are done. Cut them into 4 equal pieces. Put 1 piece onto each tortilla. Fold the tortillas up at the bottom and then over on each side. Serve with optional ingredients at the table.

NUTRITIONAL INFORMATION PER SERVING:
Carbohydrates: 13 grams • Effective Carb Count: 4 grams
Protein: 19 grams • Fat: 21 grams • Calories: 297

REDUCED-FAT VARIATION:
Use turkey bacon, reduced-fat cheese, and cooking spray.
Carbohydrates: 13 grams • Effective Carb Count: 4 grams
Protein: 20 grams • Fat: 11 grams • Calories: 209

Broccoli, Steak, and Eggs

Serves 4

Oh, so good! Sometimes it is hard for low-carbers to get their veggies in. This is one delicious way to do it!

1 onion, chopped (about 1 cup)
2 cloves garlic, minced
1 tablespoon butter
1 tablespoon lard
1 pound beef cubed steak, cut into 4 servings
1/2 teaspoon seasoning salt
1 pound broccoli, chopped (fresh or frozen)
4 eggs

1. In a large frying pan, cook the onion and the garlic in the butter and the lard over medium heat until they begin to turn golden, about 5 minutes.
2. Add the steaks to the pan, and season with seasoning salt as desired. Put the onions on the tops of the steaks and brown the steaks 3 to 5 minutes. Flip the steaks, causing the onions to go underneath, and continue to cook them until they are nicely browned, 8 to 10 minutes total. Remove the steaks to a serving platter and cover them to keep them warm.
3. Leave the onions in the pan. Stir the broccoli and seasoning salt into the onions, adding additional fat if necessary to keep it from sticking to the pan. Cook and stir about 5 minutes or until the broccoli is crisp-tender. Place the veggies in a serving dish.
4. To serve: Place each steak onto a plate. Cook the egg, sunny-side up or over-easy–fry them quickly so the yolks remain liquid, and put them on the tops of the steaks. Serve the broccoli as a side dish. Break the yolks and enjoy dipping everything in the "runny eggs"!

Nutritional information per serving:
Carbohydrates: 7 grams • Effective Carb Count: 4 grams
Protein: 30 grams • Fat: 26 grams • Calories: 381

Reduced-Fat Variation:
Use a small amount of Rich Stock (page 254) to cook the onions and garlic. Use cooking spray to keep the meat and veggies from sticking to the pan. Continue as directed.
Carbohydrates: 7 grams • Effective Carb Count: 4 grams
Protein: 30 grams • Fat: 19 grams • Calories: 327

Chubby Pancakes

Serves 2

Pancakes always remind me of Sunday mornings when I was growing up. Now they can be low-carb! These are very good served with almond butter and Sugar-Free Pancake Syrup (page 256).

2 eggs
½ cup Almond Milk (page 240) or
¼ cup cream thinned to ½ cup with water
½ teaspoon vanilla
½ cup pork rinds, ground
3 tablespoons almonds, ground
2 tablespoons soy protein (not soy flour!)
⅛ teaspoon SteviaPlus
1 packet sucralose
½ teaspoon cinnamon
Lard or butter for frying

1. Combine the eggs, Almond Milk, and vanilla in a mixing bowl. Mix them thoroughly.
2. In a separate bowl, combine the pork rinds, ground almonds, SteviaPlus, sucralose, and cinnamon. Add the dry ingredients to the wet ingredients, stirring them well. Allow this mixture to rest for a few minutes. If it is too thick, add a little more Almond Milk until the desired consistency is reached.
3. Heat a large frying pan. Add enough fat to the pan to cover the bottom. Pour the batter into the pan, pancake style. Brown the pancakes on each side and serve them hot.

NUTRITIONAL INFORMATION PER SERVING:
Carbohydrates: 5 grams • Effective Carb Count: 3 grams
Protein: 22 grams • Fat: 34 grams • Calories: 397

What oils/fats are best for cooking? While olive oil is great for salad dressings, it is not ideal to fry with, since it scorches at such a low temperature. The same goes for butter. However, if you are looking for that great buttery flavor without the scorching, simply combine a heat-stable fat, like lard, with the butter and fry.

Cookie Dough Hot Cereal

Makes about 9 servings

This fun recipe came out of some experimentation with ingredients for low-carb cookies. The dough didn't quite work for the cookies, but it was tasty, and my eldest daughter asked if she could just eat it as is. After some thought, I discovered it makes a fantastic hot cereal. It tastes like a multigrain oatmeal but is extremely rich! Garnish the cereal with blueberries, cinnamon, and half-and-half if desired.

2 cups almonds, ground
1 cup milk and egg protein
1 cup soy protein (not soy flour!)
1 teaspoon sea salt
16 packets sucralose
2 1/4 teaspoons SteviaPlus
2 eggs
1/4 cup butter, melted
1 tablespoon vanilla
1 1/2 cups buttermilk, kefir, or yogurt

1. Combine all of the dry ingredients in a large mixing bowl, stirring well.
2. In another large bowl with an electric mixer, combine the eggs, butter, and vanilla on medium speed until they are well mixed. Add the buttermilk and start mixing again on the lowest speed, gradually increasing the speed to about medium. Turn the speed back down to low; then begin to add the dry ingredients a little at a time, mixing until they are all combined.
3. Divide the dough into 1/2-cup servings and wrap with waxed paper. Place in plastic freezer bags; then freeze. The dough may be frozen up to 1 month.
4. To use: Place 1 serving in a microwave-safe cereal bowl and pour 3 to 4 tablespoons water over the dough. Cook it in the microwave on high power for about 1 minute; then stir the cereal. Cook it until the cereal just begins to bubble around the edges. Cook about 1 minute for freshly made cereal and up to 2 minutes for frozen. Do not overcook it or it will become rubbery!

NUTRITIONAL INFORMATION PER SERVING:
Carbohydrates: 8 grams • Effective Carb Count: 5 grams
Protein: 14 grams • Fat: 24 grams • Calories: 299

CRANBERRY BREAKFAST BARS

Makes about 20 bars

These are tangy but sweet–very yummy! The bars will stay fresh and tasty at room temperature for several days if they are well covered. They will not weep like a traditional coffee cake or quick bread. They are also great chilled!

Cooking oil spray

Fruit base:
*10 ounces cranberries, fresh or frozen
(about 1 1/4 cups)
4 packets sucralose
1/2 teaspoon SteviaPlus
1/2 teaspoon orange zest*

Crumble topping:
*2 eggs
1 cup kefir, yogurt, or buttermilk
3/4 cup almonds, ground
3/4 cup milk and egg protein
1 teaspoon SteviaPlus
8 packets sucralose
2 teaspoons baking powder
1/2 teaspoon baking soda
1/2 teaspoon cinnamon
1/4 teaspoon ginger*

Other:
1/3 cup butter, melted

1. Spray a 9" × 13" × 2" baking dish with cooking oil spray. Put the cranberries into the baking dish. Sprinkle them with the 4 packets sucralose, 1/2 teaspoon SteviaPlus, and orange zest. Stir them to evenly distribute the sweeteners and allow them to rest while preparing the rest of the recipe.
2. In a medium-sized mixing bowl, combine the eggs and kefir, mixing well. Set this mixture aside.
3. In another mixing bowl, combine the almonds through the ginger. Put half of the dry ingredients into the kefir/egg mixture and stir until combined. Pour this mixture over the cranberries in the pan. Spread the batter evenly over the berries. Sprinkle the remaining dry ingredients over the batter in the pan. Drizzle the butter evenly over the top of the dry sprinkle. Bake the bars for about 35 minutes at 350°F until they become golden brown on top.

NUTRITIONAL INFORMATION PER SERVING:
Carbohydrates: 3 grams • Effective Carb Count: 2 grams
Protein: 2 grams • Fat: 7 grams • Calories: 80

REDUCED-FAT VARIATION:
Use fat-free kefir and 2 1/2 tablespoons melted butter.
Carbohydrates: 3 grams • Effective Carb Count: 2 grams
Protein: 2 grams • Fat: 5 grams • Calories: 65

CREAM CHEESE
ALMOND PANCAKES

Serves 2

Oh! These are good! Instead of using vanilla and almond extracts, you may substitute 1½ teaspoons vanilla, butter, and nut extract (one item, found in the extract section of most groceries), and follow all remaining instructions. You may also make blueberry pancakes by sprinkling a few fresh or frozen blueberries onto the cakes before turning.

¼ cup cream cheese
1 teaspoon Sweet & Slender
½ teaspoon SteviaPlus
½ teaspoon cinnamon
½ teaspoon almond extract
1 teaspoon vanilla
2 eggs
¼ cup soy protein powder
¼ cup almonds, ground
¼ teaspoon baking powder
⅛ teaspoon sea salt
2 tablespoons water
Butter or lard for frying

1. In a small mixing bowl, microwave the cream cheese for 20 seconds. Add the Sweet & Slender, SteviaPlus, cinnamon, almond extract, and vanilla and mix. Add the eggs and stir well, until it is as smooth as possible—there will still be lumps. Add the soy protein, ground almonds, baking powder, salt, and water, mixing until combined. Allow the batter to rest for about 5 minutes.
2. Heat a large frying pan over medium heat with a small amount of butter; then put dollops of batter onto the hot surface. Turn the pancakes as they begin to brown, cooking for about 3 to 5 minutes total. Serve hot with cream cheese and Sweet & Slender sprinkled lightly over the top.

NUTRITIONAL INFORMATION PER SERVING:
Carbohydrates: 7 grams • Effective Carb Count: 5 grams
Protein: 17 grams • Fat: 30 grams • Calories: 367

REDUCED-FAT VARIATION:
Use reduced-fat cream cheese and omit the butter for frying.
Instead, use cooking oil spray for the frying.
Carbohydrates: 7 grams • Effective Carb Count: 5 grams
Protein: 16 grams • Fat: 17 grams • Calories: 252

CREAM CHEESE ASPARAGUS BREAKFAST PIZZA

Serves 4

You could use any sort of topping on this yummy breakfast pizza; asparagus is just particularly nice!

Base:

4 eggs
½ cup cream cheese, softened
1 tablespoon Romano cheese
1 teaspoon Italian seasonings
¼ teaspoon sea salt
Cooking oil spray

Topping:

6 spears cooked asparagus, cut into bite-sized pieces
10 black olives, sliced
4 ounces (about ½ cup) cooked meat, cut up (chicken, pork, or fish is nice)
4 ounces Monterey jack cheese, shredded
¼ teaspoon garlic salt
⅛ teaspoon oregano

1. Combine all of the base ingredients, except the cooking oil spray, in a mixing bowl and mix them as well as possible. (There will still be some lumps of cream cheese.) Spray a 9" to 10" pie pan with cooking oil spray and pour the base mixture into the pan. Bake it for about 10 minutes at 350°F or until it begins to set.
2. Layer the topping ingredients over the cooked base in the order given. Bake the pizza for another 10 minutes at 350°F, or until it is golden brown. Allow it to rest for at least 5 minutes before serving.

NUTRITIONAL INFORMATION PER SERVING:
Carbohydrates: 4 grams • Effective Carb Count: 3 grams
Protein: 19 grams • Fat: 28 grams • Calories: 343

REDUCED-FAT VARIATION:
Use reduced-fat cream cheese and reduced-fat Monterey jack cheese.
Carbohydrates: 4 grams • Effective Carb Count: 3 grams
Protein: 19 grams • Fat: 17 grams • Calories: 252

CREPES

Serves 6

Wonderful for Christmas or New Year's brunch! For a sweet treat, you could omit the Creamy Ham Filling (page 107) suggested and fill the crepes with Melt in Your Mouth Mousse (page 293). In fact, you can use your imagination and fill them with any sweet or savory filling that suits your fancy! Be very wary of the timing and heat. Be prepared to ruin a couple as you get the hang of it. After all, these are crepes!

½ cup soy protein	*4 beaten eggs*
1 cup milk and egg protein	*1½ cups half-and-half or*
1 teaspoon sea salt	*Almond Milk (page 240)*
2 teaspoons baking powder	*2 cups water*
½ teaspoon SteviaPlus	*1 teaspoon lemon zest*
½ teaspoon Sweet & Slender	*Butter for cooking*

1. Sift all of the dry ingredients into a large mixing bowl. Make a well in the top of the dry ingredients. Set this aside.
2. In another small bowl, combine the remaining crepe ingredients thoroughly. Pour them over the dry ingredients and mix them with a wire whisk until combined. Do not overbeat this mixture. Allow it to rest at least 5 minutes. While it is resting, prepare the filling.
3. To cook the crepes: Heat enough butter over medium-low heat to keep the crepe from sticking (about 1 tablespoon), and add 3 to 4 tablespoons of batter to the pan. Swirl the pan to coat it evenly with the batter. When it has browned on one side, about 1½ minutes, flip the crepe to cook the other side. The tip of a knife, rather than a spatula, works very well for flipping.
4. Fill each crepe immediately upon removing it from the heat. Use approximately ¼ cup Creamy Ham Filling, or desired filling, for each crepe. Place the filling just off center of the crepe and roll into a long tube. Eat them while they are warm!

NUTRITIONAL INFORMATION PER SERVING:
Carbohydrates: 4 grams • Effective Carb Count: 3 grams
Protein: 9 grams • Fat: 12 grams • Calories: 160

REDUCED-FAT VARIATION:
Use cooking spray instead of butter and use canned skim milk.
Carbohydrates: 8 grams • Effective Carb Count: 7 grams
Protein: 12 grams • Fat: 3 grams • Calories: 114

DEVILED EGGS WITH BACON

Serves 1

For low-carb eaters, scrambled eggs are a nearly essential part of the daily diet. This recipe came about because I didn't feel like cooking, but I did have some hard-boiled eggs already prepared. One can only eat so many scrambled eggs!

2 eggs, hard-boiled
1 piece cooked bacon, finely chopped
1 1/2 tablespoons Blender Mayonnaise (page 241) or
commercially prepared mayonnaise
1/8 teaspoon dry mustard powder
1/4 teaspoon minced onion, dried
1/2 teaspoon parsley
Dash lemon pepper

Halve the eggs and remove the yolks. Set the whites aside on a plate. Place the yolks, bacon, Blender Mayonnaise, mustard powder, onion, parsley, and lemon pepper in a small bowl. Combine thoroughly. Fill the hollows in the egg whites with the yolk mixture. Garnish with parsley if desired.

NUTRITIONAL INFORMATION PER SERVING:
Carbohydrates: 2 grams • Effective Carb Count: 1 gram
Protein: 13 grams • Fat: 30 grams • Calories: 318

REDUCED-FAT VARIATION:
Use reduced-fat mayonnaise and turkey bacon.
Carbohydrates: 5 grams • Effective Carb Count: 4 grams
Protein: 13 grams • Fat: 16 grams • Calories: 220

Eggs are an integral part of the low-carb way of life. They are an inexpensive source of protein and are part of many of the recipes in this book. If possible, choose organic, free-range eggs because they are a better source of fatty acids and won't have pesticides and antibiotics that regular storebought eggs do.

Easy Cheesy Breakfast Pizza

Makes 4 servings

Some folks may know this dish by the name of "frittata," but whatever you call it, this makes a great breakfast or lunch!

6 eggs
³/₄ teaspoon Italian seasonings herb blend
¹/₄ teaspoon seasoning salt
2 tablespoons lard

Toppings:

Black olives, sliced
Green onions, sliced
Mushrooms
Bacon, cooked and crumbled
Salad shrimp, cooked
Meat cooked and sliced, etc.
4 ounces Monterey jack or mozzarella cheese, sliced or grated

1. In a mixing bowl, combine the eggs, Italian seasonings, and seasoning salt. Set it aside.
2. Put about 2 tablespoons lard into a 10" skillet with a lid. Place over medium heat. When the skillet is hot, add the egg mixture. Once during the cooking process, lift the eggs and allow the excess uncooked eggs to flow under.
3. When the eggs are nearly set and there is no longer any excess uncooked egg, begin putting toppings of choice on egg crust. Spread them evenly so the surface area is well covered. Spread the cheese over all.
4. Cover the pizza and remove the pan from heat. Allow it to rest about 3 minutes or until the cheese is melted. If multiplying this recipe, or if many toppings are used, it may be necessary to put the entire pan, uncovered, into the oven and broil for about 3 minutes for the cheese to melt properly. Cut into wedges and serve.

Nutritional information per serving
(including only egg base and cheese):
Carbohydrates: 1 gram • Effective Carb Count: 0 grams
Protein: 15 grams • Fat: 22 grams • Calories: 263

Reduced-Fat Variation:
Omit the lard and use cooking oil spray to keep the eggs from sticking to the pan. Use reduced-fat cheese. Use lower-fat topping choices.
Carbohydrates: 2 grams • Effective Carb Count: 1 gram
Protein: 15 grams • Fat: 9 grams • Calories: 148

EASY EGG ROLL-UPS

Serves 1

I have wanted a comal, or tortilla griddle, for probably eighteen years! Recently my local discount store had a brand-new cast-iron comal on sale for $4.99. You can use a comal as you would any griddle, and it doubles as a lid for a cast-iron frying pan. If you don't have a comal, any griddle or shallow frying pan will work for this recipe.

½ teaspoon lard
2 eggs
⅛ teaspoon seasoning salt, or to taste
½ ounce cheese, shredded (Jack, Co-Jack, Cheddar, etc.)
2 tablespoons meat, cooked (sausage, chicken, ham, etc.)

Optional:

½ cup veggies, cooked (onion, asparagus, broccoli, etc.)
1 tablespoon sour cream
1 tablespoon Grown-Ups' Guacamole (page 19) or
Kids' Guacamole (page 25)
Salsa

1. Heat the lard in a large skillet or comal over medium heat until melted. Combine the eggs and seasoning salt in a small bowl and beat well. Pour all at once into the hot pan. Tip the pan gently so that the egg completely covers the bottom of the pan. Cook 1–2 minutes, or until it is set. Sprinkle the cheese on top and slide it onto a plate.
2. Put the meat (and veggies) into the center of the egg wrap, and roll, so that the finished product looks somewhat like a burrito or crepe. Add any optional toppings as desired.

NUTRITIONAL INFORMATION PER SERVING
(INCLUDING ONLY EGG BASE, CHEESE, AND MEAT):
Carbohydrates: 1 gram • Effective Carb Count: 1 gram
Protein: 15 grams • Fat: 16 grams • Calories: 207

REDUCED-FAT VARIATION:
Omit the lard and use cooking oil spray, and use reduced-fat Cheddar cheese.
Carbohydrates: 1 gram • Effective Carb Count: 1 gram
Protein: 14 grams • Fat: 10 grams • Calories: 156

FARMER'S BREAKFAST

Serves 4

During my college years, I was friends with a family that owned a farm. I have fond memories of bucking hay, picking asparagus and strawberries, and the wonderful food. The mother of the family made such delicious breakfasts! You can enjoy this hearty breakfast without having to buck any hay bales! Serve it with low-carb tortillas or High-Protein Wraps (page 225) on the side for an authentic feeling.

1 small sweet onion, finely chopped
2 tablespoons bacon grease or lard
½ pound Sharron's Pork Sausage (page 85),
1946 Pork Sausage (page 54), or commercially
prepared pork sausage, cooked and crumbled
8 eggs
1 tablespoon parsley flakes
Seasoning salt
Low-carb tortillas or High-Protein Wraps, l per serving

1. In a medium skillet, over medium heat, cook the onion in the bacon grease until it is translucent, about 3 minutes. Add the sausage and heat it through.
2. In a mixing bowl, scramble the eggs, parsley, and seasoning salt to taste. Pour the egg mixture over the sausage mixture in the skillet. Cook it through, stirring frequently. Serve hot with warmed low-carb tortillas for scooping.

NUTRITIONAL INFORMATION PER SERVING:
Carbohydrates: 15 grams • Effective Carb Count: 6 grams
Protein: 17 grams • Fat: 27 grams • Calories: 351

REDUCED-FAT VARIATION:
Use turkey sausage and omit the bacon grease.
Cook the onion in about 1 tablespoon Rich Stock (page 254).
Carbohydrates: 14 grams • Effective Carb Count: 5 grams
Protein: 13 grams • Fat: 8 grams • Calories: 155

FLAX CEREAL

Makes 6 cups, which makes 16 servings

Flax has been popping up all over the place in recipes and in newspaper head-lines. This easy recipe helps you put this great ingredient to use! While you are enjoying this yummy cereal, you can take comfort in the fact that you are also doing something really great for your body!

4 cups flax seeds, ground (3 cups whole seeds)
2 cups milk and egg protein
2 teaspoons cinnamon
½ teaspoon sea salt
4 teaspoons SteviaPlus
12 packets sucralose

1. If you are grinding your own seeds, place about ⅓ to ½ cup seeds into a blender container and pulverize them on medium-high speed. I prefer to leave some of the seeds unbroken. This gives the cereal a multigrain feel in the mouth. If you prefer a creamier cereal, pulverize the seeds completely. Repeat this process for all of the remaining seeds.
2. Combine all of the ingredients in a large bowl or gallon-size zipper-sealed bag. Mix the cereal very well and store in a covered container (or the zipper-sealed bag) in the refrigerator.
3. To mix: For 2 servings, combine ¾ cup mix, 1¼ cups water, and ¼ teaspoon extract of your choice (chocolate, maple, vanilla, etc.). Stir this mixture until it is smooth. Microwave the cereal on high for 2–3 minutes, or until it is hot and somewhat foamy across the top. Add butter or cream as desired.

NUTRITIONAL INFORMATION PER SERVING:
Carbohydrates: 11 grams • Effective Carb Count: 3 grams
Protein: 15 grams • Fat: 10 grams • Calories: 181

℃ THE SCOOP ON FLAX: Flax is one of those amazing "super foods." It is a veritable powerhouse of essential fatty acids (EFAs) and dietary fiber. It is loaded with vitamins and minerals as well. On the surface it may seem like a very carb-heavy food, but the reality is that most of those carbohydrates are in the form of dietary fiber, which is super beneficial to the digestive tract!

Some of the specifics are: Just 1 tablespoon of flaxseed contains 23 milligrams of calcium, 43 milligrams of magnesium, 59 milligrams of phosphorus, 81 milligrams of potassium, 33 micrograms of folate, plus far too many other vitamins, minerals, and fatty acids to be listed here! It contains 4.11 carbs per tablespoon, but 3.35 of those are fiber. That means it has an effective carb count of 0.76 per tablespoon!

Maple Pork Sausage

Serves 6

When my husband and I were first married, we were still in college. There was a little grocery store just down the street that made fresh sausage in their meat department. My favorite was their maple pork sausage. This recipe was inspired by that sausage. This sausage may be made into patties or just cooked and crumbled to be added to eggs, casseroles, etc. It's excellent served alongside Chubby Pancakes (page 59) with Sugar-Free Pancake Syrup (page 256)!

1 1/4 pounds ground pork
1/2 teaspoon maple extract
1 teaspoon fennel/anise seed
1 teaspoon seasoning salt
1 teaspoon minced onion, dried
1/4 teaspoon lemon pepper
1/2 teaspoon dried sage
Pinch SteviaPlus or 1/2 packet sucralose
3 drops hot chili oil or a tiny pinch of cayenne

Place all the ingredients into a deep mixing bowl and combine thoroughly. Use as desired in recipes or formed into patties or links.

Nutritional information per serving:
Carbohydrates: 1 gram • Effective Carb Count: 0 grams
Protein: 16 grams • Fat: 20 grams • Calories: 252

Reduced-Fat Variation:
Use ground chicken, turkey, or lean ground beef instead of the pork.
(Ground turkey calculated below.)
Carbohydrates: 1 gram • Effective Carb Count: 0 grams
Protein: 20 grams • Fat: 7 grams • Calories: 138

Which meat for sausage? Many folks are on restricted diets. They can't use pork for religious or health reasons. Any of the sausage recipes in this book may be made by substituting ground beef, ground chicken, or ground turkey for the ground pork, thus eliminating the problem.

MINI CHEESE SOUFFLES
Makes 12

This is a great recipe for which to let your creative juices flow—don't be afraid to experiment with ingredients such as your favorite veggies, meats, and cheeses. Try adding dried or fresh herbs and spices for some other fun variations.

½ cup cheese, shredded (Cheddar, Colby, Co-Jack, or blend)
2 tablespoons Parmesan cheese
½ cup kefir, yogurt, or buttermilk
2 tablespoons milk and egg protein
8 eggs
¾ teaspoon seasoning salt
1 teaspoon minced onion, dried
⅛ teaspoon garlic granules
1/16 teaspoon paprika (that is ½ of ⅛ teaspoon!)
Cooking oil spray

1. Preheat oven to 350°F. Combine all of the ingredients, except the cooking oil spray, in a mixing bowl and mix well using a wire whisk. Spray a standard-sized muffin tin well with the cooking oil spray. Pour the egg mixture into the muffin cups.
2. Bake the souffles for about 20 minutes, or until they are puffy and golden. Do not open the oven door to check them until toward the end of the baking time or they will fall! If you must check them, do so very, very carefully, being sure that no draft from outside the oven reaches the souffles. Remove them from the oven and slide a knife around the edges to remove them from the pan.

NUTRITIONAL INFORMATION PER SERVING:
Carbohydrates: 1 gram • Effective Carb Count: 0 grams
Protein: 6 grams • Fat: 5 grams • Calories: 80

REDUCED-FAT VARIATION:
Use reduced-fat cheese and fat-free kefir.
Carbohydrates: 1 gram • Effective Carb Count: 0 grams
Protein: 7 grams • Fat: 4 grams • Calories: 69

Parsley Eggs with
Walla Walla Sweet Sauce

Serves 4

When I was a child growing up, I lived in eastern Washington State. Those hot, arid conditions are perfect for growing big, sweet Walla Walla Sweet onions. My parents always got excited when Walla Walla Sweet season was upon us. Now that I'm an adult, I still find myself getting excited about Walla Walla Sweet season. These delicious onions seem to work their way into everything I cook.

Sauce:

*1 Walla Walla Sweet onion,
medium-sized (or other sweet onion)
2 tablespoons bacon grease
1 tablespoon butter
1/4 teaspoon garlic salt
1/8 teaspoon lemon pepper
1/2 tablespoon parsley
1/8 teaspoon seasoning salt
1/2 teaspoon arrowroot powder mixed
into 1/4 cup water*

Eggs:

*8 eggs
1/2 teaspoon seasoning salt
1/2 teaspoon chives, fresh or dried
1/2 teaspoon parsley, fresh or dried
1 tablespoon lard*

1. Slice the onion. In a medium skillet, over medium heat, cook the onion slices in bacon grease and butter. Add the garlic salt, lemon pepper, parsley, and seasoning salt. Continue cooking until the onion slices become translucent and begin to brown slightly. Add the arrowroot/water mixture and continue to cook and stir the sauce for about 1 minute. Place it in a small serving bowl.
2. In a mixing bowl, combine the eggs, seasoning salt, chives, and parsley. Mix them well. In a medium skillet over medium heat, heat the lard. Pour the eggs into the skillet and cook them through. When the eggs are no longer runny, place them into a serving dish.
3. To serve, place the desired amount of eggs on individual plates and spoon the sauce over the eggs.

Nutritional information per serving:
Carbohydrates: 4 grams • Effective Carb Count: 1 gram
Protein: 11 grams • Fat: 22 grams • Calories: 258

Reduced-Fat Variation:
Use a small amount of Rich Stock (page 254) to cook the onion.
Use cooking oil spray to keep the eggs from sticking to the pan.
Carbohydrates: 4 grams • Effective Carb Count: 3 grams
Protein: 11 grams • Fat: 9 grams • Calories: 144

Puffy Cheese and Spinach Pie

Serves 8

This great recipe is perfect for brunches, potlucks, and other special occasions where the "same ol' thing" just won't do!

Crust:

1 cup almonds, ground
1 tablespoon flax seeds (not ground)
1/3 cup soy protein powder
1/4 teaspoon Sweet & Slender
1 tablespoon Parmesan or Romano cheese
1/4 teaspoon sea salt
6 tablespoons butter

Filling:

1/2 cup onion, chopped
2 tablespoons bacon grease or lard
1/8 teaspoon seasoning salt
1 cup spinach, fresh, finely chopped
3/4 cup cream cheese
6 eggs
1/2 teaspoon seasoning salt
3 tablespoons Parmesan or Romano cheese
3 or 4 slices of bacon, cooked and chopped

Topping:

1/4 cup Monterey jack cheese, shredded
1 tablespoon Parmesan or Romano cheese
1/2 tablespoon parsley flakes, dried

Recipe continues on page 74 ➤

➤ Recipe continued from page 73

1. Preheat the oven to 350°F. Combine all of the crust ingredients in the bowl of a food processor, and pulse until they are well combined. (Or do this by hand with a pastry blender.) Dust the tips of your fingers with soy protein powder to keep them from sticking to the crust, and press the crust into a 9" pie plate. Place the crust into the refrigerator to chill while preparing the filling.

2. In a medium-sized frying pan over medium heat, cook the onion in the bacon grease and ⅛ teaspoon seasoning salt until it is golden, about 5 minutes. Stir in the chopped spinach until it begins to wilt, about 3 minutes. Set aside to cool.

3. Heat the cream cheese in a microwave-safe dish until it softens, about 30 seconds. In a medium-sized mixing bowl, beat the eggs, ½ teaspoon seasoning salt, and Parmesan cheese until they are combined. Add the cream cheese and mix as thoroughly as possible—there will still be pea-sized lumps of cream cheese in the filling.

4. Remove the crust from the refrigerator and spread the bottom with the spinach/onion mixture. Sprinkle the chopped bacon evenly on top of the spinach/onions. Carefully pour the egg/cheese mixture over the bacon and spinach. Place the pie into a 350°F oven and bake until it begins to set, about 20 minutes.

5. While the pie is baking, combine the topping ingredients. After the pie has baked for 20 minutes, remove it from the oven and sprinkle the top with the topping. Place the pie back into the oven and bake for approximately 10 more minutes, until a knife inserted near the center of the pie comes out clean. Allow the pie to rest 5 to 10 minutes before serving.

NUTRITIONAL INFORMATION PER SERVING:
Carbohydrates: 6 grams • Effective Carb Count: 4 grams
Protein: 16 grams • Fat: 35 grams • Calories: 393

REDUCED-FAT VARIATION:
Omit the bacon grease and cook the onion in a couple of tablespoons of Rich Stock (page 254), then stir in the spinach. Use low-fat cream cheese and turkey bacon. Use reduced-fat Monterey jack cheese.
Carbohydrates: 6 grams • Effective Carb Count: 4 grams
Protein: 15 grams • Fat: 26 grams • Calories: 307

𝒞 Here's how to prevent glass breakage. When you need to put hot food into a cold glass or ceramic dish, place a metal spoon in the dish first. As the hot food is poured into the dish, the metal spoon will absorb that first shock of heat and keep the glass from shattering.

PUMPKIN COCONUT MUFFINS

Makes 12

This recipe is a very yummy way to get some extra fiber into your diet. If your carb allowance is high enough, you can substitute the milk and egg protein with whole rolled oats.

Wet ingredients:

½ cup pumpkin purée
¼ cup butter, melted
1 egg
¾ cup kefir, yogurt,
or buttermilk (2%)
½ teaspoon vanilla

Dry ingredients:

½ cup unsweetened coconut, shredded
1 cup almonds, ground
½ cup milk and egg protein
½ cup soy protein (not soy flour!)
6 packets sucralose
1 teaspoon SteviaPlus
½ teaspoon cinnamon
¼ teaspoon nutmeg, ground
¼ teaspoon ginger
1 ½ teaspoons baking powder
½ teaspoon baking soda
½ teaspoon sea salt
Cooking oil spray or lard

1. In a small bowl, combine the wet ingredients and mix them well. Set them aside.
2. In a large mixing bowl, combine the dry ingredients. Mix them well.
3. Make a hollow in the center of the dry ingredients and pour the wet ingredients into the hollow. Stir this mixture until it is just combined.
4. Grease a standard 12-cup muffin tin and place the batter into the cups about ⅔ full. Bake the muffins at 400°F for about 12 minutes or until they are golden brown. Serve warm with melted butter and sugar-free jam if desired.

NUTRITIONAL INFORMATION PER SERVING:
Carbohydrates: 5 grams • Effective Carb Count: 3 grams
Protein: 16 grams • Fat: 12 grams • Calories: 189

REDUCED-FAT VARIATION:
Use nonfat buttermilk (or canned skim milk)
and applesauce instead of the butter.
Carbohydrates: 6 grams • Effective Carb Count: 4 grams
Protein: 16 grams • Fat: 8 grams • Calories: 154

PUMPKIN GRANOLA

Serves 12

This recipe is great for traveling. Make it ahead of time and store it in a large plastic bag or container. It can also be made into a hot cereal by adding 1 or 2 tablespoons of water to the dry cereal and microwaving for about 30 seconds, or until it is warm. Just add cream or half-and-half and serve as usual.

2 cups almonds, coarsely chopped
¼ cup flax seeds, whole
¼ cup unsweetened coconut
2 tablespoons soy protein (not soy flour!)
¼ cup milk and egg protein
1 teaspoon SteviaPlus
1 teaspoon ginger
1 teaspoon orange zest
1 teaspoon nutmeg
1½ teaspoons cinnamon
¼ teaspoon ground cloves
8 packets sucralose
⅛ teaspoon sea salt
¾ cup pumpkin
1 teaspoon vanilla
1 cup Roasted Pecans (page 31)

1. In a large mixing bowl, combine the dry granola ingredients, then stir in the pumpkin and vanilla. Mix it until it is evenly distributed—the mixture will be very stiff. Stir in the Roasted Pecans, mixing them well into the rest of the granola.
2. Spread the mixture on a large baking sheet and bake it at 325°F for about 25 minutes, stirring about halfway through. The granola should be golden brown and crunchy when done.
3. Cool completely on the pan; then transfer the granola to a covered container or zippered storage bag. Store unrefrigerated for up to 2 weeks. Serve with half-and-half, if desired.

NUTRITIONAL INFORMATION PER SERVING:
Carbohydrates: 9 grams • Effective Carb Count: 4 grams
Protein: 8 grams • Fat: 21 grams • Calories: 240

Pumpkin Muffins
with Crumble Topping

Makes 9 standard-sized muffins or 24 mini muffins plus 1 small loaf

A perfect winter morning treat. The mini muffins are a great treat for the kids!

Dry ingredients:

1 3/4 cups almonds, ground
1/4 cup soy protein powder (not soy flour!)
2 teaspoons baking powder
1 teaspoon Sweet & Slender
1 1/2 teaspoons SteviaPlus
3/4 teaspoon cinnamon
1/2 teaspoon ginger
1/2 teaspoon baking soda
1/2 teaspoon sea salt

Wet ingredients:

1/2 cup pumpkin purée
1 teaspoon vanilla
1/2 cup yogurt, room temperature, or cream
1/4 cup butter, melted
1 egg

Topping:

2/3 cup almonds, ground
1 teaspoon Sweet & Slender
3/4 teaspoon SteviaPlus
2 tablespoons butter
1/4 teaspoon cinnamon
1/4 teaspoon orange zest

1. In a large mixing bowl, combine the dry ingredients. Mix them well and set aside.
2. In a small mixing bowl, combine the wet ingredients. Mix them thoroughly, until they are uniform in texture.
3. Add the wet ingredients all at once to the dry ingredients, mixing the batter until it is just combined. The batter should be slightly lumpy. Spray a standard-sized muffin tin with cooking oil spray. Place the batter in the muffin cups so that they are about 2/3 full.
4. Using a food processor with a chopping blade or a pastry blender, combine topping ingredients. Sprinkle the topping evenly over the muffins.
5. Bake at 400°F for 15 minutes, or until a toothpick inserted in the center comes out clean. Allow muffins to rest in the tins for at least 1 minute; then remove by sliding a table knife around the edge of each muffin. Place muffins on a cooling rack and allow to rest about 5 minutes. Alternatively, they may be allowed to cool in the pans. They will not sweat and droop as regular muffins do! Mini muffins bake for about 8 to 10 minutes, while loaves bake for 15 to 20.

Nutritional information per serving:
Carbohydrates: 9 grams • Effective Carb Count: 6 grams
Protein: 12 grams • Fat: 27 grams • Calories: 309

PUMPKIN SPICE
MUFFINS

Makes 8

Pumpkin has so many uses! If you live in an area where pumpkins are grown as a food staple, stock up and prepare them as Baked Winter Squash (page 216). Then the flesh can be frozen and used throughout this book. This is just one recipe that uses that great all-purpose veggie!

³/4 cup almonds, ground
¹/2 cup soy protein (not soy flour!)
¹/2 teaspoon SteviaPlus
4 packets sucralose
1¹/2 teaspoons baking powder
¹/4 teaspoon sea salt
1¹/4 teaspoons pumpkin pie spice
(or 1 teaspoon cinnamon and ¹/4 teaspoon nutmeg)
¹/2 cup pecan or walnut meats, broken into ¹/4" to ¹/2" pieces
¹/2 cup Almond Milk (page 240) or ¹/4 cup cream thinned to ¹/2 cup with water
2 tablespoons olive oil or melted butter
1 egg
¹/2 cup pumpkin purée
Cooking oil spray

Topping:

6 tablespoons almonds, ground
3 tablespoons butter
¹/2 teaspoon SteviaPlus or 2 packets sucralose
¹/2 teaspoon cinnamon

Recipe continues on page 79 ❯

➤ Recipe continued from page 78

1. In a large mixing bowl, combine the ground almonds, soy protein, SteviaPlus, sucralose, baking powder, salt, pumpkin pie spice, and nut meats. Mix well and set aside.
2. In a small mixing bowl, combine the Almond Milk, olive oil, egg, and pumpkin. Mix thoroughly, until uniform in texture.
3. Add the wet ingredients all at once to the dry ingredients, mixing until just combined. The batter should be slightly lumpy.
4. Spray a standard size muffin tin with cooking oil spray. Place the batter in the muffin cups so that they are about 2/3 full.
5. Using a food processor with a chopping blade or a pastry blender, combine the topping ingredients. The topping will be sticky. Press the topping evenly over the muffins.
6. Bake them at 400°F for 15 minutes, or until a toothpick inserted in the center comes out clean. Allow the muffins to rest 1 minute in the pan; then remove them by sliding a table knife around the edge of each muffin. Place the muffins on a cooling rack and allow them to rest for about 5 minutes before serving.

NUTRITIONAL INFORMATION PER SERVING:
Carbohydrates: 7 grams • Effective Carb Count: 4 grams
Protein: 9 grams • Fat: 23 grams • Calories: 260

REDUCED-FAT VARIATION:
Use unsweetened applesauce instead of the butter in the batter.
Use Almond Milk (page 240). Use 1 1/2 tablespoons butter in the topping.
Carbohydrates: 8 grams • Effective Carb Count: 5 grams
Protein: 9 grams • Fat: 18 grams • Calories: 212

Want the secret to making moist muffins every time? If any muffin cups remain empty in the muffin pan, place about 1 tablespoon water in each cup. This keeps the muffins moist and prevents the pan from burning.

PUMPKIN WAFFLES

Makes 4 8" waffles

My in-laws served waffles every Sunday evening while my husband was growing up. These waffles are perfect for special breakfasts and Sunday evening waffles. These are excellent served with Cinnamon Butter (page 242) and Vanilla Sauce (page 261)!

⅓ cup almonds, blanched
1 ½ cups water
3 eggs, beaten
½ cup pumpkin
2 tablespoons butter, melted
⅔ cup pork rinds, ground
2 tablespoons soy protein (not soy flour!)
¼ cup almonds, ground
2 teaspoons baking powder
2 packets sucralose
⅛ teaspoon SteviaPlus
¼ teaspoon pumpkin pie spice (or ⅛ teaspoon each cinnamon and nutmeg)

1. If the almonds are not preblanched, place them into a bowl, pour in enough water to cover them, and microwave the almonds and water for about 2 minutes. The skins should become loose and peel easily. Remove and discard the skins. Place the blanched almonds into a blender container and discard the blanching water.
2. Add the water to the almonds in the blender container. Blend, beginning on low speed, then turning up to high, until the almonds are completely pulverized, about 1½ to 2 minutes. Set aside.
3. In a large mixing bowl, combine eggs and pumpkin. Stir in the pulverized almond/water mixture and butter.
4. In a small bowl, combine the pork rinds, soy protein, ground almonds, baking powder, sucralose, SteviaPlus, and pumpkin pie spice. Stir the dry ingredients into the wet ingredients until they are just combined.
5. Allow the batter to rest at least 5 minutes before baking the waffles on a hot, greased waffle iron. Bake the waffles until the steam disappears and the waffles are golden brown, about 10 minutes each.

NUTRITIONAL INFORMATION PER SERVING:
Carbohydrates: 6 grams • Effective Carb Count: 4 grams
Protein: 16 grams • Fat: 27 grams • Calories: 310

Filtered or tap water? Tap water contains chemicals such as chlorine and can contain harmful substances such as lead. Good inexpensive water filters are available everywhere. They are a worthwhile investment in your health and the quality of your food!

QUICK AND EASY SAUSAGE GRAVY

Makes 8 servings

This is a quick and easy gravy. Serve it hot over eggs, Rice-Aflower (page 227), Cauliflower Hash Browns (page 219), or low-carb bread that has been toasted. If you like things on the spicier side, you may wish to add some freshly ground black pepper or a few drops of hot chili oil to the gravy.

1 pound pork sausage
1 8-ounce package cream cheese, softened
1/3 cup half and half
1/3 cup water
1/4 teaspoon seasoning salt

1. In a medium-sized frying pan over medium heat, cook and crumble the pork sausage. Drain off the excess fat.
2. Place the cream cheese into the pan and turn the heat to medium-low. The cheese will melt as it is stirred. Add the remaining ingredients, stirring constantly to incorporate the liquid into the sausage/cheese mixture. Add additional water if necessary.

NUTRITIONAL INFORMATION PER SERVING:
Carbohydrates: 2 grams • Effective Carb Count: 1 gram
Protein: 9 grams • Fat: 34 grams • Calories: 349

REDUCED-FAT VARIATION:
Use turkey sausage, low-fat cream cheese, and canned skim milk.
Use very low heat.
Carbohydrates: 2 grams • Effective Carb Count: 1 gram
Protein: 14 grams • Fat: 11 grams • Calories: 167

Pork rinds are an essential staple of a low-carb diet. They are great to use as filler in meatballs, salmon patties, and the like. They can also be used as breading or even in some desserts. Buy a few bags, grind them, and store them in a sealed container for later use. This versatile food will be a great addition to your pantry.

SAUSAGE EGG CUPS

Makes 12

A nice treat for Sunday morning breakfast!

1 pound bulk pork sausage
(any of the sausage recipes from this book would be appropriate)
³/₄ cup cheese, shredded (Monterey jack, Colby, Cheddar, or blend)
12 eggs
Seasoning salt
1 tablespoon chives

1. Divide the sausage into 12 equal pieces. It is easiest if the sausage is in the form of a roll and partially frozen, then sliced. Place the pieces of sausage into a standard-sized 12-cup muffin tin. Bake the sausage for about 10 minutes at 350°F, or until it is done. Drain the excess fat off the sausage.
2. Sprinkle the cheese atop the cooked sausage, then break 1 egg into each cup. Sprinkle the eggs with seasoning salt, to taste. Sprinkle the chives over the tops of the eggs. Bake the Sausage Egg Cups at 350°F for about 10–15 minutes or until the eggs are cooked. Serve hot.

NUTRITIONAL INFORMATION PER SERVING:
Carbohydrates: 1 gram • Effective Carb Count: 0 grams
Protein: 12 grams • Fat: 22 grams • Calories: 252

REDUCED-FAT VARIATION:
Use chicken or turkey sausage instead of pork,
and reduced-fat cheese instead of regular.
Carbohydrates: 1 gram • Effective Carb Count: 0 grams
Protein: 14 grams • Fat: 8 grams • Calories: 135

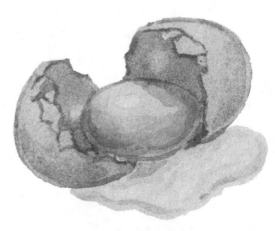

SAUSAGE 'N' CHEESE BAKE

Serves 8

This zesty, hearty breakfast is sure to stick to your ribs! Just stir it, bake it, and enjoy.

1 pound pork sausage, cooked
(one of the recipes from this book, or commercial type)
6 eggs
½ teaspoon seasoning salt
¼ teaspoon paprika
¼ teaspoon lemon pepper
2 tablespoons minced onion, dried
½ teaspoon garlic granules
⅓ cup milk and egg protein
1 cup cheese, shredded (Cheddar, Colby, Monterey jack, or a blend)
¼ cup almonds, ground

1. Place the cooked, crumbled sausage into a 9" × 13" baking dish, spreading it evenly across the bottom.
2. In a large mixing bowl, whisk the eggs and the seasonings. Add the remaining ingredients to the bowl and stir them well. Pour the egg-and-cheese mixture over the sausage and bake it for about 30 minutes at 375°F until it is golden brown and tests clean with a knife or toothpick inserted slightly off center. Serve warm.

NUTRITIONAL INFORMATION PER SERVING:
Carbohydrates: 3 grams • Effective Carb Count: 2 grams
Protein: 19 grams • Fat: 33 grams • Calories: 384

REDUCED-FAT VARIATION:
Use turkey sausage and reduced-fat cheese.
Carbohydrates: 3 grams • Effective Carb Count: 2 grams
Protein: 21 grams • Fat: 11 grams • Calories: 201

SAVORY OMELETTES
WITH OR WITHOUT CHEESE

Serves 1

Omelettes are delicious with or without cheese, and the possibilities are endless! Eat 'em up–they are yummy and a great source of protein. Load 'em up! The only limit to omelettes are what is in your fridge and your imagination!

3 eggs
Seasoning salt to taste
1/2 teaspoon chives, fresh or dried
1/2 teaspoon parsley flakes
1/2 tablespoon butter or bacon grease

Filling ingredients (choose one or several!):

2 ounces cheese (Monterey jack, Colby, Swiss, Cheddar, etc.)
Bacon, cooked and chopped
Shrimp, cooked
Turkey, chicken, or pork, cooked and cut up
Zucchini, celery, peppers, onions, asparagus,
mushrooms, etc., cooked and cut up
Sausage, cooked and crumbled

1. In a small bowl, beat the eggs with the seasoning salt, chives, and parsley until they are very well combined. Melt the butter in a small skillet over medium heat. Pour the eggs into the skillet, and cook them until they are set. As the eggs are cooking, lift the edges so the uncooked portions will run under the cooked part.
2. Cover half of the cooked eggs with your choices of meats, cheese, and veggies. Fold the empty half over the full half and slide it onto a plate.

NUTRITIONAL INFORMATION PER SERVING
(INCLUDING ONLY THE EGGS, SEASONINGS, AND CHEESE):
Carbohydrates: 2 grams • Effective Carb Count: 1 gram
Protein: 30 grams • Fat: 36 grams • Calories: 460

REDUCED-FAT VARIATION:
Omit the butter and use cooking oil spray. Use reduced-fat cheese.
Carbohydrates: 3 grams • Effective Carb Count: 2 grams
Protein: 30 grams • Fat: 17 grams • Calories: 295

Sharron's Pork Sausage

Makes 12 servings

Sausage is a cinch to freeze! Just crumble the sausage and precook it. Place the cooked sausage on a baking sheet sprayed with cooking spray and freeze. Once it is frozen, store it in freezer bags for a precooked addition to recipes. You can also freeze uncooked formed patties in the same manner to make breakfast in a snap on busy mornings. If you prefer Italian sausage, simply add ¹/₂ tablespoon Italian seasonings. If you like spicy sausage, double the lemon pepper and add ¹/₂ tablespoon red pepper flakes.

2 pounds ground pork
2 cloves garlic, minced (or ¹/₂ teaspoon garlic granules,
but fresh is always best!)
¹/₂ to 1 teaspoon fennel or anise seed (some like less, I like more!)
1 teaspoon seasoning salt
1 tablespoon minced onion, dried
¹/₂ teaspoon lemon pepper
¹/₂ teaspoon sage, dried
¹/₄ teaspoon SteviaPlus or ¹/₂ packet sucralose
¹/₂ teaspoon hot chili oil or a pinch of cayenne
¹/₄ teaspoon thyme
¹/₄ teaspoon marjoram

Place all the ingredients into a deep mixing bowl and combine thoroughly. This may be made into patties or just cooked and crumbled to be added to eggs, casseroles, etc.

Nutritional information per serving:
Carbohydrates: 1 gram • Effective Carb Count: 0 grams
Protein: 13 grams • Fat: 16 grams • Calories: 204

Reduced-Fat Variation:
Use ground chicken, turkey, or lean ground beef. (Turkey calculated below.)
Carbohydrates: 1 gram • Effective Carb Count: 0 grams
Protein: 16 grams • Fat: 6 grams • Calories: 113

SKILLET SQUASH BREAKFAST

Makes 6 servings

With big chunks of ham and cheese, this recipe can be a surprising kid pleaser! Just be very careful not to let the cheese melt completely, or it will be very messy to serve.

$1/3$ cup fresh onion, minced
2 cloves garlic, minced
2 tablespoons lard or bacon grease
2 cups Baked Winter Squash (page 216), cut into $1/2$" cubes
$1/2$ teaspoon seasoning salt
$1/4$ teaspoon lemon pepper
6 eggs
$1/2$ teaspoon seasoning salt (or to taste)
$1/2$ tablespoon parsley, dried
1 cup ham, cut into $1/2$" cubes
$3/4$ cup Monterey jack and/or Cheddar cheese, cut into $1/2$" cubes

1. Place onion, garlic, and lard in a large skillet with a snug-fitting lid. Cook them over medium heat until the onions are translucent, about $1/2$ minutes. Add the winter squash, seasoning salt, and lemon pepper. Cook it uncovered about 5 minutes, until the squash is golden. Turn it and cook it another 3 to 5 minutes. Be careful not to overcook the squash at this stage. It should stay fairly firm and in cubes.
2. Meanwhile, in a medium bowl, beat the eggs with the seasoning salt and parsley. Set them aside.
3. Add the ham to the squash mixture and heat it through. Stir it well and spread it evenly over the bottom of skillet. Pour the egg mixture over all and cook it, turning occasionally, until it is almost set.
4. Drop the cheese cubes evenly over the surface of the egg mixture. Remove the pan from the heat and cover it. Allow it to rest about 5 minutes or until the cheese melts.

NUTRITIONAL INFORMATION PER SERVING:
Carbohydrates: 6 grams • Effective Carb Count: 5 grams
Protein: 14 grams • Fat: 15 grams • Calories: 218

REDUCED-FAT VARIATION:
Use about 2 tablespoons Rich Stock (page 254) instead of the lard to cook the onion and garlic. Use cooking oil spray to keep the rest of the food from sticking to the pan. Use lean ham and reduced-fat cheese.
Carbohydrates: 6 grams • Effective Carb Count: 5 grams
Protein: 14 grams • Fat: 7 grams • Calories: 140

Sour Cream Pumpkin Pancakes

Serves 4

For a special breakfast, try dropping a few frozen berries onto the batter as it is cooking, then flip the pancakes. Enjoy these with Cinnamon Butter (page 242).

2/3 cup canned pumpkin purée
1/2 cup sour cream or yogurt
1/2 tablespoon vanilla
1/2 teaspoon almond extract
1 egg
1 cup water
1 tablespoon olive oil
2/3 cup pork rinds, crushed
1/3 cup almonds, ground
3 tablespoons soy protein
2 packets sucralose
1/4 teaspoon SteviaPlus
2 teaspoons baking powder
1/2 teaspoon baking soda
Cooking oil spray

1. In a large mixing bowl, combine the pumpkin, sour cream, vanilla, almond extract, egg, water, and olive oil. Stir well using a wire whisk or fork.
2. In a small mixing bowl, combine the pork rinds, ground almonds, soy protein, sucralose, SteviaPlus, baking powder, and baking soda.
3. Gradually stir the dry ingredients into the wet ingredients, mixing until just combined. Allow the batter to rest for about 5 minutes before cooking over a hot griddle. Use cooking oil spray as needed to keep the pancakes from sticking to the griddle.

Nutritional information per serving:
Carbohydrates: 8 grams • Effective Carb Count: 6 grams
Protein: 14 grams • Fat: 23 grams • Calories: 277

Reduced-Fat Variation:
Use fat-free yogurt and omit the olive oil.
Carbohydrates: 7 grams • Effective Carb Count: 5 grams
Protein: 15 grams • Fat: 14 grams • Calories: 208

SPINACH PUFF FOR ONE

Serves 1

This makes a yummy breakfast, brunch, or lunch when you need to cook only for yourself. Enjoy!

¼ cup cream cheese, softened
2 eggs
¼ teaspoon seasoning salt, or as desired
1 tablespoon Parmesan or Romano cheese
1 tablespoon sweet onion, minced
1 ½ teaspoons butter
⅛ teaspoon seasoning salt
½ cup spinach, chopped (fresh preferred)
1 tablespoon parsley flakes
2 tablespoons Monterey jack cheese, shredded

1. In a small mixing bowl, combine the cream cheese, eggs, ¼ teaspoon seasoning salt, and Parmesan cheese and mix well. Set the egg mixture aside.
2. In a very small (5") frying pan with a lid, cook the onion in the butter with ⅛ teaspoon seasoning salt over medium heat until the onion is golden, about 5 minutes. Stir in the spinach and cook it until it is warmed, about 3 minutes. Carefully pour the egg mixture over the spinach mixture in the frying pan. (The spinach mixture forms the "crust.") Cover the pan and cook the Puff over low heat until it is set, about 5 minutes.
3. Remove the lid and sprinkle the top of the Puff with the parsley and Monterey jack cheese. Cover the pan again and allow it to rest about 2 minutes, or until the cheese is melted.

NUTRITIONAL INFORMATION PER SERVING:
Carbohydrates: 5 grams • Effective Carb Count: 4 grams
Protein: 22 grams • Fat: 41 grams • Calories: 469

REDUCED-FAT VARIATION:
Use low-fat cream cheese and Monterey jack cheese. Omit the butter.
Cook the onion in a small amount of Rich Stock (page 254).
Carbohydrates: 4 grams • Effective Carb Count: 3 grams
Protein: 20 grams • Fat: 18 grams • Calories: 261

SPINACH QUICHE

Serves 4

There are so many variations on quiche, you're sure to find one the whole family enjoys. Try a broccoli quiche by substituting 1 cup chopped, cooked broccoli for the spinach. Cooked shrimp or crab can also be added for a terrific change of pace. This recipe can be served hot, although it's a tasty treat served warm or cold as well.

½ tablespoon butter
⅓ cup onion, chopped
1 cup spinach, raw
4 eggs
½ teaspoon seasoning salt
Pinch of nutmeg (ever so much less than ⅛ teaspoon!)
½ tablespoon parsley flakes
5 drops hot chili oil
2 cups Almond Milk (page 240) or 2 cups cream
5 pieces bacon, cooked
Cooking oil spray
½ cup Swiss or Monterey jack cheese, shredded (optional)

1. In a small frying pan, melt the butter over medium heat. Add the onion and cook it until it is translucent, about 3 minutes. Set the onion aside and allow it to cool.
2. Chop the spinach, and set it aside. In a large mixing bowl, using a wire whisk or fork, beat the eggs. Add the cooled onion, seasoning salt, nutmeg, parsley, hot chili oil, Almond Milk, and spinach, mixing thoroughly.
3. Spray a 9" or 10" pie plate with cooking oil spray. Cut the bacon up into ½" pieces and lay it evenly in pie plate. Add the cheese and pour the egg/milk mixture carefully over all. Bake the quiche at 375°F for 40 minutes or until a knife inserted off center comes out clean. Cool it for 10 minutes before serving.

NUTRITIONAL INFORMATION PER SERVING:
Carbohydrates: 4 grams • Effective Carb Count: 1 gram
Protein: 10 grams • Fat: 15 grams • Calories: 186

REDUCED-FAT VARIATION:
Omit the butter and cook the onion in a little bit
of Rich Stock (page 254) and use turkey bacon.
Carbohydrates: 4 grams • Effective Carb Count: 3 grams
Protein: 11 grams • Fat: 13 grams • Calories: 171

WONDERFUL WAFFLES

Makes 3 8" waffles

Fall mornings, lazy Saturdays . . . any time is the perfect time for Wonderful Waffles! Serve with Sugar-Free Pancake Syrup (page 256).

1 cup Almond Milk (page 240) or
½ cup cream thinned to 1 cup with water
1 teaspoon vanilla
2 eggs, separated
3 tablespoons butter, melted
1 cup pork rinds, crushed
2 tablespoons soy protein (not soy flour!)
¼ cup almonds, ground
1 teaspoon baking powder
½ teaspoon SteviaPlus
2 packets sucralose
1½ teaspoons cinnamon

1. In a large mixing bowl, combine the Almond Milk, vanilla, egg yolks, and melted butter. Set it aside.
2. In a small bowl, combine the pork rinds, soy protein, ground almonds, baking powder, SteviaPlus, sucralose, and cinnamon. Stir the dry ingredients into the wet ingredients until they are just combined.
3. In a small bowl with an electric mixer, whip the egg whites until stiff peaks form. Fold the beaten egg whites into the batter until they are just combined. There should still be a few egg white "puffs" left visible. Allow the batter to rest while the waffle iron heats up.
4. Bake the waffles on a well-greased, hot waffle iron until they stop steaming and are golden brown. Serve hot.

NUTRITIONAL INFORMATION PER SERVING:
Carbohydrates: 5 grams • Effective Carb Count: 3 grams
Protein: 22 grams • Fat: 35 grams • Calories: 393

ZUCCHINI NUT MUFFINS

Makes 8

Late summer and zucchini are synonymous. This sometimes dainty, often huge late-summer veggie is incredibly versatile. From side dishes to dinners to desserts, zucchini has endless possibilities. These delicious muffins are just one example.

3/4 cup almonds, ground
1/2 cup soy protein (not soy flour!)
1/2 teaspoon SteviaPlus
4 packets sucralose
1 1/2 teaspoons baking powder
1/4 teaspoon sea salt
1/2 teaspoon cinnamon
1/4 teaspoon nutmeg
1/2 teaspoon orange or lemon zest
1/2 cup pecan or walnut meats, broken into 1/4" to 1/2" pieces
1/2 cup Almond Milk (page 240) or 1/4 cup cream thinned to 1/2 cup with water

2 tablespoons butter, melted
1 egg
1/2 cup zucchini, shredded
Cooking oil spray

Topping:
6 tablespoons almonds, ground
3 tablespoons butter
1/2 teaspoon SteviaPlus or 2 packets sucralose
1/4 teaspoon orange or lemon zest
1/4 teaspoon cinnamon

1. In a large mixing bowl, combine the ground almonds, soy protein, SteviaPlus, sucralose, baking powder, salt, cinnamon, nutmeg, orange zest, and nut meats. Mix them well and set aside.
2. In a small mixing bowl, combine the Almond Milk, butter, egg, and zucchini. Mix them thoroughly, until they are uniform in texture. Add the wet ingredients all at once to the dry ingredients, mixing until just combined. The batter should be slightly lumpy.
3. Spray a standard-sized muffin tin with cooking oil spray. Place the batter into the muffin cups so that they are about 2/3 full.
4. Using a food processor with a chopping blade, combine the topping ingredients. Press evenly over muffins. Bake at 400°F for 15 minutes or until a toothpick inserted in the center comes out clean. Serve warm with butter.

NUTRITIONAL INFORMATION PER SERVING:
Carbohydrates: 6 grams • Effective Carb Count: 4 grams
Protein: 9 grams • Fat: 22 grams • Calories: 244

REDUCED-FAT VARIATION:
Use applesauce instead of the butter in the batter.
Use 1 1/2 tablespoons butter in the topping.
Carbohydrates: 6 grams • Effective Carb Count: 4 grams
Protein: 9 grams • Fat: 17 grams • Calories: 201

Main Courses

Beef and Meats

BACON CAULI JUMBLE

Serves 8

What do you do with some leftover meat, a package of bacon, a bit of cauliflower, and an onion? This is the answer! *Note:* Just about any leftover cooked meat will work in place of the Barbecue Pork (page 95). It is just especially nice!

<table>
<tr><td>

½ sweet onion, chopped
3 cloves garlic, minced
1 tablespoon butter
¼ teaspoon lemon pepper
¼ teaspoon celery seeds
2 teaspoons snipped chives
1 12-ounce package bacon, cut up
into bite-sized pieces

</td><td>

2 pounds Barbecue Pork (page 95)
½ head cauliflower, cut up into
bite-sized pieces (about 4 cups)
½ tablespoon parsley flakes
3 mint leaves (about 1 teaspoon
chopped or about ½ teaspoon
from a mint tea bag)

</td></tr>
</table>

1. Cook the onion and the garlic in the butter over medium heat in a large skillet until they are just becoming golden, about 8 minutes. Add the seasonings and bacon to the pan and cook them for about 10 minutes. The bacon will not crisp up like one would expect, but it will be done. (Or you may partially precook the bacon if you want it to be crispy.)
2. Add the Barbecue Pork, cauliflower, parsley, and mint, stirring them well to combine. Cover the pan and cook the Jumble for about 10 minutes, or until the cauliflower is cooked. Serve hot.

NUTRITIONAL INFORMATION PER SERVING:
Carbohydrates: 1 gram • Effective Carb Count: 0 grams
Protein: 24 grams • Fat: 25 grams • Calories: 332

REDUCED-FAT VARIATION:
Use turkey bacon and cook it at the same time with
the onion and the garlic. Omit the butter.
Carbohydrates: 2 grams • Effective Carb Count: 1 gram
Protein: 24 grams • Fat: 23 grams • Calories: 315

℘ Thicken sauces the low-carb way: While flour is traditionally used to thicken sauces, it is not a smart choice for the low-carb way of life. Arrowroot is a great thickening agent–it has only half the carbs of flour and uses less to thicken than cornstarch. Some other great low-carb alternatives to use as thickening agents are vegetable gums such as guar, carob bean, and xanthan. To thicken soups and stews, try Jerusalem artichokes, squash, or even okra, all of which are low-carb.

BARBECUE PORK

Serves 4

Have you ever wondered how barbecued meat in Asian restaurants gets the lovely red edging? It's all in the smoking process! Serve this Barbecue Pork with Egg Rolls (page 15) or Sesame Slaw (page 47) for an Asian-style meal! Save the leftovers and use for either Fried Rice-Aflower (page 111) or "Ham" Salad (page 113).

4 pork loin chops or ribs, boneless
Seasoning salt
Lemon pepper
Mesquite charcoal briquettes or chips

1. Season both sides of the meat liberally with seasoning salt and lemon pepper. Using a barbecue with a cover, place the meat on the highest rack setting (about 5" to 6" away from coals) over medium-hot coals. Cover the barbecue and allow the meat to smoke, turning it occasionally. Cook it for about 30 minutes. The meat should have a deep reddish appearance and be firm to the touch when done. Using the meat thermometer is discouraged when barbecuing because those precious juices are lost!
2. Remove from heat and slice thinly. Serve hot with sauces of choice. Offer sesame seeds alongside the sauces for dipping.

NUTRITIONAL INFORMATION PER SERVING:
Carbohydrates: 0 grams • Effective Carb Count: 0 grams
Protein: 21 grams • Fat: 6 grams • Calories: 144

When the weather is warm outside, who wants to heat up the house? Barbecuing is a simple alternative that yields terrific results. If you have a barbecue grill that uses charcoal, there are so many choices! Pure mesquite briquettes are available. Just combine 3 or 4 chunks of mesquite charcoal with your normal briquettes for a terrific Texas flavor. If you can't find the mesquite briquettes, most stores carry wood chips for barbecues. Simply follow the instructions on the package. Apple wood chips lend a particularly nice flavor to barbecued food!

BEEF GRAVY SUPREME

Makes 8 servings

Serve this over Baked Winter Squash, spaghetti (page 216) for a yummy dinner! If you like it stroganoff style, just add ½ cup sour cream right before serving.

½ large sweet onion, chopped
1 tablespoon lard
2 pounds ground beef
2 stalks celery, chopped
4 cloves garlic, minced (or ½ teaspoon garlic salt and omit seasoning salt)
2 tablespoons fresh parsley, chopped (or 1 tablespoon dried)
1 mint leaf (½ teaspoon, approximately), chopped (or ½ teaspoon of mint from an unused mint tea bag would work)
½ teaspoon fresh lemon thyme, chopped (or ¼ teaspoon dried thyme would work if no lemon thyme is available)
½ teaspoon lemon pepper
⅛ teaspoon dry mustard powder
1 teaspoon seasoning salt
⅛ teaspoon SteviaPlus or ½ packet sucralose
⅛ teaspoon hot chili oil or a few grains of cayenne
1 ½ cups water or beef or pork Rich Stock (page 254)
1 tablespoon arrowroot mixed into ½ cup water

1. In a small skillet, cook the onion in the lard until translucent and it begins to brown around the edges.
2. Meanwhile, in a large skillet with a lid, brown the ground beef. Drain it.
3. Add the cooked onion with its juices. Stir in the celery, garlic, parsley, mint, lemon thyme, lemon pepper, mustard powder, seasoning salt, SteviaPlus, chili oil, and water or stock. Cover and simmer 45 minutes to 1 hour.
4. Just before serving, add the arrowroot/water mixture to the boiling gravy and stir.

NUTRITIONAL INFORMATION PER SERVING:
Carbohydrates: 3 grams • Effective Carb Count: 2 grams
Protein: 19 grams • Fat: 32 grams • Calories: 382

REDUCED-FAT VARIATION:
Use lean ground beef and brown the onion at
the same time as the beef. Omit the lard.
Carbohydrates: 3 grams • Effective Carb Count: 2 grams
Protein: 21 grams • Fat: 24 grams • Calories: 316

BEEF PECAN

Makes 10 servings

The original high-carb version of this recipe called for rice and cream of mushroom soup. Not exactly low-carb fare! This variation has the same feel as the original without all the carbs.

Sauce:

½ small onion, chopped
4 tablespoons butter
3 stalks celery, chopped
¾ teaspoon sea salt
¼ teaspoon marjoram
1 teaspoon parsley flakes
½ teaspoon seasoning salt
Pinch pepper
½ cup beef Rich Stock (page 254) or
commercially prepared stock
1¾ cups half-and-half, cream, or
Almond Milk (page 240)
¼ cup half-and-half, cream, or
Almond Milk mixed with
1½ teaspoons arrowroot powder

Casserole base:

1⅓ pounds ground beef
½ teaspoon seasoning salt
1 6" head cauliflower, including peeled stem
Cooking oil spray

Topping:

¾ cup almonds, ground
⅓ cup soy protein powder
½ teaspoon sea salt
¼ teaspoon Sweet & Slender
¼ teaspoon SteviaPlus
4 tablespoons butter, chilled
¾ cup pecan pieces, broken

Recipe continues on page 98 ➤

➤ Recipe continued from page 97

1. In a 4-quart saucepan with a lid, cook the onion in the butter over medium heat until golden, about 10 minutes. Add the celery, sea salt, marjoram, parsley, seasoning salt, pepper, and stock to the pan, cover it, and bring it to a boil over medium heat. Reduce the heat to low and simmer it for 10 minutes, until the celery becomes soft. Remove the lid, pour in the 1 ¾ cups half-and-half, and heat it over medium-low heat until it is steaming. It is very important that you not boil your half-and-half. Add the half-and-half/arrowroot mixture and set the sauce aside.

2. While the onions and celery are cooking, brown the ground beef in a medium-sized frying pan over medium heat with the seasoning salt. When the beef is thoroughly browned, drain it, and set it aside.

3. Using a food processor with a chopping blade, finely chop the cauliflower into small pieces that resemble rice. A pulsing action works best for this task. Put the chopped cauliflower into a large bowl and set it aside. (You should end up with about 6 cups of chopped cauliflower.)

4. To make the topping, add all of the topping ingredients EXCEPT the pecans to the food processor bowl, and pulse until well combined. Pour the topping into a small mixing bowl and add the broken pecan pieces. Set it aside.

5. When the sauce is done, add the ground beef and mix it well. Spray a 9" × 13" baking dish with cooking oil spray, and spread the cauliflower evenly over the bottom of the dish. Pour the beef and cream mixture over the cauliflower, making sure that all of the cauliflower is covered with the sauce. Sprinkle the topping evenly over the beef mixture. Bake at 350°F for 35 to 40 minutes, or until the sauce is bubbling and topping is golden brown. Remove the casserole from the oven and allow it to rest 5 to 10 minutes before serving.

NUTRITIONAL INFORMATION PER SERVING:
Carbohydrates: 8 grams • Effective Carb Count: 6 grams
Protein: 16 grams • Fat: 42 grams • Calories: 466

REDUCED-FAT VARIATION:
Omit the butter in the sauce and use canned skim milk.
Cook the onions with the rest of the vegetables in the broth.
Use lean ground beef in the casserole base.
Use 2 tablespoons olive oil instead of the butter in the topping.
Carbohydrates: 11 grams • Effective Carb Count: 9 grams
Protein: 19 grams • Fat: 25 grams • Calories: 342

BEEF STEW WITH PUMPKIN

Serves 8

Super hearty! Warm and satisfying for those cold winter nights. Note: There is no additional cooking liquid added to this recipe. It is very important to have a tightly fitting lid for your pan! Also, avoid opening the pan until after at least the first hour, or you will lose too much of the precious steam.

2 pounds beef stew meat	2 small turnips, cut into 3/4" cubes
2 tablespoons lard	2 carrots, cut into 1/2" chunks
1/2 teaspoon seasoning salt	(optional)
1 medium sweet onion, chopped	1/2 head cabbage, cut into 1 1/2" cubes
1 clove elephant garlic or 2 cloves	1/2 teaspoon seasoning salt
garlic, minced	1/4 teaspoon basil
2 bay leaves	1/4 lemon pepper
4" tops from 1 bunch celery or 2 large	1 cup pumpkin purée
stalks celery, chopped	

1. Place the stew meat and lard into a 5-quart stockpot. Season it with 1/2 teaspoon seasoning salt. Cook over medium heat until the meat loses most of its redness, about 5 minutes.
2. Add the onion and garlic, and continue to cook until the onion is translucent, about 3 to 4 minutes. Add the bay leaves, celery, turnips, carrots, cabbage, 1/2 teaspoon seasoning salt, basil, and lemon pepper. Cover tightly and allow to simmer on low 4 to 6 hours.
3. After that time, remove the bay leaves and add the pumpkin to the pot. Simmer uncovered 5 minutes.

NUTRITIONAL INFORMATION PER SERVING:
Carbohydrates: 7 grams • Effective Carb Count: 5 grams
Protein: 33 grams • Fat: 27 grams • Calories: 406

REDUCED-FAT VARIATION:
Omit the lard and use cooking spray to brown lean beef.
Cook the onions at the same time as the beef.
Carbohydrates: 7 grams • Effective Carb Count: 5 grams
Protein: 23 grams • Fat: 16 grams • Calories: 273

CARING FOR YOUR HERBS: In order to encourage new growth in your herbs, you need to give them a "haircut." For maximum growth and health, trim your herbs every couple of months. Keep the tender cuttings for drying or immediate cooking, and discard any brown leaves or flowers. Wash the trimmings carefully to remove dirt and dry them—this is perfect for winter use when your plants are dormant!

BONFIRE BARBECUE STEAK

Serves 6

This recipe can be used with any large out-of-doors cooking fire or barbecue. While the meat is cooking, sit back, enjoy the fire, and relax!

1 1/2 pounds London broil, or
other boneless beef steak suitable for broiling
4 large cloves garlic
1/2 teaspoon seasoning salt
1/4 teaspoon lemon pepper
Foil
Large bonfire, or other outdoor cooking fire

1. Before building your bonfire, slice the beef into 1/4"-thick pieces, and place it into a container with a lid. Mince the garlic and stir it into the beef along with the seasoning salt and lemon pepper. Cover and allow the meat to rest while building the fire.
2. When the coals are red-hot, it's time to do the cooking! Place 2 large sheets of foil crosswise, one on top of the other. Lay the meat out as thinly as possible across the wide middle part of the foil. Wrap it up tightly, pressing out any air and making sure there are no gaps in the wrapping. If necessary, place another sheet of foil around the meat.
3. Place the meat bundle into the hot coals, and allow it to cook approximately 45 minutes, turning once partway through. Using a shovel or some other implement, remove the meat bundle from the fire. Allow the meat to rest 5 minutes. Carefully open the bundle, allowing the steam to escape. Serve hot with Roasted Veggies over a Bonfire (page 231).

NUTRITIONAL INFORMATION PER SERVING:
Carbohydrates: 1 gram • Effective Carb Count: 0 grams
Protein: 20 grams • Fat: 27 grams • Calories: 333

Which pans are the best? While nonstick pans are great for those who are on low-fat diets, they often leave a lot to be desired in terms of cooking quality! On the other hand, an inexpensive wok and cast iron skillets are easy to care for and forgiving. They will not pit and degrade like nonstick cookware, as long as they are well seasoned.

BROILED LAMB CHOPS

Serves 4

Lovely accompanied by Rice-Aflower Pilaf (page 229)!

4 lamb blade chops
4 teaspoons Braggs Liquid Aminos, divided
½ teaspoon seasoning salt, divided
¼ teaspoon garlic granules, divided
¼ teaspoon lemon pepper, divided
1 tablespoon fresh rosemary, chopped, divided (or 1½ teaspoons dried)

1. Place the chops on the rack of a broiler pan. Season with half of the seasonings in the order given. Broil the chops a few inches away from the broiler element for about 5 minutes, or until they are browned and the fat is beginning to sizzle around the edges.
2. Remove the pan from the oven and turn the chops over. Season the chops with the remaining seasonings. Return the pan to the oven and continue to broil the chops for about 3 more minutes or until they test 160°F with a meat thermometer for medium.

NUTRITIONAL INFORMATION PER SERVING:
Carbohydrates: 1 gram • Effective Carb Count: 0 grams
Protein: 16 grams • Fat: 25 grams • Calories: 302

What does "seasoning a pan" mean? That is the process that turns a yucky old pan to which everything sticks, into a wonderful cooking utensil! To season the wok or cast-iron pan, begin with a clean pan. Scrub it as clean as possible. If there are any really stuck-on bits, don't worry, they will burn off during the seasoning process. Using a folded-up paper towel (or more if they are thin), rub a small amount of oil onto the entire cooking surface, so that the oil is absorbed by the pan. Turn the heat on "high" and continue to rub the oil into the pan. Be very careful not to burn your fingers! Keep that towel between you and the hot pan, or you'll end up with a nasty burn. When the pan begins to smoke slightly, turn off the heat and allow the pan to cool. When it is completely cooled, repeat the process. Continue to repeat the above process until the pan has achieved a deep-black, shiny appearance. Once a pan is seasoned, cleanup is quite simple. Wipe the pan clean with a towel, rub a little oil into the surface, bring it to smoking-heat again, and allow it to cool again. Occasionally the pan will need to be soaked and scrubbed, but then simply repeat the seasoning steps a couple of times and it will be good to go again!

CABBAGE SOUP

Serves 4

This simple soup is a hit even with cabbage haters! The variations are many: Instead of the beaten egg, slices of hard-cooked egg may be used as a garnish. You can garnish it with cheese or toasted low-carb bread. Use this simple formula and create a variety of interesting soups!

4 to 6 cups Rich Stock (page 254), any flavor
1 to 1 1/2 cups cooked pork, cut up into bite-sized pieces
2 cups cabbage, chopped
1/2 cup celery, chopped (optional)
1/2 tablespoon parsley flakes
Seasoning salt, to taste
Lemon pepper, to taste

Optional ingredients:

A few drops of hot chili oil
1 egg, beaten
Sour cream or yogurt for a garnish

Combine all ingredients except egg in a stock pan with a lid. Cover and simmer for at least 25 minutes, or until cabbage is tender. Uncover and pour egg in, stirring in only one direction. Garnish as desired.

NUTRITIONAL INFORMATION PER SERVING:
Carbohydrates: 3 grams • Effective Carb Count: 2 grams
Protein: 11 grams • Fat: 9 grams • Calories: 142

A good set of measuring cups and spoons is absolutely essential to any kitchen, especially if you're low-carbing! Be sure your spoon set includes a 1/2 tablespoon and 1/8 teaspoon size. Measuring cups should have flat bottoms that can rest on a counter without tipping over when empty. A glass liquid measure with both ounces and cups shown is very useful; either 1 or 2 cups will do. A small dietary scale is also a helpful kitchen item.

CARNE

Serves 6

This meat can be used in a variety of dishes. It can be eaten alone with a dollop of sour cream or a sprinkling of cheese as a garnish. It can be wrapped up in a lettuce leaf with guacamole and olives. It can be placed into low-carb tortillas for a taco or burrito, or it can be made into Enchiladas, Sharron-Style (page 109).

1 tablespoon garlic powder
1 tablespoon ground cumin
2 teaspoons seasoning salt
3/4 teaspoon lemon pepper
1/4 teaspoon dried oregano
2 pounds boneless or 3 pounds bone-in
* meat (pork, beef, chicken, or turkey;*
* bone-in preferred), cut into pieces that*
* will easily fit into the pot*

2 tablespoons lard
2 cups water
1 small onion, minced
1 teaspoon lime juice
(fresh is always best!)
6 drops (about 1/4 teaspoon)
* hot chili oil*

1. In a very small bowl, combine the spices. Sprinkle them over the meat and allow it to rest while the lard is melting over medium heat in a large (5-quart) nonaluminum pot with a lid. Place the meat into the pot and brown it on all sides. Add more cooking fat if needed to prevent the meat from sticking to the bottom of the pot.
2. Add the water so that it nearly covers the meat. Add the onion to the pot, and cover it. Bring it to a slow boil and reduce the heat so it is just bubbling. Skim off any foam that rises to the surface. These are impurities that will adversely affect the taste of your broth. Also be sure your meat remains completely covered in broth for the entire cooking time. Add more liquid if necessary.
3. Cook the meat until it is beginning to fall off the bone, from about 1½ hours for a chicken, up to 4 hours for beef. Toward the end of the cooking time, add the lime juice and hot chili oil.
4. Transfer the meat and broth to the refrigerator and allow it to cool until the fat has become a hard layer on the top, usually overnight. Remove the fat and warm up the meat on the stove top. Remove the bones and other inedible parts and shred the meat, returning it to the broth so that it will stay moist.

NUTRITIONAL INFORMATION PER SERVING:
Carbohydrates: 4 grams • Effective Carb Count: 3 grams
Protein: 22 grams • Fat: 29 grams • Calories: 368

REDUCED-FAT VARIATION:
Use cooking spray to brown the meat instead of the lard and follow the instructions given for removing the fat from the meat.
Carbohydrates: 4 grams • Effective Carb Count: 3 grams
Protein: 31 grams • Fat: 22 grams • Calories: 340

CHUNKY BEEF SOUP

Serves 4

Sometimes you just need a warm, satisfying, homemade soup. This is a good choice!

2 tablespoons lard
1 1/2 pounds beef stew meat
1 onion, cut into 3/4" cubes
4 cloves garlic, minced
1 carrot, cut into 1/2" cubes (optional)
1 small turnip, cut into 3/4" cubes
1 1/2 cups cabbage, cut into 3/4" cubes
1 bay leaf
1 1/2 teaspoons fresh lemon thyme, minced, or dried thyme flakes
2 tablespoons parsley, minced
2 cups water or beef Rich Stock (page 254)
1 teaspoon sea salt
1/2 teaspoon seasoning salt
1/4 teaspoon lemon pepper

1. In a large pot, place the lard, meat, onion, and garlic. Cook over medium heat, stirring often, until the meat begins to brown and the onion becomes translucent. Add the remaining ingredients.
2. Cover and simmer for 1 hour. Some of the vegetables will have dissolved by this time, but this creates a very rich broth, which does not need a thickener. Remove the bay leaf and serve hot in bowls.

NUTRITIONAL INFORMATION PER SERVING:
Carbohydrates: 10 grams • Effective Carb Count: 7 grams
Protein: 18 grams • Fat: 18 grams • Calories: 283

REDUCED-FAT VARIATION:
Omit the lard and use cooking spray to brown
the meat and the onions and garlic.
Carbohydrates: 10 grams • Effective Carb Count: 7 grams
Protein: 18 grams • Fat: 12 grams • Calories: 225

TIP TO REMOVE THE SKIN FROM GARLIC: To remove the skin easily from a clove of fresh garlic, lay it on a cutting board and place the flat blade of a butcher knife across it. Give it a good thump with your fist, and then pick it up. The skin should virtually fall off, and the garlic is ready for mincing!

CORNED BEEF WITH VEGETABLES

Makes 8 servings

It doesn't have to be St. Patrick's Day to enjoy a good corned beef! Slice the meat thinly and serve with "Honey" Mustard Dipping Sauce (page 251) or Fiery Hot Mustard (page 246), if desired.

*2 1/2 pounds fresh corned beef with
seasoning herb packet
3 carrots, peeled and
cut into 2" chunks, optional
3 large stalks celery,
cut into 3" chunks*

*1 large sweet onion, sliced
4 cloves garlic, chopped
2 tablespoons lard
1/4 teaspoon seasoning salt
Water
1/3 head cabbage*

1. Place the beef, herb packet, carrots, and celery in a 5-quart stockpot with a lid. In a small frying pan, cook the onion and garlic in the lard with the seasoning salt over medium heat. When the onions are translucent and becoming golden, add them to the beef and veggies. Add enough water to completely cover the beef. Bring it to a boil, cover, and simmer 2 hours. During the cooking time, skim off any of the impurities that come to the top as foam and discard.
2. When the 2 hours have just about passed, cut cabbage into wedges about 5" long and 2" wide. Place into the simmering pot, cover, and cook 15 minutes. Continue to remove any impurities as they float to the top. Place the meat and veggies onto a large serving platter.

NUTRITIONAL INFORMATION PER SERVING:
Carbohydrates: 5 grams • Effective Carb Count: 4 grams
Protein: 21 grams • Fat: 24 grams • Calories: 329

REDUCED-FAT VARIATION:
Don't cook the onions and garlic in the lard, simply add them to the veggies in the pot. Chill the meat and veggies in the broth in the refrigerator overnight and remove the fat that forms in a hard layer at the top.
Carbohydrates: 5 grams • Effective Carb Count: 4 grams
Protein: 21 grams • Fat: 21 grams • Calories: 301

A really great item to have in your "kitchen arsenal" is a meat thermometer. With all the meat we eat in this way of life, it is a really important tool! How else will you know if that burger is cooked past the point where e-coli or other bacteria will live? Thermometers with temperature guidelines on the face of the dial are easiest to read. Ham cooks to 160°F. Well-done beef, as well as veal, pork, and lamb, cook to 170°F. Poultry needs to register 180°F to be done, unless you are just cooking breasts, and they are done at 170°F.

CREAM OF LEFTOVER SOUP

Makes 4 servings

This is incredibly versatile! Use whatever you have in your fridge. Makes a great lunch on a cold, rainy day!

1 to 1 1/2 pounds cooked meat,
cut into 1" cubes (beef, pork, chicken, meatloaf, whatever!)
1 to 2 cups cooked vegetables, diced
1 small carrot, diced
1 cup cauliflower, finely chopped
1/2 medium sweet onion, diced
2 cloves garlic, minced
2 stalks celery, or the leafy tops from 1 bunch, chopped
1 tablespoon parsley
1 teaspoon sea salt, or to taste
1/2 teaspoon lemon pepper
1/8 teaspoon basil
1/8 teaspoon celery seed
3 cups Rich Stock (page 254)—beef, chicken, or turkey,
depending on what meat was chosen—or commercially prepared stock
1/2 cup almonds, blanched
2 cups water (or instead of almonds/water, 1 cup cream
plus an additional cup of Rich Stock may be substituted)
1 tablespoon butter

1. Place the meat, vegetables, and seasonings into a 5-quart stockpot with a lid. Pour the stock over all. Cover and bring it to a boil over medium heat. Reduce the heat and simmer for 30 minutes or until vegetables are tender.
2. Meanwhile, place the water and almonds into a blender container and blend on high for approximately 1 1/2 minutes, or until the almonds are completely pulverized and the mixture is smooth. Pour it into the soup. Add the butter. Simmer, uncovered, 5 minutes. Serve hot.

NUTRITIONAL INFORMATION PER SERVING
(CALCULATED WITH ALMONDS/WATER):
Carbohydrates: 9 grams • Effective Carb Count: 5 grams
Protein: 5 grams • Fat: 12 grams • Calories: 156

CREAMY HAM FILLING

Serves 6

This is great in Crepes (page 64)! It can also be thinned slightly and served over Rice-Aflower (page 227) or Slurp 'Em Up Cabbage Noodles (page 233) as an entree.

1 small onion, finely chopped
1 tablespoon lard
1 tablespoon butter
½ teaspoon seasoning salt
3 cups ham, diced
½ tablespoon parsley flakes (or fresh if available; same amount)
¼ teaspoon lemon pepper
1 8-ounce package cream cheese, softened
⅓ cup water

In a medium-sized saucepan, cook the onion in the fat and seasoning salt over medium heat until it is golden, about 8 minutes. Add the remaining ingredients, cooking and stirring over medium-low heat until they are well combined and heated through.

NUTRITIONAL INFORMATION PER SERVING:
Carbohydrates: 5 grams • Effective Carb Count: 4 grams
Protein: 15 grams • Fat: 24 grams • Calories: 299

REDUCED-FAT VARIATION:
Use lean ham. Cook the onion in a little bit of Rich Stock (page 254) and omit the butter and lard. Use low-fat cream cheese.
Carbohydrates: 3 grams • Effective Carb Count: 2 grams
Protein: 17 grams • Fat: 12 grams • Calories: 194

EGG SALAD

Makes 6 servings

When one has candida, it makes it very difficult to make even the most basic things. It does until you start thinking creatively, anyway! Traditional egg salads usually rely heavily on commercial mayonnaise and pickles. Those are both "vinegar" foods, which must be eliminated while one is on candida treatment. This great-tasting egg salad is excellent for folks with candida, and also for those without! It is delicious as a stuffing for celery sticks or eaten on Crackers (page 10).

6 eggs
1/3 cup Blender Mayonnaise (page 241) or
commercially prepared mayonnaise
1/2 tablespoon onion flakes
Seasoning salt, to taste
Lemon pepper, to taste
1 teaspoon parsley flakes
5 drops hot chili oil

1. Place the eggs into a pot filled with enough cold water to cover the eggs. Put a pinch of salt into the water. This helps keep the shells from cracking. Bring the pot to a boil over medium heat; then turn off the heat and allow them to rest undisturbed for about 10 minutes. Drain the hot water off the eggs and immerse them in cold water.
2. Peel the eggs and mash them using a potato masher or a fork. Stir in the rest of the ingredients. Adjust seasonings to taste.

NUTRITIONAL INFORMATION PER SERVING:
Carbohydrates: 1 gram • Effective Carb Count: 0 grams
Protein: 6 grams • Fat: 15 grams • Calories: 155

REDUCED-FAT VARIATION:
Use reduced-fat mayonnaise.
Carbohydrates: 3 grams • Effective Carb Count: 2 grams
Protein: 6 grams • Fat: 7 grams • Calories: 98

ENCHILADAS, SHARRON-STYLE

Makes 12 servings

This is a wonderfully special meal! Serve it with Kids' Guacamole (page 25) or Grown-Ups' Guacamole (page 19) and sour cream. Yummm! For a special treat, add a can of well-drained Mexican-style canned tomatoes (watch for the sugar) and some sliced jalapeños before topping with the cheese. Bake as directed. You can even turn this into Mexican pizzas by laying the tortillas–High-Protein Wraps (page 225) would be good here–onto baking sheets and garnishing with the toppings listed and diced tomatoes, jalapeños, olives, etc., and baking until the cheese is melted. Be creative!

1 prepared recipe of Carne (page 103)
12 low-carb tortillas, small corn tortillas, or High-Protein Wraps
¾ pound Monterey jack cheese, shredded

1. If the *Carne* is cold, warm the *Carne* so that it is steaming. Spoon just enough of the broth to cover the bottom of a 9" × 13" baking dish.
2. Place about ½ to 1 cup of the steaming broth into another shallow dish that has a curved edge. Dip the tortillas one at a time into the warm broth to soften them. Keep the broth warm by adding fresh broth as the tortillas are being soaked. The warmed broth makes the tortillas more pliable.
3. As the tortillas are soaked, place each onto a plate or other work surface and fill with about ⅓ to ½ cup of the prepared meat. Roll the tortilla, overlapping the sides, leaving the ends open, and place "flaps down" into the baking dish. Continue in this fashion until all of the enchiladas are assembled.
4. Cover them with the cheese. Bake them at 350°F for about 25 minutes, or until the cheese is melted and becoming golden in places.

NUTRITIONAL INFORMATION PER SERVING:
Carbohydrates: 14 grams • Effective Carb Count: 4 grams
Protein: 28 grams • Fat: 22 grams • Calories: 338

REDUCED-FAT VARIATION:
Use reduced-fat cheese. See the tip below.
Carbohydrates: 15 grams • Effective Carb Count: 5 grams
Protein: 28 grams • Fat: 15 grams • Calories: 281

What's the best way to bake low-fat cheese? Brenda Czaya shared this tip with me: Low-fat cheese doesn't melt and brown the same as regular cheese does. If you are using low-fat cheese on a casserole, just bake it until it begins to melt; then take the dish out of the oven. Spray it with cooking oil spray; then return it to the oven to finish baking. It will brown and crisp up as you would expect cheese to do.

FAKE-ARONI AND CHEESE CASSEROLE

Serves 6

Think of that timeless kids' favorite, macaroni and cheese, and you've got it! This recipe doubles, even triples, quite easily, just be sure to allow for extra baking time!

1 1/2 cups sour cream
2 eggs
1 1/4 cups cheese, shredded (Colby, Monterey jack, Cheddar, mozzarella, etc.)
1/4 teaspoon paprika
1 1/2 tablespoons minced onion, dried
1 teaspoon seasoning salt
1/4 teaspoon lemon pepper
1 pound cauliflower, chopped into 1/2" pieces
(approximately 5 cups, either fresh or frozen)
1 pound beef franks, cut into bite-sized pieces
1 tablespoon parsley flakes
Cooking oil spray

1. In a large mixing bowl, stir together the sour cream, eggs, cheese, and spices (except the parsley). Mix thoroughly with a wire whisk, if available. Stir the cauliflower and franks into the cheese mixture.
2. Spray a 9" × 13" × 2" pan with cooking oil spray and pour the cauliflower-and-cheese mixture into the pan. Spread the mixture evenly and sprinkle it with the parsley flakes. Bake it at 350°F for about 25 to 35 minutes, or until it is bubbly and golden.

NUTRITIONAL INFORMATION PER SERVING:
Carbohydrates: 8 grams • Effective Carb Count: 6 grams
Protein: 18 grams • Fat: 38 grams • Calories: 440

REDUCED-FAT VARIATION:
Use chicken hot dogs, low-fat sour cream, and reduced-fat cheese.
Carbohydrates: 12 grams • Effective Carb Count: 10 grams
Protein: 19 grams • Fat: 18 grams • Calories: 284

FRIED RICE-AFLOWER

Makes 6 servings

Fried rice is a staple in many Asian households. Most Americans love it as well, but rice is not on most low-carb plans! Try this next time you get a hankering for some delicious fried rice. This makes a meal by itself!

½ head cauliflower
(about 4 cups, chopped)
1 carrot
½ 10" zucchini
2 stalks celery
1¼ pounds pork or chicken, cooked
(directions also given if meat is raw)
2 eggs

1 teaspoon seasoning salt, divided
Lard
½ tablespoon chopped chives, fresh
½ teaspoon lemon pepper
1 ½ teaspoons sesame oil
¼ teaspoon hot chili oil or a tiny
pinch of cayenne
1 teaspoon lemon juice

1. Have a large mixing bowl available in which to place prepared veggies. Using a food processor with chopping blade, finely chop cauliflower florets with pulsing action, so they are the consistency of rice. Place the chopped cauliflower into the bowl. Using a shredding disk, shred the carrot and zucchini. Using the slicing disk, slice celery. (Or follow the same steps by hand.) Place all in the bowl.
2. If the meat is cooked, use the slicing disk and slice meat. (If it is raw, cut it up by hand into ½" pieces.) Place the meat in a separate bowl.
3. Break the eggs into a small dish and season with a small amount of the seasoning salt, beat, and set aside.
4. Heat a large wok or other large skillet over high heat with about 2 tablespoons of lard to begin. When it is hot, add eggs to the wok, cooking until solid. Place the cooked eggs back into the bowl they had been in previously, and set aside. (If using raw meat, add a small amount of lard and the meat to the wok and cook until meat is no longer pink.) Add another 2 tablespoons of lard to the wok and the prepared vegetables. Cook, using a scooping and lifting motion, bringing the cooked veggies up from the bottom so they become thoroughly mixed during the process. Cover and allow vegetables to steam for a total of about 5 minutes, stirring about every 1½ minutes. Add additional fat as necessary, so the vegetables don't scorch.
5. When they are steaming and smelling good, add the egg, breaking it up as it is being added in. Stir. Add the meat and stir well. Season with remaining seasoning salt, lemon pepper, sesame oil, hot chili oil, and lemon juice. Taste and adjust seasonings if necessary (some like it hot, some like it saltier!).

NUTRITIONAL INFORMATION PER SERVING:
Carbohydrates: 6 grams • Effective Carb Count: 4 grams
Protein: 22 grams • Fat: 11 grams • Calories: 216

HAMBURGER STEW

Makes 6 servings

Sometimes at the end of the pay period I look into my refrigerator and all I have left is some bits and pieces of this and that. It always seems that this is the time when I make this dish. It is hearty and satisfying. I don't feel quite so much like it is the end of a pay period then!

1 1/2 pounds ground beef
2 tablespoons lard
1 large Walla Walla Sweet onion, or
any sweet onion, chopped
1 carrot, grated
2 cups cabbage, cut in 3/4" cubes

1 1/2 cups beef Rich Stock (page 254)
or commercially prepared stock
Lemon pepper, to taste
Garlic salt, to taste
1/2 tablespoon arrowroot
mixed into 1/4 cup water

1. In a large skillet that has a cover, brown the ground beef over medium heat until it is no longer pink. Drain and set aside.
2. Place the lard into the skillet, add the onion, and cook until the onion is translucent and is beginning to become golden brown around the edges, about 5 minutes. Stir in the grated carrot; cook for 1 minute. Put the meat back into the pan and add the cabbage, stock, lemon pepper, and garlic salt to taste.
3. Cover and simmer over medium-low heat for 30 minutes. When almost ready to serve, pour the arrowroot/water mixture into the stew, stirring until well combined. Serve in bowls.

NUTRITIONAL INFORMATION PER SERVING:
Carbohydrates: 5 grams • Effective Carb Count: 4 grams
Protein: 20 grams • Fat: 35 grams • Calories: 418

REDUCED-FAT VARIATION:
Use lean ground beef and omit the lard.
Cook the onion and carrot in with the beef, then drain.
Carbohydrates: 5 grams • Effective Carb Count: 4 grams
Protein: 21 grams • Fat: 24 grams • Calories: 327

There are ways to test meat besides a thermometer. If you are cooking a steak, for instance, and want it to be rare, use your own hand as a guide. Ball your hand up into a fist. Don't squeeze it, just hold it loosely. The big muscle between your index finger and thumb is the gauge. With the hand in a fist and relaxed, poke that muscle with the index finger of your other hand. That muscle feels like what "rare" meat feels like. With the muscle slightly tightened, that is what "medium-rare" feels like. When the fist is squeezed tight, that is how a "well done" piece of meat feels. Another simple way is to poke something, like a metal skewer, into the center of the piece of meat and put it against your lip. If it feels hot to the touch, it is most likely done.

"Ham" Salad

Serves 4

If you are trying to avoid foods processed with nitrates, but still have cravings for ham, try this tasty alternative. Serve it with sliced cauliflower, celery sticks, zucchini or cucumber slices, or pork rinds for scooping.

1 pound Barbecue Pork (page 95)
2/3 cup Blender Mayonnaise (page 241) or
commercially prepared mayonnaise
1/2 tablespoon parsley
1 tablespoon onion flakes
1/4 teaspoon basil
1/2 teaspoon garlic salt
1/4 teaspoon dry mustard powder
1/4 teaspoon lemon pepper
1/4 teaspoon SteviaPlus or 1/2 packet sucralose

Remove any visible fat from the Barbecue Pork. Place it into a food processor with a chopping blade, and process until the meat resembles fine crumbs. Place the chopped meat into a large mixing bowl. Add the remaining ingredients, and mix well.

Nutritional information per serving:
Carbohydrates: 2 grams • Effective Carb Count: 1 gram
Protein: 6 grams • Fat: 9 grams • Calories: 115

Reduced-Fat Variation:
Use a lean piece of pork and reduced-fat mayonnaise.
Carbohydrates: 2 grams • Effective Carb Count: 1 gram
Protein: 7 grams • Fat: 3 grams • Calories: 66

Some thoughts about barbecuing: The best part of barbecuing is the smoke! The smokier it is, the more flavorful the food will be. Season the food directly over the coals, so that the excess herbs and seasonings will fall on the hot coals for an extra smoky flavor. If it is smoking excessively, check the meat. If the coals are too hot, the meat can either be moved to the edges of the barbecue, where the heat is less intense, or the fire can actually be "turned down" by closing the air vents on the bottom of the barbecue for a couple of minutes. Just don't forget to reopen them, otherwise the fire will smother and the food will be raw.

Ham Salad Spread

Serves 4

This is good for a picnic! Cooked chicken or turkey work equally as well as the ham.

1 cup cooked ham or pork roast, chopped
1 large rib celery (leaves are okay)
1 teaspoon minced onion, dried
⅛ teaspoon celery seed
1/16 teaspoon lemon pepper (that is ½ of ⅛ teaspoon!)
½ tablespoon parsley flakes
⅛ teaspoon basil, dried
1/16 teaspoon dry mustard or hot chili oil
2 tablespoons Blender Mayonnaise (page 241) or
commercially prepared mayonnaise
¼ teaspoon Sweet & Slender

Combine all of the ingredients in a large food processor bowl. Pulse until they are all well combined. Spread on sliced veggies or low-carb crackers.

Nutritional information per serving:
Carbohydrates: 2 grams • Effective Carb Count: 1 gram
Protein: 6 grams • Fat: 9 grams • Calories: 115

Reduced-Fat Variation:
Use lean ham or equivalent roasted chicken. Use low-fat mayonnaise.
Carbohydrates: 2 grams • Effective Carb Count: 1 gram
Protein: 7 grams • Fat: 3 grams • Calories: 66

HERBED PORK CUTLETS

Serves 4

Rosemary is such a wonderful herb. Not only is the plant lovely to look at, but food cooked with it has that "something extra." Serve this alongside Rice-Aflower Pilaf (page 229).

¹⁄₃ cup almonds, ground
¹⁄₃ cup pork rinds, crushed
2 tablespoons soy protein (not soy flour!)
¹⁄₂ teaspoon seasoning salt
¹⁄₂ teaspoon rosemary (dried, but not crushed)
¹⁄₄ teaspoon lemon pepper
¹⁄₈ teaspoon thyme
1 pound pork cutlets, cubed (the kind
that have been "tenderized" like cube steaks)
2 to 4 teaspoons lard

1. Combine all of the dry ingredients in a small shallow dish. Rinse the cutlets in cold water; then dip them into the coating mixture.
2. Melt enough lard in a large fying pan with a lid to keep the meat from sticking. Place the meat into the hot fat and cook it, covered, over medium heat about 10 minutes per side, about 20 minutes total. The cutlets should be golden-brown when done.

NUTRITIONAL INFORMATION PER SERVING:
Carbohydrates: 2 grams • Effective Carb Count: 1 gram
Protein: 25 grams • Fat: 22 grams • Calories: 304

REDUCED-FAT VARIATION:
Spray the coated cutlets with cooking spray directly on
each side before cooking. Do not use the lard.
Carbohydrates: 2 grams • Effective Carb Count: 1 gram
Protein: 25 grams • Fat: 20 grams • Calories: 285

Homemade Lunch Meat

Makes 8 servings

In the book *The Little House on the Prairie,* by Laura Ingalls Wilder, she describes her mother's making "head cheese." This is a modern version, without the head! It offers folks with chemical sensitivities an option when they need luncheon meat. It cannot be sliced thinly like deli meat, but is more like a meatloaf in texture.

2 pounds pork (a fatty cut like country-style ribs or pork steaks preferred)
Water to cover

Seasonings (adjust to taste):

1 tablespoon minced onion, dried
1 ½ teaspoons seasoning salt
½ teaspoon lemon pepper
½ teaspoon basil
A few drops of hot chili oil

1. Place the meat into a pan; cover it with water. Simmer, covered, for about 3 hours on low heat. The meat should be falling off the bone. Reserve cooking liquid.
2. Cool the meat to room temperature; then remove the bones and huge chunks of fat from the meat. Some of the fat needs to remain so the lunch meat will stick together. By hand or with a food processor, finely chop the meat and fat so that they are uniform in texture.
3. Place the meat into a bowl and pour in about 1 cup of the cooking liquid. Season with dried onion, seasoning salt, lemon pepper, basil, and hot chili oil. Combine thoroughly and taste. Adjust the seasonings as necessary.
4. Place the meat into a bowl with a flat bottom. Be sure to flatten the top of the meat. Chill it at least an hour, until the meat is solid. Remove the meat from the container, slice, and serve.

Nutritional information per serving:
Carbohydrates: 1 gram • Effective Carb Count: 0 grams
Protein: 21 grams • Fat: 19 grams • Calories: 261

Reduced-Fat Variation:
Use chicken instead of pork. Remove the skin and large chunks of fat.
Carbohydrates: 1 gram • Effective Carb Count: 0 grams
Protein: 16 grams • Fat: 6 grams • Calories: 123

Josephine's Spicy Spaghetti Sauce

Makes 6 servings

This is not an Italian-type sauce, so be warned! For a special meal, serve with Parmesan cheese over Slurp 'Em Up Cabbage Noodles (page 233) or Baked Winter Squash, spaghetti (page 216).

2 cloves garlic
½ medium onion (not the sweet variety)
1 stalk celery
½ green bell pepper
1¼ pounds lean ground beef
1 cup beef Rich Stock (page 254) or 1 teaspoon Worcestershire sauce
2 8-ounce cans tomato sauce
1 15-ounce can diced tomatoes (no sugar!)
¼ teaspoon salt
5 fennel seeds (anise seeds will work as well)

Heat:

Either ⅛ teaspoon red pepper flakes or
1 jalapeño pepper, finely minced or
Several dashes Tabasco sauce, or
3 chili peppers (½" long), dried or
All of the above if you like to eat fire!

Mince the garlic. Chop the onion, celery, and pepper into ¼" pieces. Crumble the beef into a large skillet and add prepared vegetables. Brown over medium heat, stirring frequently, until most of the red is gone from the meat, about 8 minutes. Add the Rich Stock or Worcestershire sauce, tomato sauce, diced tomatoes, fennel seeds, salt, and "heat" of your choice. Simmer uncovered over medium-low heat until it is thickened, about 45 minutes.

Nutritional information per serving:
Carbohydrates: 13 grams • Effective Carb Count: 9 grams
Protein: 20 grams • Fat: 21 grams • Calories: 316

LAMB WITH ROSEMARY GRAVY

Serves 2

How delightful to find some inexpensive pieces of lamb! This recipe makes them taste almost as good as the more expensive cuts. It makes my mouth water just thinking about it! Serve over Slurp 'Em Up Cabbage Noodles (page 233) or Rice-Aflower (page 227).

1 small onion, chopped
¼ teaspoon seasoning salt
½ tablespoon butter
½ tablespoon lard
1¹/₃ pounds lamb pieces (shoulder, neck, etc.)
½ teaspoon seasoning salt
½ teaspoon rosemary (dried, but not ground)
1 teaspoon lemon juice
³/₄ cup water

1. In medium-sized frying pan with a lid, cook the onion and ¼ teaspoon seasoning salt in the butter and lard over medium heat until it is beginning to become golden, about 8 minutes.
2. While the onion is cooking, place the lamb in a dish and sprinkle with ½ teaspoon seasoning salt and rosemary. Allow it to rest about 5 minutes, then place the meat seasoned side down into the pan and brown it 3 to 5 minutes. Drizzle the meat with the lemon juice while it is browning. Turn the meat to brown the other side for 3 to 5 more minutes. Add the water, cover, and simmer the lamb over medium-low heat for about 2 hours, or until it is tender. The broth will cook down and can be served as a gravy over your favorite low-carb veggies.

NUTRITIONAL INFORMATION PER SERVING:
Carbohydrates: 3 grams • Effective Carb Count: 2 grams
Protein: 20 grams • Fat: 29 grams • Calories: 355

REDUCED-FAT VARIATION:
Use a bit of Rich Stock (page 254) instead of the
butter and lard to brown the onion.
Carbohydrates: 3 grams • Effective Carb Count: 2 grams
Protein: 20 grams • Fat: 26 grams • Calories: 328

LEMONY BEEF
AND ASPARAGUS STIR-FRY

Serves 6

This recipe is *very* versatile. Substitute any meat for the beef and any appropriate veggies instead of the asparagus. Imagination and a great sauce are wonderful companions!

Sauce:

2 teaspoons arrowroot powder
½ large lemon, juiced (or about 1½ tablespoons bottled lemon juice, but fresh is SO much better!)
¾ cup beef Rich Stock (page 254) or commercially prepared stock
¼ teaspoon ginger powder
¼ teaspoon SteviaPlus or ½ packet sucralose

Stir-fry ingredients:

Cooking oil or lard
4 large cloves garlic, minced
1½ pounds beef sirloin steak, thinly sliced
Seasoning salt
1½ pounds asparagus
3 carrots, optional

1. Combine the ingredients for the sauce in a small bowl, and set aside.
2. Heat a wok or large frying pan with about ¼ cup of cooking oil over high heat. Quickly stir-fry the garlic, then the meat. Add more oil if necessary and season the meat well with seasoning salt. Add the veggies to the wok and stir-fry until crisp-tender, again adding oil if necessary, about 5 minutes. Add the sauce, turn off the heat, and stir thoroughly.

NUTRITIONAL INFORMATION PER SERVING:
Carbohydrates: 8 grams • Effective Carb Count: 6 grams
Protein: 28 grams • Fat: 18 grams • Calories: 310

LIVER AND ONIONS

Makes 4 servings

This is a traditional southern recipe. Even if you've never liked liver and onions, you should try this one! It is succulent!

1 pound beef or calf liver, sliced ¼" thick
1 cup yogurt, cultured buttermilk, or kefir
½ medium sweet onion, sliced
1 tablespoon bacon grease or lard
1 tablespoon butter
¼ teaspoon seasoning salt
2 tablespoons bacon grease or lard
2 tablespoons butter
¾ cup soy protein powder
¾ teaspoon lemon pepper
1 ½ teaspoons seasoning salt

1. Place the sliced liver into a bowl and cover completely with cold water. Allow the liver to soak refrigerated in this manner for 6 to 12 hours, changing the water every hour or so.
2. About 1 hour before mealtime, drain the liver. Cut it into serving-sized pieces, put it back into the bowl and pour the yogurt over the top, being sure all the surfaces of the liver are covered in the yogurt.
3. In a large frying pan with a lid, cook the onion in 1 tablespoon bacon grease and 1 tablespoon butter, seasoned with ¼ teaspoon seasoning salt, until it is golden, about 8 minutes. Put the cooked onion, along with the juices, into a small dish and set it aside.
4. Melt 2 tablespoons bacon grease and 2 tablespoons butter in the frying pan over low heat. Combine the soy protein, lemon pepper, and 1½ teaspoons seasoning salt in a shallow dish. Dredge the liver pieces in the seasoned soy protein mixture and place them into the frying pan. Cover the pan and cook the liver over low heat for about 30 minutes, turning the pieces over after about 20 minutes. At that time, spread the cooked onion slices over the turned liver. The liver is done when it is fork-tender. Serve hot.

NUTRITIONAL INFORMATION PER SERVING:
Carbohydrates: 10 grams • Effective Carb Count: 9 grams
Protein: 34 grams • Fat: 25 grams • Calories: 415

LOW-CARB STROGANOFF STEW

Makes 8 servings

This recipe is great for busy days. You can even cut up the meat and veggies ahead of time and keep them in the fridge until you are ready to use them. This also makes a great slow cooker dish. Just put everything into the slow cooker and cook it on low for about 8 hours. Add the sour cream just prior to serving. This makes a nice all-in-one meal!

1 medium onion, chopped
3 cloves garlic, minced
3 stalks celery, chopped
2 turnips, cut up
2 pounds beef stew meat, cubed
1 ½ cups cabbage, chopped
1 teaspoon seasoning salt
½ teaspoon lemon pepper
¼ teaspoon paprika
½ teaspoon dill weed, dried
1 ½ teaspoons lime juice (fresh is always best!)
½ cup water
1 ½ cups sour cream

Combine all of the ingredients, except the sour cream, in a large pot with a lid. Cover the pot and bring the stew to a simmer. Simmer over medium-low heat for about 20 to 30 minutes, or until the vegetables are becoming tender. In the last 5 minutes of cooking, add the sour cream.

NUTRITIONAL INFORMATION PER SERVING:
Carbohydrates: 7 grams • Effective Carb Count: 6 grams
Protein: 34 grams • Fat: 33 grams • Calories: 461

REDUCED-FAT VARIATION:
Use low-fat sour cream.
Carbohydrates: 7 grams • Effective Carb Count: 6 grams
Protein: 33 grams • Fat: 24 grams • Calories: 384

Marinated Lamb Barbecue

Makes 6 servings

Enjoy this meat hot with a lot of napkins! *Note:* An unused mint tea bag may be opened and put into the marinade, if no fresh or dried mint is available.

2 to 3 pounds lamb shoulder chops or ribs
1 teaspoon seasoning salt
2 tablespoons fresh mint leaves, finely chopped (see note above)
2 cups beef Rich Stock (page 254) or commercially prepared stock
Lemon pepper
Mesquite briquettes or chips, if using gas or electric barbecue

1. Place the meat into a large bowl with a tightly fitting lid, and sprinkle with the seasoning salt. Add the mint and Rich Stock. Marinate for 4 hours to overnight.
2. Prepare the barbecue using mesquite briquettes if you have a charcoal barbecue. When the coals are heated to a white powder (or add soaked mesquite chips on the rocks of a gas grill over medium heat), place the meat about 5" over the coals. Lightly season both sides of the meat with lemon pepper. Cover and smoke the meat about 30 minutes.

Nutritional information per serving:
Carbohydrates: 1 gram • Effective Carb Count: 0 grams
Protein: 20 grams • Fat: 25 grams • Calories: 320

Parsley, chives, and mint are extremely easy to grow and are also inexpensive to purchase fresh in the produce section. To add a special touch to just about any meal, try adding fresh herbs to your meats and veggies. These three specifically are also very good in Spinach Salad with Lemon Dressing (page 49), adding a Middle Eastern flare!

MARVELOUS MEATBALLS

Makes about 26 meatballs

This easy meal can be served with your choice of dipping sauces. Freeze leftover meatballs for a quick meal! Reheat at 375°F for about 25 minutes or until hot.

1 pound Sharron's Pork Sausage (page 85),
1946 Pork Sausage (page 54), or commercially prepared sausage
1 1/2 pounds ground beef
3/4 cup pork rinds, ground
1/4 cup onion, minced
2 tablespoons parsley flakes
1/4 teaspoon dry mustard powder
1 teaspoon seasoning salt
3 cloves garlic, minced
1/4 teaspoon lemon pepper
2 eggs
1/3 cup Almond Milk (page 240), unsweetened, or cream

1. Combine all of the ingredients in a large mixing bowl. Mix well and allow the meat mixture to rest at least 5 minutes.
2. Form the meat into 2" balls. Bake them in a 9" × 13" × 2" baking pan about 20 minutes at 375°F, or barbecue over medium coals the same amount of time. They are done when they feel firm to the touch, no longer mushy.

NUTRITIONAL INFORMATION PER SERVING (PER MEATBALL):
Carbohydrates: 1 gram • Effective Carb Count: 0 grams
Protein: 11 grams • Fat: 17 grams • Calories: 205

REDUCED-FAT VARIATION:
Use turkey sausage instead of pork and use lean ground beef.
Carbohydrates: trace • Effective Carb Count: 0 grams
Protein: 13 grams • Fat: 10 grams • Calories: 145

MEATBALL SOUP

Makes about 10 servings

This is one of those great "clean out the fridge" soups. Use whatever fresh or frozen veggies you have available in addition to or instead of those listed. It is sure to be a winner!

½ medium onion, chopped
4 cloves garlic, minced
1 to 2 tablespoons lard
Seasoning salt, to taste
6 cups beef Rich Stock (page 254)
1 carrot, chopped (optional)
3 stalks celery, chopped
3 cups cabbage, chopped into 1" cubes
1 ½ cups broccoli (or cauliflower) stems,
peeled and chopped or chopped zucchini
1 bay leaf
½ teaspoon marjoram, dried
⅛ teaspoon fennel/anise seed
½ tablespoon parsley
Salt and lemon pepper to taste
48 1" Marvelous Meatballs (page 123)

1. In a 5-quart pot with a lid, cook the onion and the garlic in the lard with seasoning salt until they are beginning to become slightly golden, about 10 minutes. Add all of the remaining ingredients, except the meatballs, cover the pot, and simmer while preparing the meatballs, about 30 minutes.
2. Meanwhile, prepare the meatballs. Bake them on a baking sheet for about 15 minutes. Add the cooked meatballs to the soup and simmer covered for another 20 minutes.

NUTRITIONAL INFORMATION PER SERVING:
Carbohydrates: 5 grams • Effective Carb Count: 3 grams
Protein: 30 grams • Fat: 46 grams • Calories: 588

MEXICAN BEEF STEW

Serves 6

Enjoy this authentic Mexican stew with low-carb tortillas or High-Protein Wraps (page 225) for scooping. It is sure to make your mouth water as it is cooking!

2 large cloves garlic (½" × 1")
1 medium onion
2 stalks celery
1 medium turnip
1 medium carrot, optional
1½ pounds beef stew meat
2 tablespoons lard
½ of an 8-ounce can tomato sauce (do not use the whole thing!)
½ teaspoon seasoning salt
⅛ teaspoon lemon pepper
1 teaspoon ground cumin
½ tomato
1 cup beef Rich Stock (page 254) or commercially prepared stock
Low-carb tortillas or High-Protein Wraps (page 225), optional

1. Mince the garlic, and chop the other veggies into ¾" cubes. Set them aside.
2. In a skillet that has a tightly fitting lid, brown the beef in lard over medium heat until the red is gone, about 3 minutes. Add the garlic and onions, continuing to cook and stir until the onions are translucent. Add the celery, turnip, and carrot, cooking and stirring 2 minutes. Add the remaining ingredients, stirring to combine. Cover and simmer over low heat 1 hour. Remove the lid. Continue to simmer, and cook the sauce down until it is a thick gravy, about 20 minutes.

NUTRITIONAL INFORMATION PER SERVING:
Carbohydrates: 7 grams • Effective Carb Count: 5 grams
Protein: 33 grams • Fat: 28 grams • Calories: 418

REDUCED-FAT VARIATION:
Omit the lard and use cooking spray to brown the meat.
Carbohydrates: 7 grams • Effective Carb Count: 5 grams
Protein: 33 grams • Fat: 24 grams • Calories: 380

MINI CORN DOGS, LOW-CARBED

Makes 18

Rather like going to the fair without the crowds or the carb hangover! Serve hot with Pumpkin Ketchup (page 253) or other favorite dipping sauce.

²/₃ cup almonds, ground
½ cup soy flour (or use ¼ cup soy flour and ¼ cup cornmeal)
½ cup soy protein isolate
1 ½ teaspoons baking soda
1 teaspoon seasoning salt
½ teaspoon Sweet & Slender or 1 packet sucralose
1 egg
½ cup cream thinned to ¾ cup with water, or ¾ cup Almond Milk (page 240)
2 tablespoons melted lard
1 pound hot dogs, cut into thirds
Lard for frying

1. Place the dry ingredients into a mixing bowl. Set them aside.
2. In a small bowl, combine the egg and cream until uniform. Pour the cream/egg mixture and melted lard all at once into the dry ingredients. With slightly dampened hands, scoop the dough out onto the sections of hot dog, rolling until the hot dog piece is covered with dough and smooth. Set it aside on waxed paper. Repeat for the remaining hot dog pieces.
3. Fry the corn dogs in hot fat until dark golden brown. Do not undercook them or there will be gooey uncooked batter inside!

NUTRITIONAL INFORMATION PER SERVING:
Carbohydrates: 3 grams • Effective Carb Count: 2 grams
Protein: 6 grams • Fat: 15 grams • Calories: 174

TWO ESSENTIAL KITCHEN APPLIANCES: A blender and a food processor are absolutely indispensable. The blender can be used to make salad dressings, Almond Milk, and smoothies. The food processor is great for grinding pork rinds, almonds, and cheese. A full-sized food processor with chopping blade as well as slicing and shredding blades is the best type. Small ones just don't have the necessary power to grind the nuts. Often they can be found inexpensively at yard sales or secondhand stores for about $5.00.

Minted Lamb Chops

Serves 3

Lamb is such a special treat! Serve this the next time you want to feel special and pampered.

1 pound lamb rib chops
¾ cup beef Rich Stock (page 254) or commercially prepared stock
2 tablespoons fresh mint leaves, chopped
Seasoning salt
Lemon pepper

Place the chops into an 8" or 9" baking dish. Pour the stock over the top of the chops. Season liberally with seasoning salt and lemon pepper. Spread the chopped mint leaves over the top of the meat. Bake at 400°F for 25 minutes, until the juices run clear or a thermometer tests at 170°F.

Nutritional information per serving:

Carbohydrates: trace • Effective Carb Count: 0 grams
Protein: 20 grams • Fat: 25 grams • Calories: 318

A MEAT THERMOMETER TIP: When testing a small or thin cut of meat with a thermometer, please remember to never let the thermometer touch the baking dish. It may be necessary to put the thermometer into the meat horizontally in order to have it test properly.

Nightshade-Free Taco Meat

Makes about 6 servings

Nightshades are a group of plants that are all related to the toxin nightshade. They are: potatoes, tomatoes, eggplant, all forms of peppers except peppercorns, and paprika. They are a very common allergen and can cause violent reactions in many people. This wonderful recipe satisfies the urge for a taco while avoiding nightshades. Serve on Nightshade-Free Taco Salad (page 129).

1 1/2 pounds ground beef
1/2 medium onion, chopped (about 1/2 cup)
2 cloves garlic, minced
2 tablespoons butter
1/4 cup water
2 teaspoons hot chili oil
1 teaspoon lemon pepper
1/2 teaspoon oregano
1 teaspoon sea salt
1/2 teaspoon cumin, ground
1/2 teaspoon Sweet & Slender (or the same of SteviaPlus)

In a large skillet, brown the ground beef and drain it in a large colander. While the beef is draining, cook the onion and garlic in the butter until golden, about 5 minutes. Add the beef and remaining ingredients. Simmer until most of the moisture has evaporated, about 5 minutes.

Nutritional information per serving:
Carbohydrates: 2 grams • Effective Carb Count: 1 gram
Protein: 19 grams • Fat: 36 grams • Calories: 409

Reduced-Fat Variation:
Use lean ground beef and cook the onion and garlic along with the beef.
Carbohydrates: 2 grams • Effective Carb Count: 1 gram
Protein: 20 grams • Fat: 25 grams • Calories: 323

NIGHTSHADE-FREE TACO SALAD

Serves 1

This is rather like going to a Mexican restaurant without the bill! If you would like to have a fancy taco salad shell to put this in, follow the instructions given in Cheese Crisps (page 5).

3 cups Romaine lettuce, chopped (or other dark green mixed salad greens)
4 black olives, sliced
½ cup cucumber slices
2 radishes, thinly sliced
2 teaspoons lemon juice, fresh
1 tablespoon olive oil
Seasoning salt
Lemon pepper
4 to 6 ounces Nightshade-Free Taco Meat (page 128)
2 tablespoons sour cream

1. Combine the lettuce, olives, cucumber, and radishes in a salad bowl. Drizzle the lemon juice and olive oil over the top (the amounts given are approximate, as tastes will vary). Sprinkle lightly with seasoning salt and lemon pepper. Toss the salad thoroughly.
2. Place the taco meat on the top of the salad and garnish with a dollop of sour cream.

NUTRITIONAL INFORMATION PER SERVING:
Carbohydrates: 11 grams • Effective Carb Count: 6 grams
Protein: 25 grams • Fat: 45 grams • Calories: 544

REDUCED-FAT VARIATION:
Use extra-lean ground beef for the taco meat. Use low-fat sour cream.
Carbohydrates: 11 grams • Effective Carb Count: 6 grams
Protein: 25 grams • Fat: 36 grams • Calories: 458

PARSLEY PORK STEAKS MACADAMIA

Serves 2

Great for a change of pace from the same old pork! You can also try it with chicken. This is excellent served with Creamed Spinach with Macadamia Garnish (page 221).

¹/₃ cup macadamia nuts, ground
¹/₃ cup pork rinds, crushed
¹/₄ teaspoon lemon pepper
1 teaspoon chives, dried
1 tablespoon parsley, dried
¹/₂ teaspoon seasoning salt
1 egg
1 tablespoon water
Cooking oil spray
2 pork steaks

1. In a small shallow dish, place the ground macadamias, crushed pork rinds, lemon pepper, chives, parsley, and seasoning salt. In another small shallow dish, combine the egg and water. Spray a 9" × 13" baking dish with cooking oil spray.
2. Coat steaks first in the egg/water mixture, then in the macadamia mixture. Be sure they are well coated. Gently place the coated steaks in the prepared baking pan. Bake at 375°F for about 30 minutes, or until meat thermometer tests at 170°F.

NUTRITIONAL INFORMATION PER SERVING:
Carbohydrates: 4 grams • Effective Carb Count: 2 grams
Protein: 29 grams • Fat: 36 grams • Calories: 442

PERFECT POT ROAST

Makes about 8 servings

The lemon juice and sweeteners used in this recipe serve to enhance the flavor of the meat and tenderize it as well. Enjoy the gravy served over Rice-Aflower (page 227) or Slurp 'Em Up Cabbage Noodles (page 233).

4- to 5-pound chuck or 7-bone beef roast
2 to 3 teaspoons lemon juice (fresh is best)
1 ½ teaspoons Sweet & Slender or 1 teaspoon SteviaPlus
Seasoning salt
Lemon Pepper
1 medium sweet onion, thinly sliced
1¼ cups beef Rich Stock (page 254)
¼ cup water mixed with 1 teaspoon arrowroot powder

1. Place the roast into a large roasting pan with a lid. Drizzle it with lemon juice over the top. Sprinkle it with the SteviaPlus, and seasoning salt and lemon pepper as desired. Layer the onion slices over the entire surface of the roast and pour the stock into the bottom of the pan. Cover the pan and place it into a 325°F oven and bake it for 2 hours.
2. After that time, remove the roast from the pan to a serving dish and slice it as you desire. Pour the pan juices into a medium-sized saucepan and heat over medium heat until bubbling. Add the arrowroot/water and stir slightly until the gravy is thickened. Serve the gravy over the roast and your favorite low-carb veggies.

NUTRITIONAL INFORMATION PER SERVING:
Carbohydrates: 2 grams • Effective Carb Count: 1 gram
Protein: 36 grams • Fat: 35 grams • Calories: 487

PORCUPINES

Serves 6

This is a variation on a recipe from my childhood. Porcupines are meatballs with rice in them. Though rice may be out for the low-carb way of life, Porcupines are still in, thanks to this great recipe. If you don't want to use these right away, put the meatballs, along with the cooking juices, into a covered container and refrigerate. The meatballs will reabsorb the liquid, but not the fat that was released. Reheat them on a baking sheet for about 8 minutes at 375°F. They may also be grilled for the original cooking method. Serve with Sweet and Zingy Mustard Sauce (page 258).

1 ½ pounds ground beef
1 ½ cups broccoli slaw (found in the bagged salad section of the grocer)
¼ cup soy protein (not soy flour!)
1 tablespoon lime juice, fresh
½ teaspoon Sweet & Slender
½ teaspoon ginger
½ teaspoon lemon pepper
1 teaspoon seasoning salt
½ cup water

In a large mixing bowl, combine all of the ingredients and mix them well. Form the mixture into 2" balls and gently place them into a large skillet with a well-fitting lid. Cover and cook them for about 10 minutes over medium heat, until they are just beginning to brown. Turn the meatballs. Cover them and cook for another 5 minutes.

NUTRITIONAL INFORMATION PER SERVING:
Carbohydrates: 1 gram • Effective Carb Count: 0 grams
Protein: 8 grams • Fat: 11 grams • Calories: 144

REDUCED-FAT VARIATION:
Use ground chicken or turkey instead of beef.
Carbohydrates: 1 gram • Effective Carb Count: 0 grams
Protein: 9 grams • Fat: 3 grams • Calories: 72

PORK CHOPS MARIE

Serves 4

Think of these as pork chops with a kick! Enjoy the sauce on its own with the chops or served over Rice-Aflower (page 227).

4 large pork chops, ³/₄" thick
1 tablespoon lard
1 large green bell pepper
4 large or 6 small cloves garlic
3 bay leaves
1 15-ounce can tomato sauce (no sugar added!)
Salt and pepper to taste

1. Place the pork chops and lard into a large skillet. Cook over medium heat until the chops are beginning to brown, about 8 minutes.
2. Meanwhile, cut the bell pepper into 1" cubes and coarsely chop the garlic. Add the bell pepper, garlic, bay leaves, tomato sauce, and salt and pepper to the pork chops in the skillet. Simmer over medium-low heat until thickened, about 45 minutes.
3. Prior to serving, remove the bay leaves.

NUTRITIONAL INFORMATION PER SERVING:
Carbohydrates: 11 grams • Effective Carb Count: 9 grams
Protein: 25 grams • Fat: 18 grams • Calories: 305

REDUCED-FAT VARIATION:
Omit the lard and brown the chops by using cooking spray.
Carbohydrates: 11 grams • Effective Carb Count: 9 grams
Protein: 25 grams • Fat: 15 grams • Calories: 276

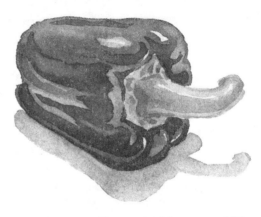

Pork Chops with Apples

Serves 4

Serve gravy with apple slices over the chops for a low-carb alternative to pork chops with applesauce! Great served over Rice-Aflower (page 227).

½ sweet onion, thinly sliced
3 cloves garlic, minced
Seasoning salt
2 tablespoons bacon grease or lard
4 pork chops
Lemon pepper
1 tablespoon bacon grease or lard
1¼ cups Rich Stock (page 254)
1 teaspoon parsley flakes
½ medium apple, peeled and thinly sliced
¼ cup water mixed with 2 teaspoons arrowroot powder

1. In a large frying pan with a lid, cook the onion and garlic, seasoned with seasoning salt, in 2 tablespoons bacon grease until they are translucent, about 5 minutes. Pour the onion mixture into a small dish and set aside.
2. Season the pork chops well on both sides with seasoning salt and lemon pepper. Add 1 tablespoon bacon grease to the frying pan and brown the chops over medium heat for about 10 minutes. Return the onion mixture, with its juices, to the pan, and add the stock. Cover the pan and allow it to simmer for about 30 minutes over medium-low heat.
3. Remove the cover, bring the stock to a slow boil, and add the parsley flakes, apple slices, and arrowroot/water mixture, stirring to combine. Cover the pan and allow it to simmer for 2 minutes.

Nutritional information per serving:
Carbohydrates: 6 grams • Effective Carb Count: 5 grams
Protein: 23 grams • Fat: 24 grams • Calories: 342

Reduced-Fat Variation:
Use a small amount of Rich Stock to cook the onions and garlic.
Omit the bacon grease. Brown the chops using cooking oil spray.
Add additional stock to cook the chops.
Carbohydrates: 6 grams • Effective Carb Count: 5 grams
Protein: 23 grams • Fat: 15 grams • Calories: 255

PUFFY PORK AND ASPARAGUS BAKE

Serves 6

This may also be made with chicken instead of pork, and broccoli or cauliflower instead of asparagus. Experiment! Get creative! Eat good food!

2/3 cup sweet onion, chopped
2 tablespoons butter
1 pound asparagus, fresh
Pinch sea salt
4 ounces cream cheese, softened
1/4 cup sour cream
1/2 teaspoon sea salt
1/3 cup grated Parmesan cheese
2 eggs
1 cup half-and-half

1 1/2 teaspoons arrowroot powder
3 cups cooked pork, cut into bite-sized cubes

Topping:

1 cup Monterey jack cheese, shredded
1/4 teaspoon oregano, dried
1 teaspoon parsley flakes
1 tablespoon Parmesan cheese, grated
Cooking oil spray

1. In a small pan, cook the onion in the butter over medium heat until the onion is translucent and beginning to become golden, about 5 minutes. Set aside to cool.
2. Blanch the asparagus: Fill a 3- to 4-quart saucepan with water and a pinch of salt and bring to a full boil. Cut the asparagus into 1" to 1½" pieces and carefully put it into the boiling water. Boil the asparagus for 3 minutes; then pour it into a colander to drain. Run cold water over the asparagus until it is cooled. Set the asparagus aside.
3. In a small mixing bowl with an electric mixer, combine the cream cheese and sour cream, beating on medium speed until smooth. Add the sea salt, Parmesan cheese, eggs, and half-and-half, mixing well. Add the cooled onions and the arrowroot powder, mixing until they are combined.
4. In another small bowl, combine the topping ingredients, mixing well.
5. Spray a 9" × 13" pan with cooking oil spray. Spread the cut-up pork and asparagus evenly into the pan. Pour the sauce evenly over the top of the meat and asparagus. Sprinkle the cheese mixture over all. Bake at 350°F for about 30 minutes, or until it is golden brown on top.

NUTRITIONAL INFORMATION PER SERVING:
Carbohydrates: 7 grams • Effective Carb Count: 6 grams
Protein: 26 grams • Fat: 30 grams • Calories: 401

REDUCED-FAT VARIATION:
Cook the onion in a bit of Rich Stock (page 254), use chicken instead of pork, and low-fat dairy products.
Carbohydrates: 10 grams • Effective Carb Count: 9 grams
Protein: 28 grams • Fat: 13 grams • Calories: 276

RAINBOW EGG SALAD

Makes 2 servings

Yum! A nice change from ordinary egg salad.

2 eggs, hard-boiled
3 tablespoons Blender Mayonnaise (page 241) or
commercially prepared mayonnaise
Lemon pepper
Seasoning salt
Pinch celery seed
2½ teaspoons of mixed dried veggies
(includes spinach, celery, tomatoes, red bell peppers)

Mash the eggs in a small bowl. Add the remaining ingredients. Serve with celery, zucchini slices, cucumber slices, etc., for scooping.

NUTRITIONAL INFORMATION PER SERVING:
Carbohydrates: 1 gram • Effective Carb Count: 0 grams
Protein: 6 grams • Fat: 22 grams • Calories: 214

REDUCED-FAT VARIATION:
Use reduced-fat mayonnaise.
Carbohydrates: 4 grams • Effective Carb Count: 3 grams
Protein: 6 grams • Fat: 9 grams • Calories: 118

"Help! I'm stalled!" is a common cry that is heard from many who follow low-carb eating plans. A stall is when no pounds or inches have been lost for four or more weeks. There are a few common culprits, the biggest of which are Carb Creep and Efficiency. Carb Creep is when we allow stray carbs back into our diets—sugar-free candies, too many servings of squash, etc. Efficiency is when our bodies just get too good at using the fuel given. That requires a change of approach. I've done everything from three-day egg- or veggie-only fasts to actually switching to another low-carb program. All have worked. The bottom line is, just because a body has stopped losing for the moment, doesn't mean the program is a failure. We may just need to shake things up!

RANCH CHOPS

Serves 8

This is so easy! Even the most reluctant chef can make this simple recipe. This may also be done with chicken for Ranch Chicken! Just bake the chicken for about 45 minutes or until the chicken tests at 180°F.

8 pork chops
⅓ to ½ package Ranch salad dressing mix
1 teaspoon lemon pepper

Rinse the chops with running water and place them on a baking sheet. Sprinkle the tops of the chops with Ranch salad dressing mix and lemon pepper. Bake them for about 20 minutes at 400°F, or until they are golden or test at 170°F.

NUTRITIONAL INFORMATION PER SERVING:
Carbohydrates: 1 gram • Effective Carb Count: 0 grams
Protein: 23 grams • Fat: 15 grams • Calories: 237

Is it best to weigh or measure? Actually, it is good to do both! Often, folks find that even though the scale may not be moving downward, they are actually smaller. For instance, one gal lost no *pounds* for four months, but she went from a size 12 to a size 8! By doing both, you can have an accurate picture of what is happening in your body. And what about those fluctuations? It is common to gain 3 pounds overnight for no apparent reason! As long as you are seeing a continuing downward trend, there is no cause for concern.

ROAST LEG OF LAMB

Serves 10

This is a low-carb variation on a holiday favorite. Try it at your next holiday feast—it's sure to be a hit!

6- to 7-pound leg of lamb (bone in)
1 clove elephant garlic or 2 large cloves of garlic, slivered
¼ cup olive oil
2 cups beef Rich Stock (page 254) or commercially prepared stock
¾ cup lemon juice, bottled
2 tablespoons lime juice, fresh
1 large sweet onion, sliced
1 carrot, sliced into ¼" pieces
3 tablespoons parsley flakes
2 teaspoons oregano, dried (not ground)
¼ teaspoon ground cloves
1 packet sucralose
¼ teaspoon SteviaPlus (use ¾ teaspoon if your onion is hot)
1 teaspoon sea salt
1 teaspoon seasoning salt

1. Rinse the meat under running water; then place into a large baking dish. With a sharp paring or utility knife score the meat in many places. Insert a sliver of garlic into each score. Do this all over the meat on both sides.
2. In a small bowl, combine the remaining ingredients. Pour them over the lamb. Pile the vegetables on top of the meat. Allow it to marinate at least 24 hours, turning occasionally.
3. Bring the meat to room temperature prior to roasting. Roast the lamb, fat side up, at 325°F for about 3 hours, basting occasionally, until a meat thermometer inserted in the fleshy part reads 145°F.
4. Remove the lamb from the oven and allow it to rest about 20 minutes before slicing. Serve the vegetables and broth as a side dish.

NUTRITIONAL INFORMATION PER SERVING:
Carbohydrates: 4 grams • Effective Carb Count: 3 grams
Protein: 39 grams • Fat: 42 grams • Calories: 562

REDUCED-FAT VARIATION:
Use 2 tablespoons olive oil.
Carbohydrates: 4 grams • Effective Carb Count: 3 grams
Protein: 39 grams • Fat: 39 grams • Calories: 539

SAUSAGE CASSEROLE

Makes 8 servings

This versatile casserole can be made for either breakfast or dinner and can be easily doubled or tripled. When doubling or tripling, please be sure to allow for extra baking time!

*1 pound bulk pork sausage (one of the recipes from
this book or commercially prepared)
1 pound cauliflower, chopped (may be fresh or frozen)
1 8-ounce package cream cheese
2 eggs
½ tablespoon dried onion, minced
½ teaspoon seasoning salt
½ teaspoon garlic granules
1 teaspoon parsley flakes
2 tablespoons cream or Almond Milk (page 240)
1 ½ cups cheese, shredded (Monterey jack, Cheddar, or
a packaged Mexican-style blend)
Cooking oil spray*

1. Cook the sausage and drain it. Spray a 9" × 13" baking dish with cooking oil spray. Put the sausage and the cauliflower into the baking dish. Set it aside.
2. Warm the cream cheese in the microwave until it has started to melt, about 1 minute. Put the cream cheese, eggs, seasonings, and cream into a mixing bowl and whisk them with a wire whisk until they are smooth. Pour this mixture over the sausage and cauliflower in the baking dish. Stir the ingredients in the dish lightly until they are uniform. Smooth the top of the mixture with the back of a spoon to flatten.
3. Sprinkle the shredded cheese over the sausage/cauliflower mixture. Bake the casserole at 350°F for about 25 minutes, or until the cheese is thoroughly melted and beginning to become golden brown in places.

NUTRITIONAL INFORMATION PER SERVING:
Carbohydrates: 5 grams • Effective Carb Count: 4 grams
Protein: 17 grams • Fat: 41 grams • Calories: 456

REDUCED-FAT VARIATION:
Use turkey sausage, low-fat cream cheese, low-fat cheese, and canned skim milk.
Carbohydrates: 5 grams • Effective Carb Count: 4 grams
Protein: 22 grams • Fat: 13 grams • Calories: 227

SESAME SEED BEEF

Serves 4

This traditional Asian dish is wonderful broiled in the oven, but even better done on the barbecue! Serve with Fiery Hot Mustard (page 246) or Sweet and Zingy Mustard Sauce (page 258). This recipe multiplies very well! Thank you, Linnea Olsen, for sharing your recipe!

1 pound beef steak, boneless (round, skirt, top sirloin, etc.)
¼ cup sesame seeds
¼ teaspoon SteviaPlus
4 packets sucralose
½ teaspoon ginger
1 tablespoon olive oil
1 tablespoon sesame oil
4 to 6 drops hot chili oil
½ tablespoon minced onion, dried, or 1 fresh green onion
1 clove garlic
6 tablespoons Bragg's Liquid Aminos or soy sauce

1. Slice the beef into strips about 4" or 5" long, about 1" wide, and about ¼" thick. It is easier to slice the beef if it is partially frozen.
2. Place the steak strips into a container with a lid for marinating. Combine the remaining ingredients in a blender container. Blend on medium speed until they are well combined. Pour this mixture over the steak strips and stir them to coat the meat evenly. Cover the container and allow the meat to marinate 30 minutes at room temperature up to overnight in the refrigerator.
3. Lay the marinated meat out on a broiling pan, leaving any sesame seeds in place. Broil a few inches from the element for about 5 minutes or until the meat reaches the desired doneness. Alternatively, the meat may be barbecued for a wonderful flavor!

NUTRITIONAL INFORMATION PER SERVING:
Carbohydrates: 5 grams • Effective Carb Count: 4 grams
Protein: 25 grams • Fat: 25 grams • Calories: 347

REDUCED-FAT VARIATION:
Omit the olive oil.
Carbohydrates: 5 grams • Effective Carb Count: 4 grams
Protein: 25 grams • Fat: 22 grams • Calories: 317

SEVEN-EGG VEGGIE LASAGNA

Makes 6 servings

This is a yummy lasagna variation! If you like things with more intense seasonings, add ½ tablespoon Italian seasonings and an additional ½ teaspoon garlic salt to the filling.

Filling:

¾ cup cream cheese, softened, or
ricotta cheese
2 tablespoons Romano cheese
(or Parmesan)
½ tablespoon parsley flakes
½ teaspoon garlic salt
4 eggs

Other ingredients:

1 medium zucchini
1 bunch spinach, washed
and trimmed
6 ounces minced ham,
chicken, or pork
3 hard-cooked eggs, sliced
½ cup Monterey jack cheese, shredded
¼ teaspoon basil, dried
¼ teaspoon seasoning salt

1. Place the filling ingredients into a mixing bowl and mix well with a wire whisk. Set the filling mixture aside.
2. Prepare the zucchini "noodles": Using a vegetable peeler, peel long strips of zucchini. Continue peeling the zucchini until it is down to the pithy core. Discard the core if it is mushy. Reserve the noodles for use as layers in the lasagna.
3. Begin layering the lasagna: Use half of the spinach as the first layer. Place half of the zucchini noodles over the spinach. Add half of the cheese filling, spreading it evenly over the spinach layer. Sprinkle half of the meat over the cheese filling.
4. For the second layer, again begin with spinach, zucchini noodles, then the cheese filling. Sprinkle the remaining meat over the cheese filling, then place the sliced hard-cooked eggs over the meat.
5. For the top: Sprinkle first the shredded cheese over the eggs, then the basil and seasoning salt.
6. Bake the lasagna at 350°F for about 35 minutes, or until the top is golden. Remove it from the oven and allow it to rest about 5 minutes before serving.

NUTRITIONAL INFORMATION PER SERVING:
Carbohydrates: 4 grams • Effective Carb Count: 3 grams
Protein: 17 grams • Fat: 22 grams • Calories: 278

REDUCED-FAT VARIATION:
Use low-fat cream cheese and low-fat Monterey jack cheese.
Carbohydrates: 3 grams • Effective Carb Count: 2 grams
Protein: 16 grams • Fat: 13 grams • Calories: 195

Seven Hills' Chili

Serves 8

Sometimes you just "need" some good, homemade chili! For those times, this is the one!

1 pound ground pork
1 pound ground beef (coarse ground for chili, if possible)
2 tablespoons minced onions, dried
1 tablespoon garlic granules
3 bay leaves
Salt and pepper to taste
3 or 4 tablespoons chili powder
1 teaspoon oregano
2 teaspoons cumin
1 large (14- to 16-ounce) can chopped tomatoes (without sugar)
½ red bell pepper, chopped finely
1 small can (8 ounces) tomato sauce
2 tablespoons fresh parsley, chopped

1. In a large skillet with a lid, cook the pork and beef over medium heat until it is no longer red. Drain.
2. Return the meat to the pan and add the remaining ingredients except the parsley (unless using dried; then add it at this time). Mix well.
3. Cover and simmer over medium-low heat for 30 minutes. Add the fresh parsley and simmer 5 minutes. Serve hot in bowls.

NUTRITIONAL INFORMATION PER SERVING:
Carbohydrates: 8 grams • Effective Carb Count: 6 grams
Protein: 21 grams • Fat: 28 grams • Calories: 365

REDUCED-FAT VARIATION:
Use lean ground beef and ground turkey.
Carbohydrates: 8 grams • Effective Carb Count: 2 grams
Protein: 23 grams • Fat: 17 grams • Calories: 271

All the soup and stew recipes in this book are slow-cooker adaptable. Simply follow the instructions in the recipe. Place the ingredients in the slow cooker, less any thickener (as would be indicated in the recipe), and cook on low for about 10 to 12 hours (high about 6 to 8 hours). If the recipe uses arrowroot and water as the thickener, simply make sure the soup or stew is bubbling, and add it right in at the very end of the cooking time. If a recipe calls for no thickener on a conventional stove, you may wish to add ½ to 1 teaspoon arrowroot mixed into ¼ cup water.

Spaghetti Squash with Cream Gravy

Serves 2

This quick and easy meal is rather like something from an Italian restaurant! It makes a great lunch on a rainy day.

Sauce:

2 cloves garlic
¼ teaspoon rosemary
1 tablespoon bacon grease or lard
*¾ pound meat (lamb, pork, chicken, beef steak), cooked and
sliced ¼" thick and cut into bite-sized pieces*
¼ teaspoon sea salt
⅛ teaspoon lemon pepper
1 tablespoon butter
1 cup cooked Baked Winter Squash, spaghetti (page 216)
¼ teaspoon garlic salt
⅛ teaspoon lemon pepper
1 tablespoon water
⅓ cup of Almond Milk (page 240), unsweetened, or cream
Pinch nutmeg

1. In a medium skillet over medium heat, cook the garlic and rosemary in the bacon grease until the garlic begins to become translucent, about 3 minutes. Put the meat, salt, and lemon pepper into the skillet. Cook and stir over medium-low heat until the flavors are well combined, about 10 minutes.
2. Meanwhile, in a medium saucepan over medium-low heat, melt the butter. Add the spaghetti squash, garlic salt, lemon pepper, and water. Heat and stir until warmed through.
3. A few minutes before serving, pour the Almond Milk (or cream) into the pan with the meat. Cook and stir until the mixture is bubbling and beginning to thicken, about 2 or 3 minutes. Serve on individual plates with the spaghetti squash on the bottom and the gravy over the top. Garnish with the nutmeg.

Nutritional information per serving:
Carbohydrates: 4 grams • Effective Carb Count: 3 grams
Protein: 15 grams • Fat: 28 grams • Calories: 328

Reduced-Fat Variation:
Cook the garlic and rosemary in about 1 tablespoon Rich Stock (page 254) and omit the bacon grease. Use canned skim milk for the sauce, and use a small amount of Rich Stock to heat the squash instead of the butter.
Carbohydrates: 7 grams • Effective Carb Count: 6 grams
Protein: 17 grams • Fat: 13 grams • Calories: 213

STEAM BOAT

Serves 10

This traditional Chinese feast, also called Hot Pot, is great for holidays, birthdays, and other festive occasions. It's a fun "interactive" meal.

Broth:

1 gallon Rich Stock (page 254) or commercially prepared vegetable or chicken stock

Meat choices:

Chicken, pork, beef, shrimp, scallops, tofu, baby squid, lamb, duck, ham, sole

Veggie choices:

Celery, napa (Chinese) cabbage, cabbage, carrots, green onions, spinach, bamboo shoots, snow peas, jicama, mushrooms, zucchini

Optional:

2 10-ounce packages mung bean noodles (also called bean thread or cellophane noodles)

Condiments:

Fiery Hot Mustard (page 246), sesame oil, hot chili oil, minced garlic, sesame seeds, grated gingerroot, chopped scallions, chopped cilantro, soy sauce or Bragg's Liquid Aminos, vinegar, fish sauce, salsa, Tabasco sauce, and sherry

Equipment needed:

Soup bowls, soup spoons, chopsticks, at least 2 wire mesh strainers per participant (available at Asian markets), 1 or 2 electric frying pans, large plastic tablecloth

Recipe continues on page 145 ➤

➤ Recipe continued from page 144

1. Cut the meat and veggie choices into ½" pieces. (Do not chop spinach.) The meat and veggie choices may be prepared the day before and stored in individual zipper-sealed plastic bags or other covered containers.
2. Just before serving time, place the meats and veggies into serving dishes. Allow approximately ⅓ pound meat and at least 2 cups chopped vegetables per person. (Optional: Open mung bean noodles and soak in 2" cold water to soften.) In a large stockpot, warm stock over medium heat until hot.
3. Cover the table with a plastic tablecloth for easy cleanup! Place the electric frying pan onto the dining table and fill with warmed stock to ½" below the rim of the pan. Turn the pan on medium-low heat, so that the stock remains hot. Place the meat and vegetable choices and condiments in serving dishes on the table.
4. For the meal, each person fills his or her wire baskets with meats and veggies (a different basket for each item), and places them into the steaming stock. The filled baskets remain in the stock until cooked–1 to 3 minutes, depending upon the item in the basket. If using pork, be especially careful to cook it completely.
5. The host places spinach, napa cabbage, and noodles into the electric frying pan without baskets. Each person places their cooked items plus any loose veggies or noodles desired in their soup bowls, with some additional broth and the condiments of their choice. Continue this way until everyone has just about eaten their fill, about 1 to 2 hours. The host needs to keep the pan full of broth and ample supplies of noodles, cabbage, and spinach.
6. At this point, there should be a lot of loose, cooked food floating in the broth. Beat the eggs in a small dish and pour into the steaming broth, stirring only one way for a final course of Egg Drop Soup. Use any leftover meats, veggies, and broth to make some yummy soup.

NUTRITIONAL INFORMATION PER SERVING:
Carbohydrates: 13 grams • Effective Carb Count: 8 grams
Protein: 23 grams • Fat: 18 grams • Calories: 324

STUFFED CABBAGE ROLLS

Makes 4 servings

If you do not wish to use the stewed tomatoes or tomato sauce listed below, you may steam the Cabbage Rolls in a steamer for about 20 to 25 minutes or until they test at 170°F with a meat thermometer. And another yummy way to fix this is to add a 1-pound can of sauerkraut to the top of the rolls before adding the tomato sauce, and bake as directed.

1 pound lean ground beef
1 egg
¼ cup cream or Almond Milk (page 240)
2 tablespoons minced onion, dried, or ¼ cup fresh
½ teaspoon seasoning salt
¼ teaspoon lemon pepper
½ teaspoon Italian seasonings
4 large cabbage leaves
Optional: 1 14-ounce can Italian herb stewed tomatoes
(be sure sugar is one of the very last ingredients, or preferably no sugar at all!),
or equivalent tomato sauce plus 1 teaspoon Italian seasonings.

1. Combine the beef, egg, cream, and seasonings well in a mixing bowl. Divide the meat into 4 equal parts and form each into a small loaf shape. Set them aside.
2. Bring a medium-sized pot of water to a boil. Turn it off and place the cabbage leaves into the pot for 5 minutes, until they are soft and pliable. Place the leaves on a large plate or cutting board. Put a piece of meat on a cabbage leaf and wrap it end over end, tucking the ends, as if it were a small burrito.
3. Place the rolls into an 8" square baking dish, and pour the stewed tomatoes or tomato sauce over the top. Bake at 350°F for about 45 minutes to 1 hour, or until they test at 170°F with a meat thermometer.

NUTRITIONAL INFORMATION PER SERVING:
Carbohydrates: 3 grams • Effective Carb Count: 2 grams
Protein: 22 grams • Fat: 28 grams • Calories: 363

REDUCED-FAT VARIATION:
Use extra-lean ground beef and canned skim milk.
Carbohydrates: 4 grams • Effective Carb Count: 3 grams
Protein: 24 grams • Fat: 21 grams • Calories: 305

Sue's Pizza Sans Bread

Makes 8 servings

Sans is just a French word that means "without." Enjoy this tasty pizza without guilt! My friend who tested this recipe thought it was simply wonderful!

Sauce ingredients:

1 8-ounce can tomato sauce
1 teaspoon Italian seasonings (the combination that was used contains basil, sweet marjoram, parsley, garlic, and red pepper flakes)
1/4 cup fresh onion, finely chopped, or 1 tablespoon minced onion, dried
1 bay leaf
1/4 teaspoon seasoning salt
Tiny pinch SteviaPlus or sucralose

Crust ingredients:

1 1/4 pounds ground beef, extra lean
1 teaspoon Italian seasonings (see above)
2 teaspoons minced onion, dried
1/4 teaspoon seasoning salt

Optional topping suggestions:

Black olives, sliced
Bell pepper, thinly sliced
Sweet onion, thinly sliced
Bacon, cooked and crumbled
Salami, thinly sliced
Pepperoni, thinly sliced
Mushrooms

Cheese:

1/2 pound mozzarella cheese, shredded
1/4 cup Parmesan cheese, freshly grated

Recipe continues on page 148 ➤

➤ Recipe continued from page 147

1. In a small saucepan, combine the sauce ingredients. Simmer 15 minutes. Remove the pan from the heat and allow the sauce to cool completely.
2. In a mixing bowl, combine the crust ingredients. Mix well. Press the beef mixture onto a round baking sheet with a rolled edge to make the crust. Be careful to form a rim around the edge so the toppings don't slide off as they bake!
3. Pour the sauce on top of the crust and spread it evenly to the edges. Top with desired toppings. Sprinkle the mozzarella and Parmesan cheeses evenly over the top. Bake at 375°F for 15 to 20 minutes or until the cheese is bubbly and the meat is browned. Allow the pizza to rest for 3 to 5 minutes before cutting it into slices.

NUTRITIONAL INFORMATION PER SERVING
(INCLUDING ONLY CRUST, SAUCE, AND CHEESE):
Carbohydrates: 4 grams • Effective Carb Count: 3 grams
Protein: 21 grams • Fat: 20 grams • Calories: 280

REDUCED-FAT VARIATION:
Use low-fat topping choices and reduced-fat cheese.
Carbohydrates: 4 grams • Effective Carb Count: 1 gram
Protein: 22 grams • Fat: 15 grams • Calories: 239

It is wise to pair a very high-fat, high-protein food with lighter fair such as a green salad. By filling up on the leafy, very low-carb veggies along with the good meats and fats, we encourage our weight loss and satisfy our tummies!

SURPRISE MEATLOAF

Makes 10 servings

This is a really special recipe to use for a birthday party or other special "kid-friendly" occasion! *Note:* This recipe may also be divided into 2 smaller meatloaves.

1 ¼ pounds ground pork
1 ¼ pounds lean ground beef
⅓ cup Almond Milk (page 240),
  unflavored (just the almonds
  and the water), or cream
¾ cup pork rinds, ground
2 eggs
½ teaspoon hot chili oil or
  a pinch of cayenne
1 ½ teaspoons seasoning salt
1 teaspoon lemon pepper

1 teaspoon sage, rubbed
3 tablespoons minced onion, dried
3 tablespoons parsley flakes
1 teaspoon dry mustard powder
¼ teaspoon SteviaPlus or
  1 packet sucralose
4 eggs
Salt and pepper
⅓ cup Creamy Roasted Garlic
  Salad Dressing (page 245)
1 tablespoon parsley, dried

1. In a large mixing bowl with an electric mixer, combine the first 13 ingredients. Mix on low speed until thoroughly combined.
2. Place the combined mixture into a 2-quart baking dish. Using the back of a ½-cup measure, press 4 holes into the top of the meatloaf. Break an egg into each hole and season the eggs with salt and pepper. Bake the meatloaf at 350°F for approximately 1½ hours.
3. Remove it from the oven and spread the salad dressing evenly on top, covering up the egg "surprises." Sprinkle the parsley over all. Continue baking another 15 to 20 minutes. Use a spoon to scoop any excess grease from the top of the meatloaf.

NUTRITIONAL INFORMATION PER SERVING:
Carbohydrates: 2 grams • Effective Carb Count: 1 gram
Protein: 26 grams • Fat: 35 grams • Calories: 435

REDUCED-FAT VARIATION:
Use extra-lean ground beef and ground turkey instead of those listed.
Carbohydrates: 2 grams • Effective Carb Count: 1 gram
Protein: 29 grams • Fat: 25 grams • Calories: 349

SAFETY TIP: Meatloaf must be checked with a meat thermometer and test to 170°F for safety. E-coli is not something to be messed with! A simple precaution, such as always checking cooked ground meat with a thermometer, is worth the effort to protect your and your family's safety!

TASTES LIKE MORE PORK ROAST

Makes 10 servings

A very dear friend of the family popped in for lunch a while back. I had some leftover pork roast. He thoroughly enjoyed his first sandwich and said, "This tastes like more pork roast!" Hence, the name! If a boneless roast is used, the meat may also be thinly sliced for deli-style lunch meat. Less expensive and better for us—what a deal!

1 4-pound pork shoulder blade roast or boneless pork roast
(If frozen, roast does not need to be thawed.)
Seasoning salt
Lemon pepper
1 large Walla Walla Sweet onion, or other sweet onion,
sliced into 1/4" slices
3/4 cup beef Rich Stock (page 254) or commercially prepared stock
1 tablespoon arrowroot powder mixed into 1/2 cup water

1. Season all sides of the roast liberally with seasoning salt and sprinkle lightly with lemon pepper. Place the roast, fat side down, in a large slow cooker (preferably with a removable crock). Spread the onion slices evenly over surface of the roast. Pour the stock into the bottom of the slow cooker. Cover and cook on low for 12 hours.
2. Allow roast to cool 1 hour at room temperature; then place the entire slow cooker and its contents into the refrigerator overnight. About 1 hour before serving time, remove the crock from the refrigerator, and remove the fat that has separated from the roast and broth. Remove any large "debris" from the broth, and place the gelled broth and onion pieces into a medium saucepan.
3. Bring the broth to a boil over medium heat. Meanwhile, slice the roast on a plastic cutting board. Add the meat to the boiling broth, reduce heat to simmering, and pour in arrowroot/water mixture, stirring lightly. Heat through, about 3 to 5 minutes.

NUTRITIONAL INFORMATION PER SERVING:
Carbohydrates: 2 grams • Effective Carb Count: 1 gram
Protein: 24 grams • Fat: 25 grams • Calories: 330

TEENY FOOD

Serves 4

This is a great kid-friendly meal. Choose a couple of the protein choices and a couple of the veggie choices. Eat the olives off the ends of your fingers! Have fun—this is the ultimate kid food. For a real treat, serve this off a child's tea set!

Protein choices (choose at least 2):

3/4 cup "Ham" Salad (page 113)
Tuna salad: 1 can tuna, drained, mixed with 2 tablespoons
Creamy Roasted Garlic Salad Dressing (page 245)
6 slices (ounces) cheese, cut into 1 1/2" pieces
6 slices deli-style lunch meat, cut into 1 1/2" pieces
3 hot dogs, sliced
Rainbow Egg Salad (page 136)
Egg Salad (page 108)
Sardines
Macadamia Nut Butter Cookies (page 291)
Mini Cheese Balls (page 27)

Veggie choices (choose at least 2):

1/2 cup olives
1/4 pound baby carrots
3 stalks celery, cut into sticks
1/2 small zucchini, sliced
1 cup cauliflower, sliced
1/2 cucumber, sliced
1 cup radishes, sliced
Cabbage wedges, cut 1 1/2" × 2"

Prepare the protein choices. For example: Tuna Salad and deli-style lunch meat. Prepare the veggie choices. For example: Cauliflower and cabbage wedges. Arrange each person's choices on their plate. The celery, zucchini, cauliflower, cucumber, radishes, and cabbage wedges may all be used instead of crackers for bases for the protein choices. *Note:* Pork rinds or Crackers (page 10) may also be used as bases. Fill 1 celery stick with Nut Butter for each person.

NUTRITION INFORMATION PER SERVING:
Varies according to choices made.

TENDER BEEF AND GRAVY

Makes 12 servings

Serve over Rice-Aflower (page 227) or Slurp 'Em Up Cabbage Noodles (page 233). This can easily be made into Tender Beef Stew. Simply add veggies for stew. For instance, 2 stalks celery, 1 turnip, 2 cups shredded cabbage, 1 medium zucchini, 2 cups cauliflower, 1 onion. If you want it to be Tender Beef with Creamy Gravy, just add ½ to 1 cup sour cream after the pot has been removed from the heat, just before serving.

¼ cup soy protein (not soy flour!)
¼ cup milk and egg protein
½ teaspoon lemon pepper
½ teaspoon seasoning salt
3 pounds beef stew meat, cubed
1 tablespoon lard
1 head garlic—about ¼ cup chopped (not clove, the whole head!)
1 cup water
½ teaspoon seasoning salt

1. Combine the soy protein, milk and egg protein, lemon pepper, and seasoning salt in a large plastic bag or bowl. Put the meat into the protein powder mixture and shake or stir to coat evenly.
2. Melt the lard in a large pot with a lid and add the meat. Brown the meat over medium heat, stirring occasionally for about 10 minutes. When it is nearly all brown, add the chopped garlic and cook 3 to 5 minutes more. The garlic should be fragrant at this point.
3. Add the water, cover, and cook the meat over low heat for about 1 hour or until it is tender. Uncover the pot, add the seasoning salt, and cook the gravy down to the consistency desired, 10 to 30 minutes.
4. At this point the beef and gravy may be refrigerated overnight or until chilled, and the fat can be lifted off in one hard layer, if desired.

NUTRITIONAL INFORMATION PER SERVING:
Carbohydrates: trace • Effective Carb Count: 0 grams
Protein: 25 grams • Fat: 11 grams • Calories: 207

REDUCED-FAT VARIATION:
Chill and remove the fat, as directed.
Carbohydrates: trace • Effective Carb Count: 0 grams
Protein: 25 grams • Fat: 9 grams • Calories: 191

VEGGIE BEEF STEW

Serves 6

This makes a really nice hot lunch for cold, rainy days! *Note:* Please notice there is no additional water or thickener added to this recipe. A tightly fitting lid is an absolute essential for this dish! If your pan doesn't have a well-fitted lid, then the stew is likely to boil dry. Also, avoid opening the lid, especially in the early part of the cooking, since you don't want to lose any of the precious steam.

1 ½ pounds beef stew meat
1 tablespoon lard
½ teaspoon seasoning salt
2 carrots, thinly sliced (optional)
1 ½ cups zucchini, shredded
1 clove elephant garlic or 2 large cloves regular garlic, finely minced
¼ head cauliflower, thinly sliced
4" cut end from 1 bunch celery or 2 large stalks celery, thinly sliced
½ onion, thinly sliced
½ teaspoon seasoning salt
¼ teaspoon lemon pepper
1 teaspoon parsley (fresh if possible), chopped
⅛ teaspoon lemon thyme (or a pinch—way less than
⅛ teaspoon—of dried thyme, if no lemon thyme is available)

1. In a 4-quart pot with a tightly fitting lid, brown the beef over medium heat in the lard and ½ teaspoon seasoning salt, until the meat is no longer red. Cover the pot with a well-fitting lid and simmer on low heat for 1 hour.
2. Add the remaining ingredients, mixing thoroughly. Cover tightly, and simmer about 45 minutes. Serve hot in bowls.

NUTRITIONAL INFORMATION PER SERVING:
Carbohydrates: 5 grams • Effective Carb Count: 3 grams
Protein: 33 grams • Fat: 26 grams • Calories: 389

REDUCED-FAT VARIATION:
Omit the lard and use cooking spray.
Carbohydrates: 5 grams • Effective Carb Count: 3 grams
Protein: 33 grams • Fat: 24 grams • Calories: 369

WALLA WALLA SWEET STEAKS

Serves 2

A girl from Washington State has to have a Walla Walla Sweet recipe, doesn't she? This could easily be made with 4 or 5 steaks and still have enough gravy!

3 tablespoons lard or bacon grease
2 beef cubed steaks
Seasoning salt
1 medium Walla Walla Sweet onion
(or Vidalia, if Walla Wallas aren't available), cut into ¼" slices
1 teaspoon arrowroot powder
½ cup water

1. Melt the lard in a medium-sized skillet and heat on medium heat. Season the steaks with seasoning salt to taste and carefully place in hot oil. Brown the steaks quickly on each side. Remove the steaks from the pan and set aside.
2. Add the onion slices to the hot lard. Season them to taste with seasoning salt, and cook them until they are beginning to become translucent, about 4 minutes. Carefully place the steaks on top of the onion slices. Also, place some of the onion slices atop the steaks. Cover the pan and turn the heat to low. Simmer 30 to 45 minutes. At this point, the steaks and sauce can be put in a storage container and refrigerated until ready to use.
3. When ready to use, heat the steaks and sauce back to a simmer. In a small cup, combine the arrowroot and water. Pour it into the sauce, stirring slightly to thicken.

NUTRITIONAL INFORMATION PER SERVING:
Carbohydrates: 6 grams • Effective Carb Count: 5 grams
Protein: 23 grams • Fat: 34 grams • Calories: 428

REDUCED-FAT VARIATION:
Use cooking oil spray to brown the steaks and a bit
of Rich Stock (page 254) to cook the onion.
Carbohydrates: 6 grams • Effective Carb Count: 5 grams
Protein: 23 grams • Fat: 15 grams • Calories: 255

WINTER PORK STEW

Makes 8 servings

Serve this comfort food with a cup of tea on a cold winter evening. Garnish it with a dollop of sour cream or yogurt.

3 cloves garlic
1 medium onion
1 parsnip
2 turnips
2 carrots, optional
3 stalks celery
2 pounds pork
2 tablespoons lard
Seasoning salt to taste
1 1/2 cups Rich Stock (page 254)
1/2 teaspoon thyme flakes
1 bay leaf
8 drops (about 1/8 teaspoon) hot chili oil
1 teaspoon lemon pepper
Seasoning salt to taste
2 teaspoons arrowroot powder mixed with 1/2 cup water (optional)
Yogurt or sour cream for garnishing, optional

1. Chop all of the vegetables and cut up the meat. Cook the onion and the garlic in the lard over medium heat in a 3- to 5-quart saucepan with a lid, until they are translucent, about 3 minutes. Add the pork, season it with seasoning salt to taste, and cook it until all of the red is gone from the meat, about 5 minutes.
2. Add the parsnip, turnips, carrots, celery, stock, thyme, bay leaf, hot chili oil, lemon pepper, and seasoning salt to taste. Cover and cook for 45 minutes to 1 hour. Remove the bay leaf. If you desire the stew thickened, add the arrowroot/water mixture and cook while bubbling, about 2 minutes.

NUTRITIONAL INFORMATION PER SERVING:
Carbohydrates: 12 grams • Effective Carb Count: 9 grams
Protein: 22 grams • Fat: 22 grams • Calories: 337

REDUCED-FAT VARIATION:
Omit the lard and simply cook the onions and the
garlic with the rest of the vegetables.
Carbohydrates: 12 grams • Effective Carb Count: 9 grams
Protein: 22 grams • Fat: 19 grams • Calories: 308

Your Basic Great Stir-Fry

Serves 6

A wonderful, tasty meal. A great change of pace from everyday meat and veggies!

3 cloves garlic, minced
2 tablespoons lard
2 1/2 pounds fresh veggies, cut up (spinach, cabbage,
broccoli, cauliflower, snow peas, jicama, etc.)
2 cups raw or cooked shrimp, peeled and deveined (optional, but not really!)
1 1/4 pounds Barbecue Pork (page 95), cut up

Sauce:

1/4 cup fish sauce (available at an Asian grocery or
in the ethnic section of your local market)
2 tablespoons Bragg's Liquid Aminos
1 teaspoon seasoning salt
1/2 tablespoon sesame oil
1/8 teaspoon hot chili oil
1 teaspoon arrowroot mixed into 2 tablespoons water (optional)

1. In a large wok or skillet with a lid, over medium-high heat, cook the garlic in the lard until it is fragrant, about 2 minutes. Add the veggies to the wok according to their density. Broccoli and cauliflower are denser, so they would be first, spinach would be last. Cook, stirring frequently, using a lifting and scooping motion. After each addition of vegetables, cover the wok and let them steam for about 2 minutes. Add any additional cooking fat as necessary to prevent sticking.
2. If using raw shrimp, add it before the least-dense veggies, like the spinach and snow peas. After cooking the veggies, add the cooked meat and shrimp and cover them to heat through.
3. While the meat is heating, combine the sauce ingredients. Add the sauce to the pan and stir well. Garnish with sesame seeds, if desired.

Nutritional information per serving:
Carbohydrates: 5 grams • Effective Carb Count: 4 grams
Protein: 34 grams • Fat: 24 grams • Calories: 378

Main Courses

Fish

BACON AND SALMON BAKE

Serves 6

Canned salmon is usually inexpensive and plentiful. Besides being a yummy main dish, this may also be served as an appetizer with Crackers (page 10) or veggies for dipping.

½ cup sweet onion, chopped
½ teaspoon lemon thyme, fresh, or
dried regular thyme
1 tablespoon butter
1 8-ounce package cream cheese, softened
2 eggs
1 tablespoon parsley flakes
¼ teaspoon lemon pepper
½ cup bacon, cooked and chopped
2 cans salmon, drained, large bones
and skin removed

Topping:

2 tablespoons Romano cheese (or
Parmesan)
½ cup Monterey jack cheese, shredded
1 teaspoon chives, snipped

1. In a small frying pan over medium heat, cook the onions and thyme in the butter until the onions are golden, about 5 minutes. Set them aside to cool.
2. Combine the cream cheese, eggs, parsley, and lemon pepper in a mixing bowl and mix well. Stir in the bacon and salmon. Pour this mixture into a 9" × 13" baking dish. Sprinkle the topping over the salmon mixture. Bake at 350°F for about 25 minutes, or until the cheese is bubbling and golden.

NUTRITIONAL INFORMATION PER SERVING:
Carbohydrates: 3 grams • Effective Carb Count: 2 grams
Protein: 15 grams • Fat: 23 grams • Calories: 278

REDUCED-FAT VARIATION:
Omit the butter and cook the onion in about 2 tablespoons of Rich Stock (page 254). Use low-fat cream cheese, turkey bacon, and low-fat Monterey jack cheese.
Carbohydrates: 3 grams • Effective Carb Count: 2 grams
Protein: 16 grams • Fat: 14 grams • Calories: 207

What makes a plan low-carb? There are a lot of lower-carb plans out there, but what really makes a plan low-carb? Generally, the most basic element of low-carbing is the need to avoid "white stuff." The "white stuff" is a group of foods that cause insulin spikes, which deter weight loss and work against overall good health, in my experience. These include: sugar, potatoes, rice, pasta, flour. Even if that is the only thing changed, just avoiding those things and increasing their protein intake, often folks see great health benefits and weight loss!

BAKED FISH MACADAMIA

Serves 6

This is a simple recipe that turns plain old cod or pollock into company fare! Garnish it with fresh lemon wedges and parsley sprigs for a really pretty platter at serving time.

2 to 3 tablespoons butter, melted
2 eggs
2 tablespoons water
⅓ pound macadamia nuts, ground
Seasoning salt
4 large pieces pollock or other white fish suitable for breading
Lemon pepper
Cooking oil spray
Lemon juice, fresh, for serving

1. Pour approximately 2 to 3 tablespoons melted butter into an 11" × 17" baking pan.
2. In a shallow dish, beat the eggs and water. In another small, shallow dish, place some of the ground macadamia nuts and season to taste with seasoning salt. *Note:* Prepare the ground macadamia nuts in small batches or the ground nuts will become too sticky and you'll waste them. Only prepare enough for 2 or 3 pieces of fish at a time.
3. Cut fish into serving-size pieces about 3" to 4" long. Dip the pieces in the egg mixture; then roll in the macadamia mixture. This part of the process is very messy! Gently place the fish in the baking pan about 1" to 2" apart. When done, sprinkle the tops of the fish with lemon pepper and spray with cooking oil spray, to aid in browning.
4. Bake at 375°F approximately 15 to 20 minutes, until macadamia topping is lightly browned. To serve, squeeze fresh lemon juice on top.

NUTRITIONAL INFORMATION PER SERVING:
Carbohydrates: 4 grams • Effective Carb Count: 2 grams
Protein: 26 grams • Fat: 25 grams • Calories: 337

REDUCED-FAT VARIATION:
Omit the melted butter and simply spray the pan with cooking spray.
Carbohydrates: 4 grams • Effective Carb Count: 2 grams
Protein: 26 grams • Fat: 21 grams • Calories: 303

BAKED FISH MARGARET

Serves 6

This is good with boned whitefish or sea bass or other white-fleshed fish with a firm texture. It can be made with smallmouth bass filets if you've had a lucky day fishing.

2 tablespoons olive oil, mildly flavored
2 tablespoons olive oil, extra virgin
2 pounds white fish fillets
1 medium onion, thinly sliced
1 clove garlic, minced
1 cup tomatoes, chopped
1 bunch parsley, freshly chopped
1 teaspoon fresh oregano or 1/3 teaspoon dried
1/4 teaspoon cinnamon
Sea salt and pepper, to taste
1/2 cup red wine

1. Combine the olive oils in a small cup. Pour enough of the oil into a large baking pan to coat the bottom. Place the fish into the pan so that it lies in one layer.
2. Place the remaining oil into a medium-sized saucepan with a lid. Add the onion and garlic and cook them gently over medium heat until they are translucent, about 3 to 5 minutes. Add the remaining ingredients and bring them to a simmer. Cover the pan and cook the sauce for a minute or 2, until it is heated through.
3. Pour the sauce over the fish and bake it at 375°F until it is done, about 20 to 30 minutes.

NUTRITIONAL INFORMATION PER SERVING:
Carbohydrates: 4 grams • Effective Carb Count: 3 grams
Protein: 28 grams • Fat: 10 grams • Calories: 236

REDUCED-FAT VARIATION:
Omit the olive oil. Use olive oil cooking spray to oil the pan and use 1 tablespoon olive oil plus a little bit of Rich Stock (page 254) to cook the onions.
Carbohydrates: 4 grams • Effective Carb Count: 3 grams
Protein: 28 grams • Fat: 8 grams • Calories: 217

BAKED FISH WITH MUSHROOMS

Serves 3

For a nice variation, sprinkle ½ cup shredded Monterey jack cheese atop the fish before adding the paprika. For a delicious change of pace, try substituting fresh herbs such as thyme, parsley, or basil for the tarragon.

1 pound firm-fleshed white fish fillets, any type,
cut into serving-sized pieces
½ teaspoon seasoning salt
2 tablespoons butter
1 cup mushrooms, sliced, or spinach, chopped
½ cup sliced green onions
¼ teaspoon dried tarragon or thyme, crushed
Paprika, as garnish (approximately ¼ teaspoon)
Lemon pepper, as garnish (approximately ¼ teaspoon)

1. Arrange the fish in a baking dish with a lid, turning under any thin edges. Sprinkle with seasoning salt.
2. In a saucepan, melt the butter and add the mushrooms, onions, and tarragon. Cook them over medium heat until they are tender, about 5 minutes. Spoon the mushroom mixture over the fish and sprinkle with the paprika and lemon pepper.
3. Bake the fish, covered, at 450°F for 12 to 18 minutes or until fish flakes easily with a fork. If you don't have a baking dish with a lid, foil works just fine!

NUTRITIONAL INFORMATION PER SERVING:
Carbohydrates: 3 grams • Effective Carb Count: 2 grams
Protein: 28 grams • Fat: 9 grams • Calories: 204

REDUCED-FAT VARIATION:
Reduce the butter to 1½ teaspoons. Cook the mushrooms in a small amount of Rich Stock (page 254) plus the butter.
Carbohydrates: 3 grams • Effective Carb Count: 2 grams
Protein: 28 grams • Fat: 3 grams • Calories: 154

CHEESY SALMON CASSEROLE

Serves 6

The original recipe came from DJ Rosales. Thank you, DJ, for sharing your recipe with me. We just love it!

6 eggs
6 cloves garlic, minced
3 tablespoons butter
1½ cups half-and-half
3 tablespoons lemon juice, fresh
2 14-ounce cans salmon, skin and bones removed, juices reserved

¼ teaspoon sea salt
⅛ teaspoon lemon pepper
¼ teaspoon oregano
¼ cup soy protein
Cooking oil spray
1 cup mozzarella or Monterey jack cheese, shredded

1. Hard cook the eggs: Place the whole eggs into a medium-sized pan with a lid and cover them with water. Add a pinch of salt, cover the pan, and bring it to a boil over medium heat. Once it reaches a full, rolling boil, turn the heat off and allow the pan to rest on the burner for 10 minutes. Then place the eggs into a bowl filled with cold water to cool them, so that they are easy to handle.
2. While the eggs are resting, cook the garlic in the butter in a 4- to 6-quart pot until it is becoming translucent, about 4 minutes. Stir in the half-and-half, lemon juice, juice reserved from the canned salmon, sea salt, lemon pepper, and oregano. Bring this mixture to a boil over medium heat; then stir in the soy protein. Blend it as thoroughly as possible and remove it from the heat. Stir in the canned salmon and set the cream mixture aside.
3. Slice the eggs and place them evenly across the bottom of a 9" × 13" baking dish that has been sprayed with cooking oil spray. Carefully spread the salmon mixture atop the egg slices. Sprinkle it with the shredded cheese and bake it for about 25 minutes at 350°F, or until the cheese is bubbling and the top is golden brown.

NUTRITIONAL INFORMATION PER SERVING:
Carbohydrates: 5 grams • Effective Carb Count: 4 grams
Protein: 21 grams • Fat: 23 grams • Calories: 313

REDUCED-FAT VARIATION:
Omit the butter and use canned skim milk and low-fat cheese. Cook the garlic in the lemon juice before adding the other sauce ingredients.
Carbohydrates: 10 grams • Effective Carb Count: 12 grams
Protein: 25 grams • Fat: 9 grams • Calories: 226

CLAM CHOWDER

Makes about 4 1-cup servings

Do you ever wonder, "What can I do with those leftover broccoli and cauliflower stems?" Try this new take on the old New England favorite!

3 tablespoons butter
2 cloves garlic, minced
½ cup sweet onion, chopped
1 cup broccoli and/or cauliflower stems, peeled and cubed
(or chopped cabbage, celery, or cauliflower) and cut into ¼" to ½" pieces
1½ cups stock: Either clam broth (if it doesn't have
any sugar) or chicken, turkey, or pork Rich Stock (page 254)
½ pound fresh or frozen chopped clams with juices
(or equivalent canned if they don't have sugar)
¼ teaspoon celery seed
½ teaspoon sea salt
1 teaspoon lemon pepper
4 drops hot chili oil, or a tiny pinch of cayenne
2 teaspoons arrowroot powder mixed into 2 tablespoons water
2 pieces bacon, cooked and chopped (optional)
1 cup Almond Milk (page 240), unflavored
(just the almonds and the water), or cream

1. In a medium-sized saucepan, melt the butter over medium-low heat. Add the garlic and onion and cook until translucent, about 3 to 5 minutes.
2. Add the cubed broccoli and/or cauliflower stems, stock, clams, celery seed, salt, lemon pepper, and chili oil. Cover and cook until the veggies are tender, about 10 minutes.
3. Add the arrowroot/water mixture and bacon. Simmer, stirring lightly, until thickened. Add the Almond Milk and serve immediately.

NUTRITIONAL INFORMATION PER SERVING:
Carbohydrates: 7 grams • Effective Carb Count: 6 grams
Protein: 8 grams • Fat: 9 grams • Calories: 143

Coconut Shrimp

Serves 6

When working with shrimp, a shrimp peeler is an invaluable tool. It costs less than $3.00, usually, and even if you use it only once a year, it is well worth keeping around! To use the peeler, simply slip the pointed end up the back of the shrimp until the last joint of the shell. Give it a little twist, and ta da! The shell comes off, and so does the vein! Serve Coconut Shrimp hot with Sweet and Zingy Mustard Sauce (page 258) or other favorite dipping sauces.

1 1/2 pounds raw shrimp, peeled and deveined
(21 to 25 per pound is a good size)
2 eggs, beaten
1/2 cup kefir or buttermilk
1/2 cup soy protein (not soy flour!)
2 cups unsweetened shredded coconut
1/2 teaspoon Sweet & Slender
1 teaspoon seasoning salt
1/2 teaspoon lemon pepper
Lard for frying

1. Place the shrimp into a colander, rinse them with running water, and allow them to drain.
2. In a shallow dish, combine the eggs and kefir. In another shallow dish, combine the soy protein, coconut, Sweet & Slender, seasoning salt, and lemon pepper. Dip the shrimp first into the kefir mixture and then into the coconut mixture.
3. Fry the shrimp in hot fat that is at least 1½" deep, until they are golden brown, about 2 minutes.

NUTRITIONAL INFORMATION PER SERVING:
Carbohydrates: 8 grams • Effective Carb Count: 3 grams
Protein: 35 grams • Fat: 22 grams • Calories: 368

DIJON MUSTARD FILLETS

Serves 3

Make this simple and tasty dish with your favorite fish! For a tasty variation, try adding chopped spinach, garlic, or onions to the sauce. This would be nice served with Spinach Salad with Lemon Dressing (page 49).

1 pound white fish fillets, cut into serving-sized pieces
½ teaspoon lemon pepper
½ teaspoon seasoning salt

Sauce ingredients:

¼ cup sour cream
1 tablespoon half-and-half
1 tablespoon Dijon mustard
2 teaspoons chives, snipped
Black pepper, to taste

1. Place the fish fillets onto the rack of a broiler pan. Sprinkle them with lemon pepper and seasoning salt. Broil them for about 5 minutes or until they flake with a fork.
2. Combine the sauce ingredients in a small saucepan over medium-low heat. Heat the sauce through. Do not allow it to boil. Serve the sauce alongside the fish.

NUTRITIONAL INFORMATION PER SERVING:
Carbohydrates: 2 grams • Effective Carb Count: 1 gram
Protein: 28 grams • Fat: 6 grams • Calories: 177

REDUCED-FAT VARIATION:
Use reduced-fat sour cream and canned skim milk.
Carbohydrates: 2 grams • Effective Carb Count: 1 gram
Protein: 28 grams • Fat: 2 grams • Calories: 141

FRIED FISH

Serves 6

Serve the fish hot with Tartar Sauce I (page 259) or Tartar Sauce II (page 260) for a real taste treat!

1 ½ pounds white fish fillets (cod, catfish, etc.)
1 ½ cups pork rinds, crushed
3 tablespoons soy protein (not soy flour!)
1 tablespoon minced onion, dried
1 teaspoon dill
½ teaspoon orange or lemon zest
¼ teaspoon sea salt
1 egg
3 tablespoons water
Lard for frying

1. Cut the fish into approximately 3" chunks. Combine the pork rinds, soy protein, onion, dill, orange zest, and salt in a shallow dish, leaving at least 1½" headroom. Combine the egg and water thoroughly in another shallow dish.
2. Put enough lard into a deep fryer, wok, or other large cooking pot suitable for deep-frying. Do not skimp on the cooking oil or you will end up with soggy fish! I use 1 pound of lard in my large wok and it is just right.
3. Dip the fish a few pieces at a time first into the egg wash, then into the coating mixture. Gently shake the container with the coating mixture to completely cover the fish. Fry a few pieces at a time in deep hot fat until golden brown, about 2 to 3 minutes per side

NUTRITIONAL INFORMATION PER SERVING:
Carbohydrates: 1 gram • Effective Carb Count: 0 grams
Protein: 34 grams • Fat: 16 grams • Calories: 270

So what is all this business about "carb count, fiber, and ECC"? If you've been low-carbing for even more than a few minutes, you will understand the need to count your carbs. But what about the effective carb count figures? Where do they fit into the picture? Some low-carb plans allow their participants to deduct the dietary fiber from the total carbs of their food. The reasoning behind it is that since our bodies don't digest fiber, it shouldn't figure into the carb count. The "effective carb count" refers to those carbs that our bodies do digest.

FRIED SMELT

Serves 6

These tiny fish are the perfect finger food! Serve with lemon slices as a garnish or try the optional sauce below. Thank you Margaret Fries for sharing this very easy, very yummy recipe with us!

2 pounds smelt
1 1/2 cups soy protein
1 to 2 teaspoons sea salt
Freshly ground black pepper, to taste
Olive oil, mildly flavored, for frying (about 2 cups total)

Smelt Sauce, optional:

Remaining olive oil and juices from cooked fish
1 clove garlic, crushed
1 cup wine vinegar or lemon juice, fresh
1 teaspoon fresh thyme or 1/3 teaspoon dried
1/4 teaspoon guar gum or about 1 1/2 teaspoons arrowroot
mixed into 2 tablespoons water

1. Place the fish into a large colander and rinse them well under cold running water. Allow them to drain.
2. Meanwhile, place the soy protein, salt, and black pepper into a fairly large plastic bag. Place the fish, a few at a time, into the bag. Shake them gently, just enough to give them a light coating of soy protein, not a heavy breading.
3. Pour about 1/2" to 3/4" olive oil into the bottom of a large frying pan. Cook the fish in the oil over medium-high heat until they are browned on all sides, about 5 minutes. Do not crowd the fish! Cook them in several batches, adding more oil as necessary to keep them from sticking to the pan.
4. When the fish is cooked, cool the pan slightly and add the garlic, vinegar, and thyme to the cooking juices. Return the heat to medium-high and bring the sauce to a boil for about 2 minutes. Remove the pan from the heat and add the guar gum or arrowroot/water mixture. Pour the sauce into a serving dish and serve alongside the freshly fried fish.

NUTRITIONAL INFORMATION PER SERVING (FISH ONLY):
Carbohydrates: 0 grams • Effective Carb Count: 0 grams
Protein: 38 grams • Fat: 22 grams • Calories: 361

NUTRITIONAL INFORMATION PER SERVING (SAUCE ONLY):
Carbohydrates: trace • Effective Carb Count: 0 grams
Protein: trace • Fat: 18 grams • Calories: 169

Garlic Butter Prawns

Serves 6

Give your family a "dinner at the coast" without having to leave home! This is great served over Rice-Aflower (page 227).

¹/₂ cup butter
2 tablespoons lard
4 cloves garlic
2 pounds prawns, raw, peeled if possible
1 lemon, juiced (about 3 tablespoons fresh lemon juice)
¹/₂ teaspoon seasoning salt
1 ¹/₂ tablespoons parsley flakes (but freshly chopped would be terrific!)
1 teaspoon arrowroot powder mixed into 2 tablespoons water

1. Melt the butter and lard over medium-low heat in a large frying pan with a lid. Add the garlic and cook it until it becomes translucent, about 3 minutes.
2. Put the remaining ingredients (except the arrowroot/water mixture) into the pan, stirring well. Cover and cook, stirring occasionally about 8 to 10 minutes or until the prawns are pink. Add the arrowroot/water mixture, cooking and stirring until the sauce is thickened.

Nutritional information per serving:
Carbohydrates: 2 grams • Effective Carb Count: 1 gram
Protein: 25 grams • Fat: 21 grams • Calories: 298

Reduced-Fat Variation:
Instead of the butter and lard listed, use 2 teaspoons
butter and ¹/₂ cup white wine.
Carbohydrates: 2 grams • Effective Carb Count: 1 gram
Protein: 25 grams • Fat: 2 grams • Calories: 148

HAPPY FAMILY

Makes 8 servings

Happy Family is a popular dish at Chinese restaurants. It may also be called Four Happiness, signifying the different meats used in the dish. Unfortunately, most restaurants use ingredients in their sauces that are not low-carb. Here is my low-carb, "from scratch" variation. I hope you enjoy it!

Sauce ingredients:

³/₄ cup beef or pork Rich Stock (page 254) or commercially prepared stock
¼ teaspoon Sweet & Slender
⅛ teaspoon SteviaPlus
½ teaspoon ginger
⅛ teaspoon dry mustard
2 tablespoons lemon juice, fresh
1 ½ teaspoons arrowroot powder
1 tablespoon sesame oil

Stir-fry ingredients:

Lard
1 ¼ pounds boneless beef steak, sliced into bite-sized pieces (London broil or sirloin are good choices)
³/₄ pound boneless pork, sliced into bite-sized pieces
3 cloves garlic, minced
Seasoning salt (to taste)
3 carrots, thinly sliced (optional)
½ pound scallops, fresh or frozen
2 stalks celery, sliced
¼ pound jicama, thinly sliced, or 1 can sliced water chestnuts
¼ pound bean sprouts, fresh
¼ pound snow peas, fresh, cut into ½" pieces
¼ head cabbage, chopped (about 4 cups)
¼ pound shrimp, fresh or frozen
Lemon pepper
1 tablespoon sesame seeds (optional)

1. Combine the sauce ingredients in a small dish and set aside.
2. Melt about ¼ cup lard in a large wok or other large frying pan. Turn the heat to high, and add the beef, pork, and garlic. Season the meat with seasoning salt. Cook the meat and garlic using a lifting and stirring action for about 5 minutes, or until the meat is no longer red.
3. Add the carrots and continue to cook (use the same lifting and stirring action throughout the recipe) for about 2 minutes.
4. Add the scallops, celery, and jicama and cook for about 2 minutes. Add the bean sprouts, snow peas, and cabbage. Cook for about 3 minutes.
5. Stir in the shrimp and the sauce. Season to taste with additional seasoning salt and lemon pepper. Transfer the stir-fry to a large serving dish and garnish with the sesame seeds.

NUTRITIONAL INFORMATION PER SERVING:
Carbohydrates: 8 grams • Effective Carb Count: 5 grams
Protein: 29 grams • Fat: 27 grams • Calories: 399

KELLY'S SALMON MACADAMIA CASSEROLE

Serves 4

Enjoy this tasty casserole with nuts from the tropics. This recipe was developed with severe allergy restrictions in mind, but you don't have to be restricted to enjoy it!

¼ cup sweet onion, chopped
2 cloves garlic, minced
1 tablespoon butter or lard
1 sprig each fresh oregano, parsley,
and lemon thyme, chopped
Lemon pepper and seasoning salt,
as desired

1 16-ounce can salmon, liquid
reserved, bones and skin removed
½ cup water plus ¼ cup macadamia nuts
3 egg whites (or 3 whole eggs)
2 tablespoons Parmesan cheese, grated
2 whole grain rye crackers
2 tablespoons macadamia nuts

1. Cook the onion and garlic in the butter over medium-low heat until they are becoming golden, about 5 minutes. Stir in the fresh herbs until they are wilted, just a few seconds. Season as desired with lemon pepper and seasoning salt. Turn off the heat.
2. Place the salmon and ¼ cup of the juices into a fairly large mixing bowl and stir in the herb/onion mixture.
3. In a blender container, combine the ½ cup water and ¼ cup macadamia nuts. Blend until the nuts are completely pulverized into a "milk." Pour the macadamia milk into the salmon mixture.
4. Beat the egg whites in a small bowl with a fork until they are slightly frothy. Stir them into the salmon mixture until it is all well combined. Pour this into an 8" × 8" baking dish. Bake at 350°F for 10 minutes, or until the salmon mixture is beginning to set up.
5. Meanwhile, place the cheese, crackers, and 2 tablespoons macadamia nuts in the bowl of a food processor and process until they are well combined and uniform in size. After the casserole has baked for 10 minutes, sprinkle the topping onto the salmon mixture. Bake it for another 15 to 25 minutes, or until a knife inserted off center comes out clean. Remove from the oven and allow to rest about 5 minutes before serving.

NUTRITIONAL INFORMATION PER SERVING:
Carbohydrates: 6 grams • Effective Carb Count: 4 grams
Protein: 28 grams • Fat: 17 grams • Calories: 290

REDUCED-FAT VARIATION:
Omit the butter and lard. Use 2 to 4 tablespoons of the
canned salmon broth to cook the onion and garlic.
Carbohydrates: 6 grams • Effective Carb Count: 4 grams
Protein: 28 grams • Fat: 14 grams • Calories: 264

MAGGIE'S SWEET AND SOUR FISH

Makes 8 servings

Enjoy this traditional Lenten dish anytime for a special family get-together!

2 pounds cod, cut in 2- to
3-ounce pieces
2 cups low-carb bread crumbs or
1¾ cups ground almonds mixed with
¼ cup soy protein
¼ cup Romano cheese, grated
½ teaspoon parsley, dried
½ teaspoon thyme, dried
½ teaspoon oregano, dried
½ teaspoon sea salt

1 cup soy protein
2 eggs beaten with 1 tablespoon water
Olive oil, mild, for frying
(about 2 cups total)
1 really large onion, or 2 small onions,
sliced into thin strips (not rings)
⅓ cup red wine vinegar
⅓ cup water
¼ cup pourable sucralose or
6 packets sucralose

1. Place the fish into a large colander. Rinse it under cold running water and allow it to drain.
2. Combine the low-carb bread crumbs, cheese, herbs, and salt in a shallow dish. Set them aside. Place the soy protein into another shallow dish. Place the egg/water mixture into another shallow dish.
3. Dredge the pieces of cod first in the soy protein; then dip them into the egg mixture. Finally, coat them in the bread crumb mixture, pressing them down a bit to coat.
4. Start with 1 cup of olive oil and fry the fish over medium-high heat in a large frying pan, until golden on each side, about 3 to 5 minutes. Transfer the cooked fish to a large platter. Add more oil as needed, being sure that the oil is hot before adding the next batch of fish. Continue in this manner until all of the fish is cooked.
5. Pour the excess oil from the pan, leaving a light coating. Add the onion to the pan and cook over medium heat until golden, about 5 minutes. Add the vinegar, water, and sucralose and turn the heat to medium-high. Bring it to a boil and cook the liquid down by half. It should appear as juicy onions, not onion soup. Spread the juicy onions over the fish and allow it to cool to room temperature for serving.

NUTRITIONAL INFORMATION PER SERVING:
Carbohydrates: 8 grams • Effective Carb Count: 5 grams
Protein: 38 grams • Fat: 25 grams • Calories: 392

How do you make low-carb bread crumbs? To make the bread crumbs from a loaf of low-carb bread, put a few slices into the oven on lowest heat for about 15 minutes to dry them out. It may take more or less time according to the thickness and freshness of your bread. Grind them in a food processor and store in a zipper-sealed bag. The extras can be kept frozen for 2 to 3 months.

MARYLAND CRAB CAKES

Makes 8 servings

Maryland has long been famous for its incredible crab cakes. Now you can bring a low-carb version of that "best in the world" flavor into your own home! These would be nice served with a salad for a light lunch.

1 pound crabmeat, fresh preferred, shell pieces removed
3/4 cup pork rinds, crushed
1 egg, beaten
1 tablespoon Blender Mayonnaise (page 241)
1 teaspoon Dijon mustard or 1/2 teaspoon dry mustard
1 teaspoon Worcestershire sauce
1 tablespoon Old Bay seasoning
2 tablespoons parsley
Sea salt and pepper to taste
Butter or lard, for frying

1. Combine all of the ingredients except the butter in a mixing bowl. Form the mixture into 8½"-thick patties.
2. Melt the butter in a large frying pan over medium heat. Place the crab cakes into the butter and fry them until they are golden brown, about 8 minutes, turning partway through.

NUTRITIONAL INFORMATION PER SERVING:
Carbohydrates: trace • Effective Carb Count: 0 grams
Protein: 15 grams • Fat: 9 grams • Calories: 138

REDUCED-FAT VARIATION:
Use reduced-fat mayonnaise and omit the butter. Broil the crab cakes for 10 to 15 minutes, turning halfway through.
Carbohydrates: 1 gram • Effective Carb Count: 0 grams
Protein: 15 grams • Fat: 5 grams • Calories: 105

PARMESAN FISH

Serves 4

This is my low-carb version of a local fish house favorite. Serve it with a squeeze of fresh lemon juice and fresh asparagus on the side for a real treat!

1 ½ pounds fresh white fish fillets (halibut, cod, hoki, etc.)
¼ cup soy protein (not soy flour!)
½ teaspoon seasoning salt
¼ teaspoon dry mustard powder
¼ teaspoon paprika
¼ cup butter, melted
⅓ cup Parmesan cheese, freshly grated
½ teaspoon lemon pepper
Lemon wedges for garnish

1. Preheat the oven to 350°F. Cut the fish into serving-sized pieces, about 4" long. Place it into a colander and rinse it under running water. Allow it to drain.
2. In a plastic bag, combine the soy protein, seasoning salt, dry mustard, and paprika. Shake the fish in the coating mixture and place it into a large baking dish. Drizzle the tops of the fish with the melted butter. Sprinkle the cheese and lemon pepper evenly over all. Bake the fish at 350°F for about 15 minutes, or until it flakes easily with a fork. Garnish with lemon wedges.

NUTRITIONAL INFORMATION PER SERVING:
Carbohydrates: 1 gram • Effective Carb Count: 0 grams
Protein: 39 grams • Fat: 15 grams • Calories: 301

REDUCED-FAT VARIATION:
Omit the butter. Spray the tops of the fish with cooking oil spray.
Carbohydrates: 1 gram • Effective Carb Count: 1 gram
Protein: 39 grams • Fat: 3 grams • Calories: 200

SALMON CHOWDER

Makes 10 servings

Even if you don't live in an area where fresh salmon is prevalent, whole salmon are now available year-round in most areas. This is a terrific use for the bones! If you don't have a fresh salmon, you can use 2 14-ounce cans of salmon with the skin removed, retaining the bones and juices, instead.

Soup ingredients:

*Bones and attached meat from one
large Chinook salmon
that has had the fillets removed, or
about 1 1/2 pounds skinned salmon
6 cups water (to cover)
4 carrots, chopped (optional)
1 large onion, chopped
1 small turnip, peeled and chopped
1/2 small head cabbage, chopped
(about 3 cups)
1 Jerusalem artichoke, unpeeled,
chopped (optional)
2 stalks celery, chopped
1 tablespoon lime or lemon juice, fresh*

*1/2 teaspoon celery seed
1 bay leaf
1 tablespoon fresh chives, snipped
1/2 tablespoon fresh parsley, chopped
1 teaspoon seasoning salt
1/2 teaspoon lemon pepper*

Additional ingredients:

*4 slices bacon, cooked and chopped
2 teaspoons arrowroot mixed with
2 tablespoons water
1 cup cream or Almond Milk
(page 240), unflavored*

1. Combine all of the soup ingredients in a large stockpot with a lid. Bring to a boil over medium-high heat; then cover and simmer the soup for about an hour. The veggies should be tender and the flavors should be blending.
2. Remove the bay leaf and salmon bones from the soup and add the bacon and arrowroot/water mixture. Remove the soup from the heat and pour in the cream. Serve immediately.

NUTRITIONAL INFORMATION PER SERVING:
Carbohydrates: 6 grams • Effective Carb Count: 4 grams
Protein: 16 grams • Fat: 10 grams • Calories: 175

REDUCED-FAT VARIATION:
Use turkey bacon and canned skim milk.
Carbohydrates: 8 grams • Effective Carb Count: 6 grams
Protein: 17 grams • Fat: 4 grams • Calories: 136

SALMON LASAGNA

Makes 6 servings

The question was asked: "I have some spinach and some canned salmon. What in the world can I do with them?" Salmon Lasagna!

Filling ingredients:

³/4 cup sweet onion
¹/2 tablespoon lard
¹/2 tablespoon butter
¹/4 teaspoon seasoning salt
4 eggs
³/4 cup cream cheese, softened, or ricotta cheese
¹/2 tablespoon parsley, fresh or dried, chopped
¹/2 teaspoon garlic salt
¹/4 teaspoon dill weed, fresh or dried, chopped
3 tablespoons Parmesan cheese
2 14- to 16-ounce cans salmon, drained, with large bones and skin removed

Other ingredients:

1 bunch fresh spinach, washed and stemmed
1 cup Monterey jack cheese, shredded and divided

1. Cook the onion in the lard, butter, and seasoning salt in a small frying pan over medium heat until it becomes golden, about 5 minutes. Set the onion aside to cool.
2. While the onion is cooling, combine the remaining filling ingredients in a large mixing bowl. Add the cooled onions and stir the salmon mixture well.
3. Place half of the spinach leaves across the bottom of a 9" × 13" baking dish, evenly as if they were lasagna noodles. Pour half of the salmon mixture over the spinach and sprinkle half of the cheese over that. Repeat for the remaining ingredients. Bake the lasagna at 350°F for about 35 minutes, or until the cheese is golden and bubbling.

NUTRITIONAL INFORMATION PER SERVING:
Carbohydrates: 3 grams • Effective Carb Count: 2 grams
Protein: 18 grams • Fat: 23 grams • Calories: 287

REDUCED-FAT VARIATION:
Omit the butter and lard. Cook the onion in about 2 tablespoons Rich Stock (page 254). Use low-fat cream cheese and low-fat Monterey jack cheese.
Carbohydrates: 3 grams • Effective Carb Count: 2 grams
Protein: 17 grams • Fat: 9 grams • Calories: 167

SALMON LOAF

Makes 8 servings

The salmon in this recipe stays nice and moist. A pleasant change of pace from just the "same ol' thing"! Serve with lemon juice and Tartar Sauce I (page 259) or Tartar Sauce II (page 260).

*2 pounds cooked salmon, or the equivalent canned
salmon with skin and large bones removed
4 eggs
1 cup pork rinds, crushed
1 teaspoon dry mustard powder
2 teaspoons parsley flakes
1 teaspoon dill weed, dried
3 tablespoons onion flakes, or ½ cup fresh onion, minced
1 tablespoon lemon juice, fresh
¼ teaspoon lemon pepper
½ teaspoon seasoning salt
1 cup cheese, shredded (Colby, Monterey jack, Cheddar, or a blend)
Cooking oil spray*

1. In a mixing bowl, combine all of the ingredients except the cheese and cooking oil spray. Mix them well.
2. Spray an 8" × 4" loaf pan and pour the salmon mixture into the pan. Spread it evenly and top the loaf with the shredded cheese. Bake at 350°F for about 35 minutes or until the cheese is thoroughly melted and becoming golden.

NUTRITIONAL INFORMATION PER SERVING:
Carbohydrates: 2 grams • Effective Carb Count: 1 gram
Protein: 34 grams • Fat: 16 grams • Calories: 284

REDUCED-FAT VARIATION:
Use low-fat cheese instead of regular.
(*Note:* Whole rolled oats may be used instead of the pork rinds.
The nutritional values for this option are in parentheses below.)
Carbohydrates: 2 grams (9) • Effective Carb Count: 1 gram (8)
Protein: 34 grams (31) • Fat: 12 grams (8) • Calories: 252 (235)

❦ A NOTE ABOUT CANNED GOODS: Always be sure to rinse the tops of your canned goods. You never know what might have been crawling around on them or what chemicals they may have been exposed to before you purchased them!

SALMON PATTIES

Serves 2

Enjoy an authentic Pacific Northwest specialty right in your own home! Serve with Tartar Sauce I (page 259) or Tartar Sauce II (page 260). *Note:* This recipe multiplies very well; just add an additional egg for every third can of salmon.

1 14-ounce can salmon, skin and large bones removed
1 egg
½ cup pork rinds, crushed
½ teaspoon dry mustard powder
1 teaspoon parsley flakes
½ teaspoon dried dill weed
1 ½ tablespoons onion flakes, or ¼ cup fresh onion, minced
1 ½ teaspoons lemon juice
⅛ teaspoon lemon pepper
¼ teaspoon garlic salt
Lard

1. In a mixing bowl, combine all of the ingredients except the lard. Mix well. Shape the mixture into patties about 3" across.
2. Put enough lard into a large frying pan to completely cover the bottom, and heat on medium. Carefully place the patties into the hot oil and fry until golden brown on each side, about 8 minutes total.

NUTRITIONAL INFORMATION PER SERVING:
Carbohydrates: 3 grams • Effective Carb Count: 2 grams
Protein: 21 grams • Fat: 26 grams • Calories: 323

SCAMPI

Serves 4

Scampi is always a hit! For a yummy variation, add some sliced mushrooms cooked in butter and a little white wine to the final product.

3/4 pound shrimp or prawns, raw
2 large cloves garlic, minced
1 teaspoon seasoning salt
1 tablespoon parsley, dried or fresh, chopped
1 1/2 tablespoons butter
2 tablespoons lemon juice, fresh

1. Peel and devein the shrimp. Rinse and place them fairly close together in a single layer in a shallow baking pan that can withstand broiling temperatures. *Warning:* Do not use a glass pan!
2. Sprinkle the minced garlic, seasoning salt, and parsley over the top of the shrimp. Break the butter into tiny pieces and put it on top of the shrimp. Pour the lemon juice over all.
3. Broil for approximately 5 minutes, or until the shrimp has gone from being gray and black to being white and pink. Serve hot.

NUTRITIONAL INFORMATION PER SERVING:
Carbohydrates: 1 gram • Effective Carb Count: 0 grams
Protein: 14 grams • Fat: 5 grams • Calories: 109

Scampi in an Avocado

Serves 2

If you love shrimp and love avocado, then try this fun, elegant recipe. What a treat!

1 large avocado
2 tablespoons butter
2 small cloves or 1 large clove garlic, minced
½ tablespoon parsley, fresh
½ pound small salad shrimp, fresh, found in the deli case
½ teaspoon lemon juice, fresh
Fresh parsley and lemon wedges for garnish (optional)

1. Cut the avocado in half lengthwise. Remove the pit and gently remove the skin. Place each avocado half on a plate.
2. In a medium skillet, melt the butter over medium-low heat. Add the garlic and cook it until the garlic smells wonderful and is beginning to become translucent, about 2 minutes. Add the parsley, cooking and stirring until heated through.
3. Add the shrimp and lemon juice, continuing to cook until the mixture is heated through. Do *not* overcook the shrimp, or it will become rubbery. You just want it hot; it's already been cooked.
4. Pour the heated Scampi over the avocados, allowing the excess to spill onto the plates. Garnish with fresh parsley and lemon wedges if desired.

Nutritional information per serving:
Carbohydrates: 10 grams • Effective Carb Count: 7 grams
Protein: 25 grams • Fat: 29 grams • Calories: 389

Reduced-Fat Variation:
Use 1 teaspoon butter and 2 tablespoons white wine to cook the garlic.
Carbohydrates: 10 grams • Effective Carb Count: 7 grams
Protein: 25 grams • Fat: 19 grams • Calories: 314

SHRIMP AND BROCCOLI BAKE

Makes 8 servings

This tasty recipe can have many faces—you can use cauliflower or cabbage instead of the broccoli. You could use scallops, crab, or white fish instead of the shrimp, or in combination with it. Experiment and enjoy!

Casserole ingredients:

1 to 1¼ pounds broccoli, fresh, cut into bite-sized pieces (frozen is fine)
1 pound shrimp, cooked
3 to 4 cloves garlic, minced
½ cup sweet onion, chopped
2 tablespoons butter
1 tablespoon lard
1½ cups cream or Almond Milk (page 240), unflavored
2 eggs
½ teaspoon seasoning salt
¼ teaspoon lemon pepper
½ tablespoon parsley flakes
½ teaspoon lemon thyme or regular thyme leaves
1 teaspoon lemon zest
½ tablespoon fresh lemon juice
Cooking oil spray

Topping ingredients:

½ tablespoon soy protein
¼ cup Parmesan cheese, freshly grated
1 cup Monterey jack cheese, shredded
1 tablespoon butter

Recipe continues on page 181 ➤

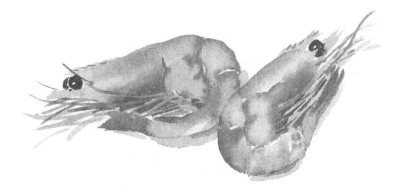

➤ Recipe continued from page 180

1. Put the broccoli into a medium-sized saucepan and add about ½" of water to the pan. Cover and bring to a boil over medium-high heat. Cook the broccoli for about 5 minutes; then pour it into a colander to drain. Pour cold running water over the broccoli to cool it thoroughly.
2. Spray a 9" × 13" baking dish with cooking oil spray and add the cooled broccoli to the dish. Add the shrimp to the dish.
3. In the same saucepan, cook the garlic and onion in the butter and lard until they are slightly golden, about 5 to 8 minutes. Set aside to cool.
4. In a mixing bowl, combine the remaining casserole ingredients, except the cooking oil spray. Add the cooled onions and mix the sauce well. Pour it over the shrimp and broccoli in the baking dish. Mix well.
5. In a small dish, combine the soy protein and Parmesan cheese. Sprinkle over the top of the shrimp and broccoli. Spread the Monterey jack cheese evenly over the top of the casserole. Dot the top with the butter, using a knife to break off bits of butter.
6. At this point the casserole may be covered tightly and refrigerated overnight. When you are ready to bake it, place the uncovered casserole into a 350°F oven. Bake it for about 35 minutes or until the top is beginning to become slightly golden and the cheeses are thoroughly melted. Remove from the oven and allow it to rest for about 5 minutes before serving.

NUTRITIONAL INFORMATION PER SERVING:
Carbohydrates: 6 grams • Effective Carb Count: 5 grams
Protein: 20 grams • Fat: 24 grams • Calories: 320

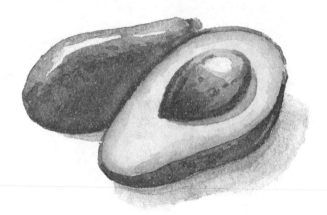

SHRIMP SALAD IN AN AVOCADO

Serves 2

This wonderful salad is great for a special luncheon with a close friend!

1 large avocado
½ pound salad shrimp, fresh, found in the deli case
2½ tablespoons Blender Mayonnaise (page 241) or
commercially prepared mayonnaise
½ teaspoon lemon juice, fresh
1 teaspoon minced onion, dried
½ teaspoon parsley flakes
¼ teaspoon lemon pepper
¼ teaspoon seasoning salt

1. Cut the avocado in half lengthwise. Remove the pit and gently remove the skin. Place each half onto a salad plate.
2. Combine all of the remaining ingredients in a small bowl. Mix well. Pile an equal portion of the shrimp salad on each avocado half, allowing the excess to spill onto the plates. Garnish each with fresh parsley or lemon wedges.

NUTRITIONAL INFORMATION PER SERVING:
Carbohydrates: 8 grams • Effective Carb Count: 5 grams
Protein: 26 grams • Fat: 31 grams • Calories: 401

REDUCED-FAT VARIATION:
Use reduced-fat mayonnaise.
Carbohydrates: 11 grams • Effective Carb Count: 8 grams
Protein: 26 grams • Fat: 20 grams • Calories: 321

SHRIMP SAUCE

Serves 2 to 3

Serve over Rice-Aflower (page 227) or Slurp 'Em Up Cabbage Noodles (page 233). For a really delicious variation, use equal parts scallops, crab, and shrimp for the meat. And, if you want a real treat, instead of the water mixed with the cream, use chicken Rich Stock (page 254) and about ½ tablespoon each fresh lemon juice and white wine. Fresh parsley or cilantro is also superb, if available.

2 to 3 cloves garlic, minced
1 tablespoon butter
2 cups shrimp, cooked (small to medium size)
½ cup cream thinned with water to 1 cup, or
Almond Milk (page 240), unflavored
1 to 1½ teaspoons arrowroot powder mixed with 2 tablespoons water
2 tablespoons Parmesan cheese
½ tablespoon parsley flakes
Seasoning salt and lemon pepper, to taste

1. In a medium-sized saucepan over medium heat, cook the garlic in the butter until it is translucent, about 2 minutes.
2. Add the shrimp and thinned cream. Heat the shrimp mixture until it is steaming, about 4 minutes.
3. Add the arrowroot/water mixture and stir slightly until the shrimp mixture is thickened. Add the Parmesan cheese and parsley, heating through. Season with seasoning salt and lemon pepper to taste.

NUTRITIONAL INFORMATION PER SERVING:
Carbohydrates: 5 grams • Effective Carb Count: 4 grams
Protein: 31 grams • Fat: 24 grams • Calories: 358

REDUCED-FAT VARIATION:
Use Rich Stock (page 254) instead of the butter and canned
skim milk instead of the cream.
Carbohydrates: 10 grams • Effective Carb Count: 9 grams
Protein: 34 grams • Fat: 3 grams • Calories: 211

Are seasonings low-carb? While most herbs and spices are quite low in carbs and high in fiber, often manufacturers sneak little "extras" into their blends. Keep an eye out for things like maltodextrin (*dextrin* is a word ending that means "sugar"), MSG (which has been reported to cause excess weight gain), sugar (which is a no-no while low-carbing and one of the most common allergens around), and other unhealthy substances in the seasoning mixes you use. Please always check your labels on your blends, especially your everyday items like seasoning salt and lemon pepper.

SMOKED SALMON

Smokes 8 to 15 pounds of fish

This tasty brine will work not only with salmon, but also with just about any firm-fleshed fish. Use the smoked fish in Smoked Salmon Dip (page 35) and Smoked Salmon Casserole (page 185). It is also great served on salads for lunch or with Crackers (page 10) for a tasty appetizer.

½ cup sea salt
½ tablespoon Sweet & Slender
¼ cup olive oil
2 tablespoons lemon juice, fresh
1 ½ teaspoons lemon pepper
½ teaspoon thyme, dried (not ground)
1 tablespoon minced onion, dried
8 cups water

Combine all of the ingredients. Completely immerse 8 to 15 pounds of salmon for 45 minutes to 6 hours. Smoke the fish according to smoker directions.

NUTRITIONAL INFORMATION PER SERVING (BRINE ONLY):
Carbohydrates: trace • Effective Carb Count: 0 grams
Protein: trace • Fat: 2 grams • Calories: 17

SMOKED SALMON CASSEROLE

Makes 6 servings

Something yummy to make with all that Smoked Salmon (page 184)!

Sauce ingredients:

1 cup sour cream
1 1/2 tablespoons minced onion, dried
1 1/2 teaspoons dried or fresh dill weed
1 teaspoon orange zest
1/2 teaspoon seasoning salt
2 eggs

Other ingredients:

1 pound cauliflower (fresh or frozen), cut up (about 4 cups)
3 cups smoked salmon
Cooking oil spray
1/2 cup Parmesan cheese, shredded
1 tablespoon parsley flakes

1. Thoroughly combine all of the sauce ingredients in a mixing bowl. Add the cauliflower and the salmon, mixing well.
2. Spray a 9" × 13" baking dish with cooking oil spray. Pour the salmon mixture into the casserole dish. Flatten the top of the casserole with a spoon and sprinkle the cheese and parsley over the top. Bake it for about 25 minutes at 350°F, or until heated through.

NUTRITIONAL INFORMATION PER SERVING:
Carbohydrates: 7 grams • Effective Carb Count: 5 grams
Protein: 20 grams • Fat: 15 grams • Calories: 327

REDUCED-FAT VARIATION:
Use low-fat sour cream.
Carbohydrates: 7 grams • Effective Carb Count: 5 grams
Protein: 19 grams • Fat: 7 grams • Calories: 168

SOLE AMANDINE

Serves 4

This is a very elegant dish. Serve it the next time you want to feel like you are eating at a restaurant, without the tab!

1 cup almonds, blanched, or slivered almonds
1 teaspoon seasoning salt
1 tablespoon parsley flakes
1 egg
2 tablespoons water
⅓ cup lard
2 tablespoons butter
1 pound Dover sole fillets
Lemon juice, fresh, for serving

1. If using whole almonds, chop almonds in a food processor until they are coarsely ground. Do *not* chop the almonds until finely ground. If using slivered almonds, do not chop. Place almonds into a shallow dish with the seasoning salt and parsley. In another shallow dish combine the egg and water.
2. Place the lard and butter into a large skillet. Melt over medium heat.
3. Meanwhile dip the fish fillets into the egg/water mixture, coating thoroughly, and quickly dip in almond mixture. This should yield a light coating of almonds. Fry the prepared fish quickly–about 1½ minutes on each side. Do not overcook the fish. The fish will fall apart as it is removed from the pan if it is overcooked. Serve hot with freshly squeezed lemon juice.

NUTRITIONAL INFORMATION PER SERVING:
Carbohydrates: 7 grams • Effective Carb Count: 4 grams
Protein: 30 grams • Fat: 28 grams • Calories: 391

SUPER SPECIAL SHRIMP SALAD

Serves 4

This is a wonderful salad to serve as an appetizer with low-carb crackers or veggies for dipping.

Dressing ingredients:

¼ cup Blender Mayonnaise (page 241) or
commercially prepared mayonnaise
¼ cup whole milk yogurt
⅛ teaspoon lemon pepper
¼ teaspoon seasoning salt
½ tablespoon minced onion, dried
⅛ teaspoon marjoram, dried
⅛ teaspoon celery seed
⅛ teaspoon dry mustard powder
1 teaspoon fresh chives, snipped
1 teaspoon parsley flakes
½ teaspoon lemon juice, fresh
¼ teaspoon Sweet & Slender or ⅛ teaspoon SteviaPlus

Salad ingredients:

2 stalks celery, cut into bite-sized pieces
1 small avocado, cut into bite-sized pieces
1½ cups shrimp, cooked
2 hard-cooked eggs, chopped
Lemon wedges, fresh (optional)
Parsley or mint sprigs, fresh (optional)

1. Combine all dressing ingredients in a small bowl and mix well.
2. Place all of the salad ingredients into a serving bowl and add the dressing. Mix well. Garnish with fresh lemon wedges and fresh parsley sprigs, if desired.

NUTRITIONAL INFORMATION PER SERVING:
Carbohydrates: 6 grams • Effective Carb Count: 4 grams
Protein: 15 grams • Fat: 23 grams • Calories: 276

REDUCED-FAT VARIATION:
Use reduced-fat mayonnaise and fat-free yogurt.
Carbohydrates: 8 grams • Effective Carb Count: 6 grams
Protein: 15 grams • Fat: 13 grams • Calories: 212

Surf 'N' Turf

Serves 4

Take the kids to the sitter and invite some close friends over for a fancy restaurant-type meal, right at home! Serve with Old-Fashioned Green Beans (page 226), or Marinated Asparagus Salad with Almonds (page 44) and Spinach Salad with Lemon Dressing (page 49) for a very special meal!

1 pound beef steak, cut into 4 equal pieces
(sirloin, tip, rib eye—a NICE steak!)
1 pound bay scallops (the large variety, 1" to 2" across)
Seasoning salt
Lemon pepper
Lard

Garlic Butter Dipping Sauce:

4 cloves garlic
½ cup salted butter
2 tablespoons lemon juice, fresh
½ tablespoon parsley, fresh
¼ teaspoon lemon pepper

1. Season the steaks and scallops with seasoning salt and lemon pepper, and have them ready for cooking.
2. To prepare the Garlic Butter Dipping Sauce, mince the garlic and place it into a small saucepan. Add the butter and cook it over medium-low heat. The garlic will cook as the butter melts. When the butter is thoroughly melted, add the remaining sauce ingredients. Keep the sauce warm over very low heat while cooking the meat.
3. Heat a large frying pan or griddle and apply lard as needed to keep the meat from sticking, about 1 teaspoon total. Cook the steaks to desired doneness, about 3 to 4 minutes per side, depending upon thickness. Place the steaks on a platter and cover them with a lid to keep them hot. Cook the scallops in the same pan in the same manner. When the scallops are done, they go from being just soft to having slight vertical lines and are fairly firm. Remove them to a platter.
4. To serve the Surf 'N' Turf, distribute the steaks and scallops amongst the guests. Give each guest a small "monkey" dish. Fill each dish with about 2 tablespoons of warm Garlic Butter Dipping Sauce for the scallops.

Nutritional information per serving:
Carbohydrates: 4 grams • Effective Carb Count: 3 grams
Protein: 40 grams • Fat: 40 grams • Calories: 549

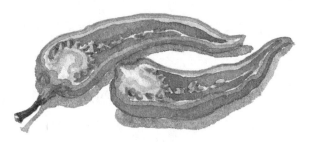

TEX-MEX FISH

Makes 6 servings

If you have access to fresh herbs and homemade salsa, this recipe will be simply astounding. It is terrific even with the canned varieties! Thank you, Connie Pritchett, for this very exciting fish recipe!

*2 pounds catfish or other firm-fleshed white
fish fillets, cut into serving-sized pieces
½ cup almonds, ground
½ cup soy protein
1 teaspoon chili powder
½ teaspoon garlic granules
½ teaspoon Cajun-style seasoning mix (with salt)
½ teaspoon sea salt
Lard for frying
1 cup salsa, drained of excess liquid
1 cup cheese, shredded (Monterey jack, Colby, Cheddar, etc.)*

1. Place the fish into a large colander and rinse it under cold running water. Allow it to drain.
2. Combine the ground almonds, soy protein, and dry seasonings in a shallow dish. Dredge the fish in the almond mixture.
3. Heat about ¼" lard in a large frying pan. Place the coated fish pieces into the hot fat and brown them quickly over medium heat. Transfer them to a large baking dish. The pieces of fish should just touch each other, but not overlap.
4. Pour the salsa evenly over the fish; then sprinkle the cheese over all. Bake it for 10 to 15 minutes at 350°F, until the fish flakes easily with a fork and the cheese is melted.

NUTRITIONAL INFORMATION PER SERVING:
Carbohydrates: 6 grams • Effective Carb Count: 4 grams
Protein: 37 grams • Fat: 25 grams • Calories: 394

What in the world is a "monkey" dish? A monkey dish is a small bowl for holding sauces and relishes. It generally holds about ¼ cup. Monkey dishes are a common item in a well-stocked kitchen. If you don't have them, you may use small mugs or bowls.

TUNA CASSEROLE

Serves 4

Tuna is a good, inexpensive protein source. Many non-low-carb families rely on tuna noodle casseroles to make it from payday to payday. Here is a low-carb choice!

Sauce ingredients:

1 cup sour cream
2 eggs
½ tablespoon minced onion, dried
1 teaspoon dill weed
½ teaspoon orange zest
½ teaspoon seasoning salt

Other ingredients:

1 pound cauliflower, cut into
bite-sized pieces (may be fresh or frozen)
1 6-ounce can of tuna, drained
Cooking oil spray
1 ½ cups cheese, shredded (Monterey jack,
Co-Jack, Cheddar, or a blend)

1. Combine the sauce ingredients in a mixing bowl with a wire whisk. Mix the cauliflower into the sauce, then the tuna.
2. Spray a 9" × 13" baking dish with cooking oil spray and pour the cauliflower mixture into the baking dish. Top it with the cheese. Bake it at 350°F for about 25 minutes or until the cheese is thoroughly melted and starting to become golden brown.

NUTRITIONAL INFORMATION PER SERVING:
Carbohydrates: 10 grams • Effective Carb Count: 7 grams
Protein: 27 grams • Fat: 28 grams • Calories: 390

REDUCED-FAT VARIATION:
Use low-fat sour cream and reduced-fat cheese.
Carbohydrates: 10 grams • Effective Carb Count: 7 grams
Protein: 26 grams • Fat: 7 grams • Calories: 202

Main Courses

Poultry

BARBECUE CHICKEN

Serves 4

This is a very simple and tasty recipe that is perfect for company coming in the summer!

1 whole frying chicken cutup, or the equivalent in pieces
Lemon pepper
Seasoning salt

1. Season both sides of the meat liberally with seasoning salt and lemon pepper. Using a barbecue with a cover, place the meat on the highest rack setting (about 5" to 6" away from coals) over medium-hot coals.
2. Cover the barbecue and allow the meat to smoke, turning it occasionally. Cook it for about 45 minutes or until the meat is golden brown and firm to the touch. Using the meat thermometer is discouraged when barbecuing because those precious juices are lost!

NUTRITIONAL INFORMATION PER SERVING:
Carbohydrates: 0 grams • Effective Carb Count: 0 grams
Protein: 32 grams • Fat: 29 grams • Calories: 397

REDUCED-FAT VARIATION:
Remove the skin from the chicken after it is cooked.
Carbohydrates: 0 grams • Effective Carb Count: 0 grams
Protein: 27 grams • Fat: 5 grams • Calories: 164

❧ Do you ever have trouble lighting the coals for your barbecue? If you live in a high humidity area, try this method: Open all the vents on the barbecue to their largest positions. Then, thoroughly soak the coals with barbecue lighter fluid. Set a timer for 5 minutes. No more, no less. When the timer goes off, light the coals. They usually light perfectly, unless of course the barbecue needs to be cleaned.

CARBONARA WITH CHICKEN

Serves 6

Have you ever had spaghetti carbonara? It is certainly not low-carb! Try this wonderful low-carb variation of that traditional Italian dish.

1 small head cabbage	*½ teaspoon lemon pepper*
2 cloves garlic, minced	*3 egg yolks*
2 tablespoons butter	*2 tablespoons cream or Almond Milk*
1½ pounds chicken, cooked and cut	*(page 240), unflavored*
up into bite-sized pieces	*2 tablespoons parsley flakes*
6 slices bacon, cooked and chopped	*½ cup Parmesan cheese, freshly grated*
1 6-ounce can olives	*Additional Parmesan cheese*
1 teaspoon seasoning salt	*for garnish, optional*

1. Prepare the cabbage "noodles": Cut the cabbage away from the core. Slice it into ¼"-wide strips. You should end up with 8 to 10 cups of cabbage strips. Place them into a 5-quart pot with a lid. Add about 1" water to the bottom of the pot, cover it, and cook the cabbage for about 8 minutes, or until tender. Drain it and let it rest in the colander while you prepare the rest of the meal.
2. In a medium-sized frying pan, cook the garlic in the butter over medium heat until it becomes fragrant, about 3 minutes. Stir in the chicken, bacon, olives, seasoning salt, and lemon pepper and heat it through. Turn the heat off, but allow the pan to remain on the burner so the chicken stays hot.
3. Since the eggs won't be cooked, coddle the eggs: Fill a small saucepan about half full with water. Bring the water to boiling; then place the whole eggs into the boiling water for 20 seconds. Remove the eggs from the boiling water and immerse them in ice-cold water to stop them from cooking any further.
4. In a small bowl, stir together the cream, egg yolks, seasoning salt, lemon pepper, and parsley. Combine them very well!
5. Place the cooked cabbage into a large serving bowl. Pour the chicken-and-bacon mixture over the cabbage and toss it well. Pour the egg/cream mixture over the cabbage/chicken mixture and toss it well. Finally, add half of the cheese to the dish and toss it well. Add the remaining cheese and toss it well. Serve it immediately, garnished with Parmesan cheese.

NUTRITIONAL INFORMATION PER SERVING:
Carbohydrates: 11 grams • Effective Carb Count: 6 grams
Protein: 23 grams • Fat: 26 grams • Calories: 361

REDUCED-FAT VARIATION:
Cook the garlic in about 2 tablespoons of Rich Stock (page 254).
Omit the butter. Use turkey bacon and canned skim milk.
Carbohydrates: 10 grams • Effective Carb Count: 6 grams
Protein: 23 grams • Fat: 21 grams • Calories: 317

CHICKEN AND BROCCOLI ALFREDO
Serves 4

A tasty, simple meal! You can also omit the chicken and serve Broccoli Alfredo as a side dish.

1 whole chicken, cut up, or 2 large breast pieces,
cut up (about 3 1/2 pounds total)
Salt and pepper
1 bunch broccoli (about 1 1/2 pounds), cut up into 1 1/2" chunks
3 cloves garlic, minced
2 tablespoons butter
1 1/2 cups whipping cream
1 1/2 teaspoons arrowroot powder mixed into 2 tablespoons water
1/2 cup Parmesan cheese
Seasoning salt and pepper to taste
Nutmeg for garnish, if desired

1. Place the chicken in a large baking dish and season with salt and pepper. Bake at 375°F for 50 to 60 minutes or until the juices run clear or the chicken tests at 180°F with a meat thermometer. (About 40 minutes for breasts, and they are done when the meat thermometer tests at 170°F.)
2. Place the broccoli into a pot with about ½" of water. Cover the pan tightly and simmer the broccoli for about 10 minutes, or until it is tender.
3. Meanwhile, make the sauce by cooking the garlic in the butter over medium-low heat in a small saucepan until garlic is translucent, about 3 minutes. Add the whipping cream and heat it until it is steaming. Add the arrowroot/water mixture, cooking until thickened. Remove it from the heat and add the Parmesan cheese, stirring to combine well. Add seasoning salt and pepper to taste.
4. Place the chicken pieces in a large serving bowl. Drain the broccoli and add it to the chicken in the serving bowl. Pour the sauce over the chicken and broccoli. Garnish with a light sprinkling of nutmeg, if desired.

NUTRITIONAL INFORMATION PER SERVING:
Carbohydrates: 11 grams • Effective Carb Count: 8 grams
Protein: 25 grams • Fat: 38 grams • Calories: 476

REDUCED-FAT VARIATION:
Use skinless chicken breasts and canned skim milk.
Carbohydrates: 18 grams • Effective Carb Count: 15 grams
Protein: 28 grams • Fat: 10 grams • Calories: 272

Chicken 'N' Vermicelli, Low-Carbed

Serves 8

My father and I used to cook this recipe together when I was a teenager. Now I've developed a tasty, low-carb version you can enjoy anytime!

½ medium head cabbage
¼ pound fresh mushrooms, sliced, or
1 cup spinach, chopped
2 tablespoons butter
2 cups sour cream
4 eggs
½ teaspoon seasoning salt
⅛ teaspoon pepper (optional)
1½ pounds chicken, cooked and cut
into bite-sized pieces
Cooking oil spray

Topping ingredients:

1 cup pecan pieces, chopped
2 tablespoons butter, melted
½ teaspoon seasoning salt
½ cup Parmesan cheese, freshly grated

1. Prepare the cabbage "noodles": Cut the cabbage away from the core. Slice it into ¼"-wide strips. You should end up with 8 to 10 cups of cabbage strips. Place them into a 5-quart pot with a lid. Add about 1" water to the bottom of the pot, cover it, and cook the cabbage for about 8 minutes, until it is just getting tender. Drain it and let it rest in the colander while you prepare the rest of the meal.
2. While the cabbage is cooking, cook the mushrooms in the butter in a frying pan over medium heat until they are cooked through, about 5 minutes. Set them aside to cool.
3. In a large mixing bowl, combine the sour cream, eggs, seasoning salt, and pepper until they are well mixed. Add the cooled mushrooms and chicken, stirring well. Set this aside.
4. Place the cooked cabbage into the bottom of a 9" × 13" baking pan that has been sprayed with cooking oil spray. Pour the sauce over the top of the cabbage, stirring just enough to coat it evenly, making sure the chicken and mushrooms are evenly distributed throughout. Smooth the top with the back of a spoon.
5. Combine the topping ingredients, except for the cheese, in a small dish. Sprinkle them over the top of the chicken-and-cabbage mixture. Sprinkle the cheese over that. Bake the casserole in a 375°F oven for about 30 minutes, or until the center is set.

Nutritional information per serving:
Carbohydrates: 9 grams • Effective Carb Count: 6 grams
Protein: 18 grams • Fat: 33 grams • Calories: 396

CHUNKY CHICKEN STEW

Serves 6

This also makes a great slow cooker recipe. Just toss everything but the sour cream and eggs into the slow cooker first thing in the morning. When you are ready for dinner, follow the remaining recipe instructions.

1 3 1/2-pound chicken cut up
1 medium turnip
1 large carrot (optional)
2 large stalks celery
1 medium onion
1 teaspoon seasoning salt
1/2 teaspoon lemon pepper
1/2 tablespoon parsley flakes
2 cups water or Rich Stock (page 254)
3/4 cup sour cream
2 eggs

1. Place the chicken into a large pot with a lid. Cut all of the veggies up into 3/4" to 1" chunks. Place them in the pot with the chicken and season them with the seasoning salt, lemon pepper, and parsley.
2. Add the water to the pot and cover it. Bring it to a boil over medium heat; then reduce the heat to simmering. Simmer the chicken and veggies over medium-low heat for about 1 hour 15 minutes total.
3. Remove the pot from the heat. In a small bowl, stir together the sour cream and the eggs. Pour them into the stew and serve immediately.

NUTRITIONAL INFORMATION PER SERVING:
Carbohydrates: 5 grams • Effective Carb Count: 1 gram
Protein: 25 grams • Fat: 27 grams • Calories: 364

REDUCED-FAT VARIATION:
Use low-fat sour cream.
Carbohydrates: 5 grams • Effective Carb Count: 1 gram
Protein: 25 grams • Fat: 21 grams • Calories: 312

Coconut Chicken

Serves 4

When Valentine's Day comes, and you want to celebrate your love, enjoy this elegant recipe.

2 pounds chicken, cut up into serving-sized pieces
1 cup coconut, unsweetened shredded (not finely ground)
½ cup almonds, ground
2 tablespoons soy protein
¾ teaspoon seasoning salt
¹/₁₆ teaspoon chipotle pepper granules, roasted, or a few grains of cayenne
½ cup kefir or buttermilk

1. Preheat the oven to 375°F. Wash the chicken and set it aside. In a shallow dish, combine the coconut, almonds, soy protein, seasoning salt, and chipotle. Pour the kefir into another shallow dish.
2. Dip the chicken one piece at a time first into the kefir, then into the coconut mixture. Coat the pieces evenly and place them into a large baking dish. Repeat this for all of the chicken.
3. Place the coated chicken pieces into the oven and bake them for 40 to 60 minutes, depending upon the size of the pieces. When the chicken is done, the juices should run clear or a meat thermometer should read 180°F (170°F for breasts).

Nutritional information per serving:
Carbohydrates: 8 grams • Effective Carb Count: 6 grams
Protein: 27 grams • Fat: 29 grams • Calories: 392

Reduced-Fat Variation:
Use skinless chicken and nonfat buttermilk or yogurt.
Carbohydrates: 8 grams • Effective Carb Count: 6 grams
Protein: 20 grams • Fat: 14 grams • Calories: 231

CREAMY COCONUT CHICKEN SALAD

Serves 4

When I created this recipe, I truly felt inspired. Enjoy this great salad, with its sweet and tangy island flavor!

Dressing ingredients:

½ cup coconut milk
1 tablespoon lime juice, fresh
½ teaspoon seasoning salt
¼ teaspoon dry mustard powder
½ teaspoon Sweet & Slender
½ teaspoon lime zest
½ teaspoon parsley flakes

Salad ingredients:

1 head Romaine lettuce, cut up
1 large cucumber, sliced
1 bunch radishes, sliced
4 green onions, chopped
1 pound chicken, cooked and cut up
4 tablespoons coconut, unsweetened, shredded
4 tablespoons sunflower seeds, roasted and salted, or
hulled pumpkin seeds, roasted and salted
Lime wedges, for garnish (optional)

1. In a small bowl, whisk together the dressing ingredients.
2. Arrange the lettuce on plates, covering each with the cucumber slices, radishes, onions, and chicken. Pour the dressing over the salads. Garnish each with the coconut, sunflower seeds, and lime wedges. Serve immediately.

NUTRITIONAL INFORMATION PER SERVING:
Carbohydrates: 13 grams • Effective Carb Count: 6 grams
Protein: 23 grams • Fat: 21 grams • Calories: 321

CREAMY LEMON CHICKEN

Makes 8 servings

This recipe is super easy and produces wonderful results. It will become a family favorite! Two cups of fresh spinach may be substituted for the mushrooms for a tasty variation.

1 3-pound chicken, cut up
Seasoning salt, to taste
1 teaspoon lemon zest
¼ pound mushrooms, sliced
2 tablespoons butter
1 cup cream
1 cup sour cream
¼ cup chicken Rich Stock (page 254)

1. Place the chicken into a large (9" × 13") baking dish. Sprinkle with seasoning salt and the lemon zest.
2. In a medium frying pan over medium heat, cook the sliced mushrooms in butter until they are softened, about 5 minutes. Cool slightly, about 3 minutes.
3. In a mixing bowl, using a wire whisk, thoroughly combine the cream and sour cream. Add the chicken broth and cooled mushrooms, mixing thoroughly. Spread all of the sauce over the chicken, so that the chicken is completely covered.
4. Bake 2 hours at 350°F (or 1 hour if you prefer bone-in breasts). To serve, place excess sauce in a small serving dish and use as a gravy over chicken and your choice of veggie.

NUTRITIONAL INFORMATION PER SERVING:
Carbohydrates: 3 grams • Effective Carb Count: 2 grams
Protein: 18 grams • Fat: 31 grams • Calories: 363

REDUCED-FAT VARIATION:
Cook the mushrooms in about 2 tablespoons of Rich Stock instead of the butter. Use canned skim milk and low-fat sour cream.
Carbohydrates: 6 grams • Effective Carb Count: 5 grams
Protein: 20 grams • Fat: 15 grams • Calories: 238

CROQUETTES

Makes 12 croquettes

This is a tasty thing to do with leftover chicken. This recipe is a real kid-pleaser and these may also be used as appetizers.

Filling ingredients:

1 cup Rich Stock (page 254)
2 tablespoons soy protein
3 tablespoons butter, melted
2 egg yolks
2 cups meat, cooked and chopped (chicken, ham, pork, or turkey)
2 teaspoons minced onion, dried
2 teaspoons parsley flakes
4 drops hot chili oil
1/4 teaspoon celery seed
1/4 teaspoon seasoning salt if meat is unseasoned

Coating ingredients:

1/2 cup pork rinds, crushed
2 tablespoons almonds, ground
2 tablespoons soy protein (not soy flour!)
1/2 tablespoon parsley flakes
1 egg
3 tablespoons water
Lard for cooking

1. In a large saucepan, heat the stock, soy protein, and butter until they are steaming. Remove them from the heat. Stir in the egg yolks until they are combined. Add the remaining filling ingredients, stirring well to combine. Form the meat mixture into 12 balls. Set them aside.
2. In a shallow dish, combine the pork rinds, almonds, soy protein, and parsley flakes. In another dish, combine the egg and water. Dip the meat first in the egg wash, then in the pork rind breading.
3. Heat the lard in a large pan suitable for frying, like a wok, and deep-fry the croquettes until they are golden brown. Serve hot with choice of dipping sauces.

NUTRITIONAL INFORMATION PER SERVING:
Carbohydrates: 1 gram • Effective Carb Count: 0 grams
Protein: 7 grams • Fat: 8 grams • Calories: 98

EASY LEMON PEPPER CHICKEN

Serves 4

This chicken is really tasty all by itself, and it is also a great way to fix most of the cooked chicken required by recipes in this book!

1 ½ tablespoons lard
1 ¼ pounds chicken, boneless and skinless legs or breasts
Seasoning salt
Lemon pepper

1. Place the lard into a large frying pan and melt it over medium heat. Season the chicken well on one side with the seasoning salt and lemon pepper. Place the chicken into the pan, seasoned side down. Season the remaining side (that is, faceup) liberally with seasoning salt and lemon pepper.
2. Cook the chicken until it browns on the first side; then turn it over. Cook it on the other side until it browns. Continue cooking and turning it as needed until it is done, about 35 minutes or until it tests at 180°F (170°F for breasts) with a meat thermometer.

NUTRITIONAL INFORMATION PER SERVING:
Carbohydrates: 0 grams • Effective Carb Count: 0 grams
Protein: 16 grams • Fat: 8 grams • Calories: 139

A sharpening steel is a very good investment. How else are you going to keep a nice slicing edge on your knives if you don't have a steel? The little "gadgets" that are available in the kitchen areas of most stores are only slightly better than worthless and have the great potential to do damage to your knives. A steel, which is a long, rough steel rod with a handle, will keep those blades nice and sharp! To use, simply slide the cutting edge down the surface of the steel, first one side then the other. For an extremely sharp edge, do the process under slowly running water. Always wash knives by hand, not in a dishwasher. This will keep them "good as new" for years to come. A good knife is a good investment.

Elegant Chicken

Makes 8 servings

This would definitely impress company! You could add chopped onions or spinach to the sauce instead of the mushrooms for a deliciously different taste.

1 3 1/2-pound chicken, cut up
Seasoning salt
1/2 pound bacon
10 medium (1 1/2") mushrooms
2 tablespoons butter
1/8 teaspoon basil, dried
Garlic salt
1 cup Swiss cheese, shredded
1 cup half-and-half
Nutmeg

1. Place the chicken into a 9" × 13" baking pan. Sprinkle the chicken with seasoning salt to taste. Cut the bacon into 3" to 4" lengths. Place the slices over the chicken so that it is completely covered. Bake, uncovered, at 375°F for 1 hour.
2. Meanwhile, slice the mushrooms. Place the butter into a medium saucepan and melt it over medium heat. Add the mushrooms and cook them until they are softened, about 5 minutes. Add the basil and garlic salt to taste.
3. Turn the heat to low and add the Swiss cheese and half-and-half to the mushroom mixture. Cook and stir over low heat until the cheese is thoroughly melted.
4. Serve on individual plates, pouring sauce on each person's plate as they desire. Garnish with a tiny sprinkling of nutmeg.

Nutritional information per serving:
Carbohydrates: 2 grams • Effective Carb Count: 1 gram
Protein: 23 grams • Fat: 28 grams • Calories: 356

Reduced-Fat Variation:
Use turkey bacon and cook the mushrooms in about
2 tablespoons of Rich Stock (page 254). Omit the butter.
Use canned skim milk and reduced-fat cheese.
Carbohydrates: 5 grams • Effective Carb Count: 4 grams
Protein: 25 grams • Fat: 18 grams • Calories: 286

"FETTUCCINI" ALFREDO

Serves 4

One of my favorite dishes before starting to low-carb was Fettuccini Alfredo. This is a low-carb, high-protein choice!

½ medium head cabbage
3 cloves garlic, minced
2 tablespoons butter
1 cup whipping cream
½ teaspoon seasoning salt
¹⁄₁₆ teaspoon pepper, if desired
1½ teaspoons arrowroot powder mixed into 2 tablespoons water
1 pound chicken, cooked and cut into bite-sized pieces
½ cup Parmesan cheese, freshly grated
¹⁄₁₆ teaspoon nutmeg

1. Prepare the cabbage "noodles": Cut the cabbage away from the core. Slice it into ¼"-wide strips. You should end up with 8 to 10 cups of cabbage strips. Place them into a 5-quart pot with a lid. Add about 1" water to the bottom of the pot, cover it, and cook the cabbage for about 15 minutes. Drain it and let it rest in the colander while you prepare the rest of the meal.
2. Cook the garlic in the butter over medium-low heat in a large saucepan until the garlic is fragrant, about 3 minutes. Stir in the cream and continue to cook it until it is steaming. Season it with the seasoning salt and the pepper. Stir the arrowroot/water mixture into the sauce and allow it to rest, unstirred, for about 1 minute.
3. Stir the sauce and add the cabbage "noodles" to the pan. Stir them until they are softened, about 2 or 3 minutes. Add the chicken and heat it through. Remove the pan from the heat and sprinkle the cheese and nutmeg over all. Stir it slightly and serve it immediately.

NUTRITIONAL INFORMATION PER SERVING:
Carbohydrates: 10 grams • Effective Carb Count: 7 grams
Protein: 15 grams • Fat: 27 grams • Calories: 337

REDUCED-FAT VARIATION:
Cook the garlic in about 2 tablespoons Rich Stock (page 254)
and omit the butter. Use canned skim milk.
Carbohydrates: 16 grams • Effective Carb Count: 13 grams
Protein: 18 grams • Fat: 7 grams • Calories: 190

KENTUCKY-STYLE SEASONING

Yields about 16 batches of seasoning mix

This is a delicious low-carb version of a restaurant favorite. It does require a little effort in pulverizing the spices, but once that has been done, the seasoning mix will be good for months. You may add 1 tablespoon of soy protein (*not* soy flour!) per cup of the pork rind breading mixture in order to make the breading coat more pieces of food. The coating doesn't turn out as thick and crunchy, but it does make it last longer and coat more pieces. This is *very* versatile. It can be used as a deep-fry coating for a variety of things: chicken or pork nuggets, fried chicken, pork chops, beef, or pork cubed steaks. It can also be used on various veggies, like eggplant, zucchini, onion rings, etc.

Spice mixture:

1 tablespoon rosemary, dried
1 tablespoon oregano, dried
1 tablespoon sage, dried
1 teaspoon ginger, dried
1 teaspoon marjoram, dried
1 1/2 teaspoons thyme, dried
2 packets sucralose
1/4 teaspoon SteviaPlus
3 tablespoons parsley, dried
1/2 teaspoon lemon pepper
1/2 teaspoon pepper
1 tablespoon garlic salt
1/2 tablespoon garlic granules
3 tablespoons minced onion, dried
1 tablespoon paprika (optional)

Coating ingredients:

Pork rinds, crushed
1 egg
2 tablespoons water
Lard

1. Place all of the ingredients for the spice mixture into a blender container. Blend on medium-high until the spices are completely pulverized into a fine powder. Store in an airtight container.
2. To use: Combine 1/2 tablespoon seasoning mix per each cup of crushed pork rinds.
3. Combine the egg and water in a shallow dish.
4. Place the desired amount of coating in a plastic bag. Coat the meat or veggies in the egg/water mixture and then place in bag with coating. Shake to coat. Bake at 375°F until done: About 45 minutes for chicken, 25 minutes for pork chops, or 10 to 15 minutes for nuggets.

NUTRITIONAL INFORMATION PER SERVING (SEASONING MIX ONLY):
Carbohydrates: 2 grams • Effective Carb Count: 1 gram
Protein: trace • Fat: trace • Calories: 7

KING'S CHICKEN

Makes 8 servings

This is a great meal to serve to company. Have this dish and you'll feel like a king!

Sauce ingredients:

1 medium onion, finely chopped
½ tablespoon butter
½ tablespoon lard
¼ teaspoon seasoning salt
1 8-ounce package cream cheese, softened
3 tablespoons sour cream
¼ teaspoon seasoning salt
⅛ teaspoon lemon pepper
4 drops hot chili oil
½ teaspoon parsley flakes

Other ingredients:

2 pounds chicken breasts, boneless and skinless
2 2.5-ounce packages beef, dried and chopped
(the inexpensive packets sold with the luncheon meats at the grocer)
Cooking oil spray
Paprika, for garnish

1. Preheat the oven to 350°F. Cook the onion in the butter, lard, and ¼ teaspoon seasoning salt in a small frying pan over medium heat until the onion is golden, about 5 to 8 minutes. In a mixing bowl with a wire whisk, combine the remaining sauce ingredients. Add the onion and mix well. Set the sauce aside.
2. Cut the chicken into 8 pieces. Divide the beef by 8 and place the slices into the bottom of a large baking dish that has been sprayed with cooking oil spray. Place a piece of chicken atop each stack of beef slices.
3. Divide the sauce evenly over the tops of the chicken. Garnish each with a tiny pinch of paprika. Bake it for about 40 minutes at 350°F, or until the sauce is golden and the chicken tests at 170°F with a meat thermometer.

NUTRITIONAL INFORMATION PER SERVING:
Carbohydrates: 3 grams • Effective Carb Count: 2 grams
Protein: 33 grams • Fat: 16 grams • Calories: 296

REDUCED-FAT VARIATION:
Omit the butter and lard. Cook the onion in a small amount of Rich Stock (page 254) and use low-fat cream cheese and sour cream instead of those listed.
Carbohydrates: 2 grams • Effective Carb Count: 1 gram
Protein: 32 grams • Fat: 7 grams • Calories: 208

Low-Carb Chicken and Noodles

Serves 4

If you like your chicken and noodles thick, the southern way, add a little less stock. If you like them more like soup, add more.

1 small onion, chopped
3 cloves garlic, minced
½ tablespoon butter
½ tablespoon lard
¼ teaspoon seasoning salt
1 large stalk celery or the leafy ends, chopped
½ cup carrots, cut up (optional)
2 cups Baked Winter Squash, spaghetti (page 216)
3 cups chicken, pork, or turkey, cooked
1 teaspoon seasoning salt
½ tablespoon parsley flakes
4 cups chicken or pork Rich Stock (page 254) or commercially prepared stock
½ teaspoon lemon pepper

1. In a medium-sized saucepan with a lid, cook the onion and the garlic in the butter, lard, and seasoning salt over medium heat until they are becoming golden, about 5 minutes. Add the celery and carrots and continue cooking about 3 more minutes.
2. Stir in the spaghetti squash, breaking up any lumps. Add the remaining ingredients, stirring them well.
3. Cover the pot and simmer the soup for about 30 to 45 minutes or until the flavors are well blended. Garnish with sour cream if desired.

Nutritional information per serving:
Carbohydrates: 8 grams • Effective Carb Count: 7 grams
Protein: 22 grams • Fat: 8 grams • Calories: 203

Reduced-Fat Variation:
Omit the butter and lard. Pour the broth into the pan and add the other veggies then. Continue as directed.
Carbohydrates: 8 grams • Effective Carb Count: 7 grams
Protein: 22 grams • Fat: 4 grams • Calories: 176

Oven-Baked Barbecue Chicken

Makes 8 servings

Thanks to *Better Homes and Gardens* for the inspiration for this yummy dish!

½ cup butter, melted
¼ teaspoon hot chili oil
1 3½-pound chicken, cut up
1 cup almonds, ground
½ teaspoon Sweet & Slender
2 teaspoons chipotle pepper granules, roasted, or 1 teaspoon chili powder
2 teaspoons garlic granules
1 teaspoon seasoning salt
½ teaspoon dry mustard powder
½ teaspoon celery seed

1. Combine the melted butter and hot chili oil and brush it onto the chicken. Combine the remaining ingredients in a shallow dish.
2. Roll the chicken in the coating mixture and place it into a large baking dish. Sprinkle any remaining coating mixture over the chicken.
3. Bake it at 375°F for about 50 minutes or until the chicken tests at 180°F with a meat thermometer.

Nutritional information per serving:
Carbohydrates: 4 grams • Effective Carb Count: 3 grams
Protein: 24 grams • Fat: 34 grams • Calories: 403

When using a cutting board or a knife, it is very important to avoid cross-contamination. For instance, if you are going to be cutting both meats and vegetables, cut the vegetables first and the meats last. Always wash and rinse your knives and cutting boards in soap and the hottest water available. You could save yourself and those you love from a nasty case of food poisoning by simply keeping your work area clean!

Peanut Butter Chicken Salad

Makes 6 servings

Enjoy this delicious salad with an Asian flare! This would be great served at a potluck or some other special luncheon.

Marinade:

⅓ cup Bragg's Liquid Aminos, or soy sauce
3 tablespoons fresh garlic, minced
3 tablespoons creamy peanut butter
¼ cup parsley, minced (fresh if possible) or 2 tablespoons dried
½ teaspoon hot chili oil

Salad ingredients:

4 chicken breasts, boneless and skinless
1 head Romaine lettuce, chopped
1 large cucumber, peeled and sliced
1 cup Roasted Pecans (page 31), prepared using peanuts if carb-allowance is high enough, otherwise use pecans

Dressing ingredients:

3 tablespoons Marinade, reserved (above)
2 tablespoons olive oil
2 tablespoons lemon juice or vinegar
¼ teaspoon Sweet & Slender
¼ teaspoon SteviaPlus
2 tablespoons Creamy Ranch Salad Dressing (page 244) or commercially prepared dressing
2 tablespoons creamy peanut butter
½ teaspoon sesame oil
⅛ teaspoon hot chili oil (adjust to taste)

1. Combine the marinade ingredients in a small saucepan and heat them over medium-low heat to combine. Cool thoroughly. Reserve 3 tablespoons of the marinade for the salad dressing.
2. Place the chicken and the remaining marinade in a large plastic container with a lid, or a zipper-sealed bag, and refrigerate for 1 hour up to overnight.
3. Broil or grill the chicken until it is done (tests at 170°F with a meat thermometer). Cut the chicken into bite-sized pieces and set aside.
4. Combine the reserved marinade and remaining dressing ingredients in a small bowl with a wire whisk. Set aside.
5. Prepare the salad. Place a bed of greens on each plate. Top each with a portion of the cucumber slices and the cooked chicken. Pour the dressing over each salad and top with the Roasted Pecans (or peanuts).

NUTRITIONAL INFORMATION PER SERVING:
Carbohydrates: 6 grams • Effective Carb Count: 5 grams
Protein: 23 grams • Fat: 16 grams • Calories: 255

SESAME CHICKEN

Makes 8 servings

Sometimes low-carbers need a change of pace from basic baked chicken. Try this golden chicken with a crunchy coating.

1 3¹/₂-pound chicken, cut up
¹/₂ cup milk and egg protein
¹/₄ teaspoon paprika
¹/₄ teaspoon chipotle pepper granules, roasted, or a pinch of cayenne
¹/₂ teaspoon lemon pepper
¹/₂ teaspoon Sweet & Slender
2 eggs
1 tablespoon Bragg's Liquid Aminos, or soy sauce
1 cup sesame seeds

1. Rinse the chicken in running water and set it aside. In a shallow dish, combine the dry ingredients (except for the sesame seeds). In another shallow dish, combine the eggs and Bragg's. Place the sesame seeds into a third shallow dish.
2. Dip each piece of chicken first into the seasoned protein powder, then into the eggs, and finally into the sesame seeds, rolling to coat the pieces well.
3. Place the coated chicken into a large baking dish. Bake it for about an hour at 350°F until the coating is crunchy and the chicken tests at 180°F (170°F for breasts) with a meat thermometer.

NUTRITIONAL INFORMATION PER SERVING:
Carbohydrates: 5 grams • Effective Carb Count: 3 grams
Protein: 34 grams • Fat: 25 grams • Calories: 373

REDUCED-FAT VARIATION:
Remove the skin from the chicken prior to coating.
Carbohydrates: 5 grams • Effective Carb Count: 3 grams
Protein: 25 grams • Fat: 14 grams • Calories: 237

A trip to your local Asian market is well worth the effort. A good soy sauce, purchased at an Asian market, is really nice to have around. Another very useful item is sesame oil. The dark sesame oil, which most of us have access to, is yet another oil that isn't good for high temperatures. It smokes at a low temperature. It is primarily used as a seasoning agent in Asian cooking. "Virgin" sesame oil doesn't smoke at high temperatures, but it isn't widely available. A bottle of hot chili oil—it is displayed with the sesame oil—is another Asian cooking necessity. A few drops will go a *long* way! Pick up some sesame seeds while you are there, because they are just so much fun to have around!

Shake It and Bake It!

Makes 6 servings

Here's a great quickie meal! This mix is enough to coat approximately 2 pounds of meat, although it could easily be multiplied and used as a make-ahead mix. It makes excellent chicken or pork nuggets as well as chops or breaded baked chicken. Try different salad dressing mixes and have a variety of flavors. Just watch out for sugar in the mixes!

Coating ingredients:

½ cup pork rinds, crushed
½ packet ranch-flavored salad dressing mix
1 tablespoon soy protein (not soy flour!)

Place all of the ingredients into a ½-gallon (or so) plastic bag and shake it well. Place the desired meat into the bag and shake it until the meat is well coated. Bake the meat at 400°F until desired doneness is reached.

Nutritional information per serving:
Carbohydrates: 1 gram • Effective Carb Count: 0 grams
Protein: 4 grams • Fat: 3 grams • Calories: 48

SUE'S ITALIAN CHICKEN

Makes 8 servings

Enjoy this delicious dish served with freshly grated Romano cheese as a garnish. You'll want to have plenty of napkins available!

2 tablespoons lard
1 3½-pound chicken, cut up
1 14- to 16-ounce can diced tomatoes
1 8-ounce can tomato sauce
3 tablespoons Italian seasonings herb blend
3 cloves garlic, chopped
1 medium onion, chopped into 1" cubes
1 stalk celery, chopped into 1" pieces
1 small can green chilies, cut into 1" cubes (or if
you like it hot, 1 jalapeño pepper diced finely)
Salt and pepper to taste

1. Place the lard into a chicken fryer or other large covered skillet. Place the chicken, top side down, into the pan, and cook it over medium heat until the meat is lightly browned, about 8 minutes.
2. Turn the chicken pieces over and add the remaining ingredients. Cover, and bring the sauce to a boil. Turn the heat to medium-low and allow the chicken to simmer about 45 minutes. Serve piping hot in bowls.

NUTRITIONAL INFORMATION PER SERVING:
Carbohydrates: 7 grams • Effective Carb Count: 5 grams
Protein: 18 grams • Fat: 18 grams • Calories: 259

REDUCED-FAT VARIATION:
Omit the lard and use cooking oil spray. Use skinless chicken.
Carbohydrates: 7 grams • Effective Carb Count: 5 grams
Protein: 9 grams • Fat: 4 grams • Calories: 95

 Though fresh is always best, try to keep canned or frozen green beans around if you should run out of fresh veggies. Along that same line, canned tuna, canned salmon, and sardines are good things to have because they provide an easy source of protein. Try sardines on zucchini or cauliflower slices, and they can be eaten on cucumber slices and pork rinds as well. Canned olives are another staple at this house because they are quick and yummy.

WALNUT SESAME CHICKEN

Serves 4

A terrific twist on stir-fry! If you've never used jicama before, be sure to choose one that is firm and even toned. It shouldn't have dark spots or any mushy places. Jicama tastes similar to water chestnuts, with a fraction of the carbs!

Marinade ingredients:

6 tablespoons Bragg's Liquid Aminos, or soy sauce
4 tablespoons lemon juice or wine vinegar
2 teaspoons ginger (freshly grated, if possible; same amount if using dried)
½ teaspoon Sweet & Slender
1 teaspoon seasoning salt
½ teaspoon hot chili oil
4 teaspoons sesame oil
4 tablespoons sesame seeds

Stir-fry ingredients:

1 ¼ pounds boneless, skinless chicken, cut into bite-sized pieces
1 cup walnuts, broken (or pecans)
2 tablespoons lard
1 cup jicama, sliced
1 cup celery, sliced
4 green onions, sliced
2 teaspoons arrowroot

1. Combine the marinade ingredients in a plastic container with a lid. Place the chicken into the marinade and stir it well. Cover the container and allow the chicken to soak in the marinade for at least an hour, up to overnight.
2. Just before dinner, cook the walnuts in the lard in a large wok or skillet over medium-high heat until they are golden, about 2 minutes. Remove them from the wok and set them aside.
3. Carefully place the chicken into the hot wok, using a lifting and stirring motion, adding more cooking fat if necessary. Cover the wok to steam the chicken as it is cooking. Remove it from the pan when it is cooked through.
4. Cook the veggies in the wok until they are crisp-tender, about 3 minutes. Cook and stir them in the same manner as above.
5. Pour the remaining marinade into a small dish and add the arrowroot, stirring to combine. Add the other cooked ingredients back to the wok and pour the marinade over all. Stir it well to combine. Be sure to bring it to a boil to kill any bacteria. Pour it into a serving platter to serve.

NUTRITIONAL INFORMATION PER SERVING:
Carbohydrates: 12 grams • Effective Carb Count: 7 grams
Protein: 18 grams • Fat: 31 grams • Calories: 380

WASHINGTONIAN'S CHICKEN

Serves 6

Even folks who don't like chicken always like this recipe! Try this dish with 1 cup fresh chopped spinach instead of the mushrooms for a great variation!

½ cup mushrooms, finely chopped (about 5 mushrooms)
2 tablespoons butter
½ cup heavy cream
¼ teaspoon sea salt
Dash cayenne (much less than ⅛ teaspoon!)
1 ¼ cups sharp Cheddar cheese, shredded

6 chicken breast halves, boneless and skinless (the largest available!)
1 egg, slightly beaten
2 tablespoons water
½ cup almonds, ground
½ cup soy protein (not soy flour!)
Seasoning salt
¼ cup butter, melted

1. Cook the mushrooms in the butter in a medium-sized skillet over medium heat until they are softened, about 5 minutes. Stir in the cream, salt, and cayenne. Cook and stir over medium-low heat until the mixture has thickened. (The cream should be reduced by half.) Turn the heat to low and add the shredded cheese, stirring until melted.
2. Pour the sauce into an 8" or 9" square dish. Chill in the refrigerator 1 hour, then cut into 6 equal pieces (3 pieces across by 2 down), shaped like french fries.
3. Place each chicken breast between 2 sheets of plastic wrap and pound out from the center with a wooden mallet to form cutlets not quite ¼" thick. Peel off the wrap and sprinkle the meat with salt, as desired.
4. Place the cheese sticks on each breast at the closest edge. Tuck in sides and roll as for jelly roll. Press to seal the chicken well—so the cheese won't run out all over the pan when it is baked!
5. Place the egg and water into a shallow dish and combine thoroughly. Set aside. Place the almonds into a food processor bowl and chop coarsely. Add the soy protein to the food processor bowl and continue chopping until the mixture is pulverized. Pour the ground almond mixture into another shallow dish and season as desired with seasoning salt.
6. First dip the rolled breast halves in the egg/water mixture; then roll them in the almond mixture. Place the chicken onto a large baking sheet, cover, and chill it in the refrigerator 1 hour or longer.
7. Just before baking, drizzle the chicken with the melted butter and bake at 325°F for 45 minutes. Serve hot.

NUTRITIONAL INFORMATION PER SERVING:
Carbohydrates: 4 grams • Effective Carb Count: 3 grams
Protein: 45 grams • Fat: 32 grams • Calories: 488

WONDERFUL CHICKEN CLUB PIZZA

Makes 8 servings

Have you ever had chicken club pizza at a pizzeria? Now you can have a low-carb version at home!

1 1/4 pounds chicken or turkey, ground
1/2 cup pork rinds, crushed
1 egg
1 tablespoon Italian seasonings
1/2 teaspoon seasoning salt
1/3 cup Creamy Roasted Garlic Salad Dressing (page 245) or
Creamy Ranch Salad Dressing, (page 244)

Toppings:

4 slices bacon, cooked and crumbled
3 mushrooms, sliced
4 olives, sliced
1/4 pound Monterey jack cheese, shredded
2 tablespoons Parmesan cheese, freshly grated

Garnish:

Garlic salt
Dried basil or oregano

1. In a mixing bowl, combine the chicken, pork rinds, egg, Italian seasonings, and seasoning salt. Mix thoroughly. Spread the mixture thinly on a round baking sheet with a rolled edge. Leave a rim around the edge so the toppings don't fall off.
2. Spread the salad dressing over the chicken and place the toppings in order listed atop the dressing. Garnish with a gentle sprinkling of garlic salt and a very light sprinkling of either basil or oregano.
3. Bake at 375°F for 15 to 20 minutes, until the cheese is bubbling and the meat is beginning to brown. Allow to cool 3 minutes. Cut into slices.

NUTRITIONAL INFORMATION PER SERVING:
Carbohydrates: 3 grams • Effective Carb Count: 2 grams
Protein: 26 grams • Fat: 20 grams • Calories: 294

Veggies and Sides

BAKED WINTER SQUASH

Servings vary according to size and type of squash

Even if you're not a squash lover, you're sure to enjoy this recipe. Any leftovers from firm-fleshed squash may be used in Skillet Squash Breakfast (page 86). Leftover spaghetti squash may be used in Spaghetti Squash with Cream Gravy (page 143). Tip: To separate the "noodles" in spaghetti squash, use a large fork to scrape the flesh from the rind of the squash.

1 medium squash (spaghetti, pumpkin, or
other winter variety squash)
Butter
Garlic salt or seasoning salt
Lemon pepper

1. Using a sharp utility knife, poke 8 to 10 holes total around the entire circumference of the squash. Place the squash on a baking sheet and bake it at 350°F for about 1 hour.
2. Allow it to rest 5 to 10 minutes before cutting it in half lengthwise. Scoop out the seeds, rinse them, and allow them to air dry to use for Roasted Pumpkin Seeds (page 32). Scoop the squash flesh into a serving dish.
3. Add a generous amount of butter, garlic salt, and lemon pepper and mix well. (The amount of butter and seasonings will vary according to the size and type of squash cooked–you will just have to taste it!)

NUTRITIONAL INFORMATION PER SERVING (1 CUP SPAGHETTI SQUASH):
Carbohydrates: 7 grams • Effective Carb Count: 7 grams
Protein: 1 gram • Fat: 4 grams • Calories: 65

A WORD ABOUT SQUASH: Squashes are great powerhouses for vitamins and minerals! Though their carb content is a bit higher than more typical low-carb veggies, they are a great replacement for yams or sweet potatoes and can be used in much the same way. They make great bases for casseroles, gravies, and several recipes that are in this book.

BAKED WINTER SQUASH HASH BROWNS

Servings vary according to size and type of squash

Way too yummy to be "diet food," but it is!

1 recipe Baked Winter Squash (page 216)
Butter
Lard
Seasoning salt
Lemon pepper
Garlic granules
Parsley flakes

1. Cut the completely cooled squash flesh into ½" cubes. Heat enough butter and lard to cover the bottom of a 10" skillet. Add the desired amount of squash (approximately 1 cup squash per person) to the pan. Season liberally with seasoning salt, lemon pepper, garlic granules, and parsley flakes.
2. Fry it over medium heat, turning every 5 minutes, until it is golden brown on all sides, about 20 minutes. Serve hot with butter or gravy of choice.

NUTRITIONAL INFORMATION PER SERVING
(1 CUP SPAGHETTI SQUASH PLUS 1 TABLESPOON BUTTER CALCULATED):
Carbohydrates: 7 grams • Effective Carb Count: 7 grams
Protein: 1 gram • Fat: 12 grams • Calories: 133

If you have a wooden cutting board, it can be seasoned nicely with olive oil to keep it in prime condition. Simply make sure it is clean and dry; then pour a small amount of olive oil onto the surface. Using a circular motion, rub the oil into the surface of the board with a clean, dry paper towel. Make sure to cover every area with oil: bottom, top, sides. Continue the process until no more oil will be absorbed by the board. Gently clean the board with soap and water and reseason when necessary, about once a month. By taking these simple steps, you'll ensure the condition and longevity of your board.

BREADED ZUCCHINI

Serves 1 as a primary side dish or 2 as appetizers

Now you can enjoy this restaurant favorite at home while keeping your carb count nice and low!

1 egg
1 tablespoon water
1 cup pork rinds, crushed
1 tablespoon soy protein
½ teaspoon garlic salt
½ tablespoon parsley flakes
¼ teaspoon thyme, dried
Lard for frying
1 cup zucchini, sliced about ⅛" thick, or
substitute 1 cup of any of the following: yellow summer squash,
chopped frozen okra, sliced mushrooms, broccoli florets, onion rings, etc.

1. In a small shallow dish, combine the egg and water. In another small shallow dish, combine the pork rinds, soy protein, garlic salt, parsley, and thyme. In a large skillet, place enough lard to cover the bottom to about ½" deep.
2. While the lard is heating, dip zucchini slices in the egg/water mixture, then into the pork rind mixture. Hold the shallow dish with the pork rinds on its edge and shake gently while dropping the veggies in. This will provide an even coating without getting the goo all over your fingers!
3. Gently place the coated pieces into the hot fat and cook on both sides until golden brown, about 3 minutes total. (If you don't want to fry the veggies, melt about ¼ cup of lard on a large baking sheet. Place the breaded veggies onto that and bake them for about 15 to 20 minutes at 375°F.) Serve hot with dipping sauces of choice.

NUTRITIONAL INFORMATION PER SERVING (AS A MEAL):
Carbohydrates: 7 grams • Effective Carb Count: 4 grams
Protein: 18 grams • Fat: 9 grams • Calories: 172

❧ INDIVIDUAL QUICK FREEZING TIP: Place the cooked Breaded Zucchini pieces (or any of the other veggies suggested) on a baking sheet sprayed with cooking oil spray. Place the filled baking sheet into the freezer until the veggies are frozen solid, usually overnight. Store tightly sealed in freezer containers for up to a month. This makes a quick-to-heat veggie dish or appetizer. Just bake about 8 minutes at 375°F and enjoy! *Caution:* Be sure to precook the Breaded Zucchini before freezing. *Note:* if zucchini is not precooked before it is frozen, it will get slimy.

CAULIFLOWER HASH BROWNS

Serves 2

This makes a great base for Quick and Easy Sausage Gravy (page 81).

1/3 cup onion, chopped
2 tablespoons lard
1 tablespoon butter
1/2 teaspoon seasoning salt
3 cups cauliflower, chopped to about 1/2" dice
Seasoning salt
Lemon pepper
1/4 teaspoon paprika

1. Cook the onion in the lard, butter, and seasoning salt over medium heat in a medium-sized frying pan for about 8 minutes or until the onion becomes golden brown.
2. Add the cauliflower to the pan and season it liberally with seasoning salt and lemon pepper and paprika. Cook over medium heat for about 15 minutes, stirring occasionally.

NUTRITIONAL INFORMATION PER SERVING:
Carbohydrates: 10 grams • Effective Carb Count: 6 grams
Protein: 3 grams • Fat: 19 grams • Calories: 215

REDUCED-FAT VARIATION:
Use about 2 tablespoons Rich Stock (page 254) to cook the onions.
Spray the pan with cooking oil spray to cook the hash browns.
Carbohydrates: 10 grams • Effective Carb Count: 6 grams
Protein: 3 grams • Fat: trace • Calories: 48

℘ At least two good knives are essential. It is well worth it to go to a professional kitchen supply store or the like to purchase an all-purpose kitchen knife and a French chef's knife. The knives should be made of high-quality steel, with either a wooden handle that shows the tang the entire length of the handle, or a professional molded plastic one. The type with a wooden handle is preferable because you can see what you are getting! The utility knife, about 10" long with a common-looking blade, can be used for almost any slicing task. The French chef's knife, about 15" long with a wedge-shaped blade, is for chopping. Grasp the handle firmly with your writing hand, and place the other hand gently on the top (flat edge) of the blade to help provide stability and control. Be sure and keep your fingers up! Chop with a rocking motion, using the point of the blade as a pivot. Finely chopped food in a snap! No more tedious paring-knife chopping!

CHEESY RICE-AFLOWER CASSEROLE

Serves 6

Try this for a different twist on au gratin potatoes!

Casserole ingredients:

½ cup onion, chopped
1 tablespoon butter
⅛ teaspoon seasoning salt
*½ head cauliflower, finely chopped
(about 4 cups)*
½ cup cream cheese, softened
2 eggs
*¾ cup cheese, shredded (Co-Jack,
Colby, Cheddar, or a blend)*
½ teaspoon sea salt
*¹⁄₁₆ teaspoon paprika (that is
½ of ⅛ teaspoon)*
*3 to 4 drops hot chili oil (or
a few grains of cayenne)*
¼ teaspoon lemon pepper

Topping:

*2 tablespoons cheese,
shredded (as above)*
1 tablespoon Parmesan cheese
½ tablespoon parsley flakes

1. In a small frying pan over medium heat, cook the onion in the butter with the seasoning salt until it is becoming golden, about 5 minutes. Set the onion aside to cool.
2. In a large mixing bowl, combine all of the remaining casserole ingredients. Add the cooled onion and stir well. Pour this mixture into a casserole dish, approximately 10" across. Flatten the top.
3. Combine the topping ingredients and sprinkle them over the top of the casserole. Bake it at 350°F for about 35 minutes or until it is set and golden.

NUTRITIONAL INFORMATION PER SERVING:
Carbohydrates: 6 grams • Effective Carb Count: 4 grams
Protein: 9 grams • Fat: 16 grams • Calories: 199

REDUCED-FAT VARIATION:
Cook the onion in about 2 tablespoons Rich Stock (page 254)
and use low-fat cream cheese and low-fat shredded cheese.
Carbohydrates: 5 grams • Effective Carb Count: 3 grams
Protein: 9 grams • Fat: 5 grams • Calories: 101

CREAMED SPINACH
WITH MACADAMIA GARNISH

Serves 4

This is a very elegant side dish! This is terrific served with Minted Lamb Chops (page 127).

1 pound spinach, washed and trimmed of stems
1/3 cup sweet onion, diced
2 tablespoons butter
1/2 cup Almond Milk (page 240) or cream
Pinch nutmeg (way less than 1/8 teaspoon)
Lemon pepper and seasoning salt, to taste

Garnish ingredients:

1 tablespoon butter
2 tablespoons pork rinds, crushed
2 tablespoons macadamia nuts, ground
1 1/2 teaspoons parsley flakes
Garlic salt, to taste

1. Place the spinach into about 1/2" of water in a 3-quart pot with a lid. Bring it to a boil over medium-high heat and turn down the heat to medium-low. Cook it until it is done, about 5 minutes.
2. Meanwhile, in a small saucepan over medium-low heat, cook the onion in 2 tablespoons butter. When the onion is translucent and beginning to brown slightly around the edges, about 2 to 3 minutes, add the Almond Milk and stir until thickened. Remove it from the heat. Add the nutmeg and season with lemon pepper and seasoning salt to taste.
3. In a small frying pan, place 1 tablespoon butter. Melt it over medium heat. Add the remaining garnish ingredients and cook and stir until golden brown, about 3 to 4 minutes. Place the garnish in a small serving dish.
4. Drain the spinach thoroughly. Place it into a serving bowl and season it with seasoning salt. Break up the spinach so that it isn't in a big ball, and pour the sauce over the spinach. Mix gently. Garnish as desired at the table.

NUTRITIONAL INFORMATION PER SERVING:
Carbohydrates: 6 grams • Effective Carb Count: 2 grams
Protein: 4 grams • Fat: 12 grams • Calories: 138

REDUCED-FAT VARIATION:
Omit the butter for cooking the onion. Instead, cook the onion in a small amount of Rich Stock (page 254). Use canned skim milk.
Carbohydrates: 9 grams • Effective Carb Count: 5 grams
Protein: 6 grams • Fat: 7 grams • Calories: 112

BEWARE OF BURNS AND SPLATTERS: Always be sure the pans are *completely* dry before putting any oil into them! A very dangerous burn could result from failing to do that simple task.

CREAM OF BROCCOLI SOUP

Serves 2 as appetizers

If you would like Cheesy Cream of Broccoli Soup, simply add 1 ounce Cheddar or Parmesan cheese before thickening.

4 tablespoons onion, chopped
1 tablespoon butter
2 cups chicken Rich Stock (page 254) or commercially prepared stock
2 cups broccoli, cut into 2" pieces
½ teaspoon thyme, dried
1 small bay leaf
¼ teaspoon sea salt
Pinch pepper (way less than ⅛ teaspoon)
⅛ teaspoon garlic powder
½ cup Almond Milk (page 240) or cream
1 teaspoon arrowroot powder mixed into 2 tablespoons water, or about ½ teaspoon guar gum

1. In a small saucepan, over medium-low heat, cook the onion in the butter until it is translucent. Pour in the chicken broth. Add the broccoli, thyme, bay leaf, salt, pepper, and garlic.
2. Bring it to a boil over medium heat; then cover and allow it to simmer for 10 minutes.
3. Remove the bay leaf and pour half of the hot mixture into a blender container. Cover the blender and place a towel over the top of the container to prevent a heat-induced blowout. (It can be very dangerous!) Blend on medium speed 30 to 60 seconds or until it is smooth.
4. Pour the soup back into the saucepan. Add the Almond Milk and arrowroot/water mixture and bring to a boil. Remove from heat and serve hot.

NUTRITIONAL INFORMATION PER SERVING:
Carbohydrates: 8 grams • Effective Carb Count: 5 grams
Protein: 3 grams • Fat: 6 grams • Calories: 107

REDUCED-FAT VARIATION:
Cook the onion in a bit of Rich Stock and use
canned skim milk instead of the Almond Milk.
Carbohydrates: 15 grams • Effective Carb Count: 12 grams
Protein: 8 grams • Fat: 1 gram • Calories: 106

FRENCH-STYLE GREEN BEANS

Serves 6

A wonderful way to serve fresh green beans! If you don't have fresh beans on hand, you can use frozen or canned beans–this recipe will make them a bit more special.

1 ½ pounds green beans, fresh
2 tablespoons butter
4 to 6 large cloves garlic, minced (about 2 tablespoons when chopped)
Seasoning salt

1. Wash the beans, and snap off the ends. On a cutting board with a very sharp utility knife, slice the beans into ¾" to 1" pieces at a 45° angle. A lot of the interior of the bean should be exposed.
2. Place the beans in about ½" of water in a 2-quart saucepan with a tight-fitting lid. Cover and cook them over medium-high heat for 8 minutes. Pour the beans into a colander. Run cold water over the beans in the colander to stop the beans from cooking any further.
3. In the same saucepan, melt the butter over medium-low heat. Add the garlic and cook it until it is just becoming golden. Do *not* overcook the garlic or it will become bitter! Add the beans back to the pan, season them to taste with seasoning salt, and cook and stir until they are thoroughly heated. If a softer bean is preferred, the lid may be place on the pan and the beans cooked for an additional 3 minutes.

NUTRITIONAL INFORMATION PER SERVING:
Carbohydrates: 8 grams • Effective Carb Count: 5 grams
Protein: 2 grams • Fat: 4 grams • Calories: 68

Golden Onions

Makes 2 servings

So simple, but so delicious! Serve them atop your favorite steak.

½ tablespoon butter
½ tablespoon lard
1 medium onion, sliced
½ teaspoon seasoning salt

In a medium-sized frying pan, melt the butter and the lard. Add the onion and the seasoning salt and cook over medium heat for about 5 to 8 minutes, or until the onion is golden. Serve warm.

Nutritional information per serving:
Carbohydrates: 5 grams • Effective Carb Count: 4 grams
Protein: 1 gram • Fat: 6 grams • Calories: 76

Reduced-Fat Variation:
Use 1 teaspoon butter and about 2 tablespoons
Rich Stock (page 254) instead of the butter and lard.
Carbohydrates: 5 grams • Effective Carb Count: 1 gram
Protein: 1 gram • Fat: 2 grams • Calories: 39

HIGH-PROTEIN WRAPS

Makes 16 wraps

Use these wraps anywhere low-carb tortillas would be appropriate. I've made them into Enchiladas, Sharron-Style (page 109), Breakfast Burritos (page 57), and mini pizzas. If you make mini pizzas, be sure to brown the wraps first. This dough also makes nice High-Protein Biscuits–just roll the dough into balls and bake them for about 12 minutes, until they are golden. Serve the biscuits hot with your favorite sugar-free jam!

1 1/2 cups cottage cheese (large curd preferred)
3/4 cup butter
1 1/3 cups milk and egg protein
1/3 cup soy protein
1/3 cup almonds, ground
1/8 teaspoon salt

1. In a large mixing bowl with an electric mixer on medium speed, cream the cottage cheese and the butter for about 2 minutes.
2. Meanwhile, in another, smaller bowl combine the remaining dry ingredients. Continue to mix the cottage cheese mixture, and add the dry ingredients little by little until they are all mixed into the dough.
3. Roll the dough into 16 equal-sized balls. Place the dough balls one at a time on parchment-lined or nonstick baking sheets, and press them flat with the palms of your hands. Form them into 6" circles. Bake them at 350°F for about 8 to 10 minutes or until they are just done. Do *not* allow them to brown, or they will not be pliable! Remove the wraps to waxed paper to cool.
4. To store, stack the wraps with waxed paper between them and wrap them well with plastic wrap. Store them refrigerated for up to 1 week.

NUTRITIONAL INFORMATION PER SERVING:
Carbohydrates: 1 gram • Effective Carb Count: 0 grams
Protein: 8 grams • Fat: 10 grams • Calories: 125

OLD-FASHIONED GREEN BEANS

Makes 4 to 6 servings

A dear lady friend who was originally from Georgia used to make delicious "brown sugar beans." This is my low-carb version!

½ cup sweet onion, chopped
2 tablespoons bacon grease or lard
1 pound green beans, fresh or frozen
⅓ cup water
¼ cup bacon, cooked and chopped
½ teaspoon Sweet & Slender
1 teaspoon sea salt
⅛ teaspoon almond extract
¼ teaspoon lemon pepper
⅛ teaspoon lemon thyme, fresh or dried thyme flakes
½ teaspoon lemon juice, fresh

1. Cook the onion in the bacon grease over medium heat in a medium-sized saucepan with a lid until the onion is golden, about 8 minutes.
2. Add all of the remaining ingredients to the pan. Cover the pan and bring it to a boil. Turn the heat down to low and simmer the beans for about 15 minutes or until they are quite tender. Serve hot.

NUTRITIONAL INFORMATION PER SERVING:
Carbohydrates: 6 grams • Effective Carb Count: 3 grams
Protein: 3 grams • Fat: 7 grams • Calories: 91

REDUCED-FAT VARIATION:
Use 1 teaspoon bacon grease or lard and about 2 tablespoons
Rich Stock (page 254) to cook the onion.
Carbohydrates: 6 grams • Effective Carb Count: 3 grams
Protein: 3 grams • Fat: 3 grams • Calories: 58

Rice-Aflower

Serves 4

This recipe is a great alternative to rice and potatoes. Serve this as a base for your gravies and sauces.

½ medium head cauliflower
3 tablespoons butter
¼ teaspoon seasoning salt
Dash lemon pepper (less than ⅛ teaspoon)

1. Cut the cauliflower in 2" chunks and place it into a small saucepan with a tightly fitting lid. Pour about ½" water into the pan. Cover and bring it to a boil over medium heat. Turn down the heat and continue to boil slowly for 8 to 10 minutes or until the cauliflower pierces easily with a fork. This will be cooked longer than the normal crisp-tender stage that would usually be done for cauliflower, *but* do not cook it until it is mushy!
2. When it is done cooking, drain the cauliflower in a colander. Place it into a small bowl with butter, seasoning salt, and lemon pepper. Mash it with a potato masher until the cauliflower is the consistency and texture of rice.

NUTRITIONAL INFORMATION PER SERVING:
Carbohydrates: 5 grams • Effective Carb Count: 2 grams
Protein: 2 grams • Fat: 9 grams • Calories: 102

REDUCED-FAT VARIATION:
Use 1½ teaspoons butter.
Carbohydrates: 5 grams • Effective Carb Count: 2 grams
Protein: 2 grams • Fat: 2 grams • Calories: 38

Rice-Aflower Au Gratin

Serves 6

Who says potatoes have to have all the fun? This super easy recipe is sure to become a family favorite!

1 small head cauliflower
1/2 cup sour cream
1/2 cup cheese, shredded (Co-Jack, Colby, or Cheddar)
2 tablespoons butter
1/8 teaspoon paprika
1/2 teaspoon minced onion, dried
1/2 teaspoon seasoning salt, or to taste
1/4 teaspoon chives, dried or fresh, for garnish

1. Break apart the cauliflower into approximately 3" florets. Place the florets into a medium-sized saucepan with 1/2" water. Cover and cook the cauliflower over medium heat for about 10 minutes until it is soft, then drain it.
2. Place the remaining ingredients except the chives into a serving dish. Put the drained cauliflower into the dish, on top of the sauce ingredients. Mash it with a potato masher until it resembles the consistency of rice. Stir it well and garnish it with the chives.

Nutritional information per serving:
Carbohydrates: 2 grams • Effective Carb Count: 1 gram
Protein: 3 grams • Fat: 11 grams • Calories: 118

Reduced-Fat Variation:
Use reduced-fat sour cream, reduced-fat cheese, and omit the butter.
Carbohydrates: 2 grams • Effective Carb Count: 1 gram
Protein: 3 grams • Fat: 1 gram • Calories: 28

RICE-AFLOWER PILAF

Serves 6

Serve this with Broiled Lamb Chops (page 101) for a nice Middle Eastern–style meal.

1 pound cauliflower (frozen is okay), chopped (about 4 cups)
1 small onion, chopped (about ³/₄ cup)
2 cloves garlic, minced
¹/₂ tablespoon lard
¹/₂ tablespoon butter
¹/₂ teaspoon seasoning salt
1 teaspoon fresh mint leaves, chopped (or ¹/₂ teaspoon dried)
¹/₂ tablespoon Bragg's Liquid Aminos
1 teaspoon parsley flakes
1 teaspoon chives, snipped
¹/₈ teaspoon hot chili oil
¹/₄ teaspoon lemon pepper

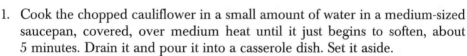

Topping ingredients:

³/₄ cup pecan pieces, broken
2 tablespoons butter, melted
¹/₄ teaspoon seasoning salt

1. Cook the chopped cauliflower in a small amount of water in a medium-sized saucepan, covered, over medium heat until it just begins to soften, about 5 minutes. Drain it and pour it into a casserole dish. Set it aside.
2. In a small frying pan, or the pot used previously, cook the onion and the garlic in the lard, butter, and seasoning salt over medium heat until they are golden, about 5 to 8 minutes. Add the mint to the pan at the last bit of cooking. Pour onion mixture into the cauliflower that is resting in the casserole dish. Add the remaining seasonings. Stir it well and smooth the top.
3. Combine the topping ingredients and pour them over the cauliflower. Bake the casserole at 350°F for about 20 minutes or until heated through.

NUTRITIONAL INFORMATION PER SERVING:
Carbohydrates: 9 grams • Effective Carb Count: 6 grams
Protein: 3 grams • Fat: 15 grams • Calories: 172

REDUCED-FAT VARIATION:
Instead of cooking the garlic and onion in fat, steam them in 2 tablespoons Rich Stock (page 254). Follow remaining instructions as given, up to the point of the topping. For the topping use 1 teaspoon butter.
Carbohydrates: 9 grams • Effective Carb Count: 6 grams
Protein: 3 grams • Fat: 11 grams • Calories: 137

ROASTED GARLIC

Yields about 10 cloves of Roasted Garlic

Why roast a head of garlic? Raw garlic has an intense bite to it, and, when it is left raw in cold foods, the flavor grows more intense and overpowering as time passes. Roasted garlic, on the other hand, has a rich, mellow flavor that doesn't compete with the food it is served alongside. This can be used as a spread for meat and vegetables or in recipes like Creamy Roasted Garlic Salad Dressing (page 245). It is also excellent spread on Barbecue Pork (page 95).

1 head garlic (yes, HEAD, not clove!)
½ tablespoon olive oil

1. With a sharp knife, cut the top ⅓ from the garlic, so that the insides of the cloves are all exposed. It may be necessary to individually cut some of the cloves if they are down farther in the head.
2. Place the garlic into the center of an 8" square of aluminum foil. Drizzle the oil over the top. Wrap the foil around the garlic, then place it onto a baking sheet or other oven-safe dish and bake it at 325°F or 350°F for about 2 hours.

NUTRITIONAL INFORMATION PER SERVING:
Carbohydrates: trace • Effective Carb Count: 0
Protein: trace • Fat: 1 gram • Calories: 6

Roasted Veggies over a Bonfire

Serves 4

You'll be amazed at how wonderful these veggies turn out—especially the onions.
You can use all of your favorite veggies for this meal—mushrooms, peppers, even
broccoli. Everything tastes so much better when it is cooked outdoors! Serve hot
with Bonfire Barbecue Steak (page 100).

Large bonfire or other outdoor cooking fire
Foil
1 large sweet onion
2 small or 1 medium zucchini, sliced (about 2 cups)
¼ teaspoon seasoning salt
⅛ teaspoon lemon pepper
2 tablespoons olive oil

1. While your bonfire is getting to the red-hot-coals stage, slice the veggies into
   ½" slices. Spread 2 large sheets of foil on a working surface, crosswise on top
   of each other. Place the veggies into the center of the foil and season them with
   seasoning salt and lemon pepper. Drizzle the oil over all. Wrap the bundle
   tightly, squeezing out any excess air. Be sure there are no gaps in the foil. If
   there are any gaps, add another piece of foil to ensure there will be no leaks.
2. When the fire has reached the red-hot-coal stage, gently place the veggie bundle into the coals for about 45 minutes, turning once partway through. Use a
   shovel or some other implement to remove the veggie bundle from the fire.
   Allow the cooked vegetables to rest about 5 minutes. Carefully open the bundle, allowing the steam to escape.

Nutritional information per serving:
Carbohydrates: 5 grams • Effective Carb Count: 3 grams
Protein: 1 gram • Fat: 7 grams • Calories: 84

Reduced-Fat Variation:
Use 1½ teaspoons olive oil.
Carbohydrates: 5 grams • Effective Carb Count: 3 grams
Protein: 1 gram • Fat: 2 grams • Calories: 40

SHARRON'S FAKE CORNBREAD

Serves 6

Most low-carb eating plans avoid cornmeal. With this recipe, you can have your cornbread and eat it, too! This is great used the southern way, as a base under other foods. You can also try it out for breakfast topped with poached eggs.

½ cup almonds, ground
¼ cup soy flour
¼ cup soy protein powder
¾ teaspoon SteviaPlus
2 teaspoons Sweet & Slender
½ tablespoon baking powder
¼ teaspoon salt
3 tablespoons butter, melted
1 egg
¼ cup cream thinned with water to make ½ cup, or
½ cup Almond Milk (page 240)
½ teaspoon almond extract or vanilla
Butter

1. Combine the ground almonds, soy flour, soy protein, SteviaPlus, Sweet & Slender, baking powder, and salt in a mixing bowl and mix well. In a small bowl, combine the melted butter, egg, thinned cream, and almond/vanilla extract well. Pour all at once into the dry ingredients and stir until the batter is just combined. Don't overmix it! The batter should be lumpy.
2. Grease a loaf pan (approximately 4" × 8") with butter and pour the batter into the pan. Bake it at 400°F for about 15 minutes. It should test clean with a toothpick. Serve warm with melted butter.

NUTRITIONAL INFORMATION PER SERVING:
Carbohydrates: 5 grams • Effective Carb Count: 1 gram
Protein: 9 grams • Fat: 15 grams • Calories: 190

REDUCED-FAT VARIATION:
Use applesauce instead of the melted butter.
Use canned skim milk instead of the cream.
Carbohydrates: 6 grams • Effective Carb Count: 4 grams
Protein: 10 grams • Fat: 7 grams • Calories: 127

SLURP 'EM UP CABBAGE NOODLES

Serves 6

Kid factor: They slurp just like noodles! Serve these under any of the sauces in this book or your favorite low-carb gravy.

½ head cabbage
¼ cup butter
¼ teaspoon lemon pepper
½ teaspoon seasoning salt

1. Slice the cabbage into strips about ¼" wide, so they resemble fettuccini noodles. Individually separate the pieces of cabbage so that they are not in clumps or chunks. This will allow the water and steam to cook them evenly.
2. Place the sliced cabbage pieces into a saucepan (or steamer) with about ½" of water. Cover the pan with a tightly fitting lid, and cook the cabbage on medium heat for about 8 minutes or until it is tender. The cabbage needs to be slightly on the soft side—not the normal crisp-tender you would want from a fresh vegetable—in order to achieve the "noodle" feel.
3. Drain the cabbage thoroughly. Place the butter into the bottom of a serving bowl and sprinkle the lemon pepper and seasoning salt over it. Add the cabbage, and mix it thoroughly with the butter and seasonings.

NUTRITIONAL INFORMATION PER SERVING:
Carbohydrates: 4 grams • Effective Carb Count: 2 grams
Protein: 1 gram • Fat: 8 grams • Calories: 87

REDUCED-FAT VARIATION:
Use 2 tablespoons butter.
Carbohydrates: 4 grams • Effective Carb Count: 2 grams
Protein: 1 gram • Fat: 4 grams • Calories: 53

SPINACH WITH
ONIONS AND GARLIC

Makes 2 servings

This is something a little different to do with that bunch of spinach that always seems to be hanging around the fridge!

1 small onion, chopped (about ½ cup)
2 cloves garlic, minced
½ tablespoon butter
½ tablespoon lard
¼ teaspoon seasoning salt
⅛ teaspoon lemon pepper
1 large bunch spinach, washed and trimmed

1. Place all of the ingredients, except the spinach, into a large pot, like a wok, and cook them over medium heat until the onions and garlic are golden, about 5 to 8 minutes.
2. Add the spinach, stirring constantly until it is wilted, about 3 to 5 minutes. Serve hot.

NUTRITIONAL INFORMATION PER SERVING:
Carbohydrates: 5 grams • Effective Carb Count: 1 gram
Protein: 1 gram • Fat: 6 grams • Calories: 78

Sweet and Sour Beets

Makes 6 servings

This recipe is not strongly flavored like pickled beets, but rather subtly seasoned, just bringing out their best! Beets aren't the lowest-carb veggie out there, but they are yummy for an occasional treat.

3 medium beets (about 1 pound)
2 teaspoons lemon juice
1/2 teaspoon Sweet & Slender
1/8 teaspoon seasoning salt
1 teaspoon butter
1/4 cup water

1. If you are starting with fresh beets, the easiest way to cook them is to place them in about 1" of water in a small saucepan with a tightly fitting lid. Cover and cook them until they are tender, about 20 to 30 minutes. They should be able to be pierced easily with a fork. Let them cool off completely–I just leave them in the water they cooked in. When they are completely cool, the skins just slip right off them!
2. Slice the beets and place all of the ingredients into a small saucepan. Heat and stir over medium heat until the beets are warmed through and coated evenly with the sauce. Serve warm.

NUTRITIONAL INFORMATION PER SERVING:
Carbohydrates: 4 grams • Effective Carb Count: 3 grams
Protein: 1 gram • Fat: 1 gram • Calories: 25

SWEET CINNAMON SQUASH

Serves 4

You can also serve this dish as squash boats. Simply cut the squash in half, season each half with the listed seasonings, and put it into a 350°F oven until the butter melts.

1 medium Baked Winter Squash (page 216), unseasoned
½ teaspoon cinnamon
¼ teaspoon orange zest
¼ teaspoon SteviaPlus or 1 packet sucralose
¼ cup butter
A tiny pinch of sea salt

Scape the inside flesh from the squash, reserving the seeds for Roasted Pumpkin Seeds (page 32). Place the flesh into a large mixing bowl and add the remaining ingredients. Mix the squash on medium speed until it is well blended. Adjust seasonings to taste.

NUTRITIONAL INFORMATION PER SERVING:
Carbohydrates: 5 grams • Effective Carb Count: 3 grams
Protein: 1 gram • Fat: 12 grams • Calories: 125

REDUCED-FAT VARIATION:
Use 1 tablespoon butter.
Carbohydrates: 5 grams • Effective Carb Count: 3 grams
Protein: 1 gram • Fat: 3 grams • Calories: 49

SWEET PUMPKIN CASSEROLE

Serves 8

Think of that traditional southern dish, sweet potato casserole, and you've got the idea! It is so yummy–what a wonderful accompaniment to a great holiday meal.

1 29-ounce can pumpkin purée (about 3 cups)
1 teaspoon SteviaPlus
8 packets sucralose
¼ teaspoon sea salt
2 eggs
1 ½ teaspoons vanilla
1 cup Almond Milk (page 240) or cream
Cooking oil spray

Topping:

½ teaspoon SteviaPlus
6 packets sucralose
½ cup soy protein (not soy flour!)
½ cup pecans (or any nuts)
3 tablespoons butter
½ teaspoon vanilla

1. In a large mixing bowl, combine the pumpkin, sweeteners, salt, eggs, vanilla, and Almond Milk. Mix thoroughly. Spray a casserole dish, pie pan, or 8" square baking dish with cooking oil spray. Pour the pumpkin mixture into the dish.
2. Place the topping ingredients into the bowl of a food processor and process until the mixture resembles coarse crumbs. (Alternatively, chop nuts by hand; then combine all of the ingredients with a pastry blender until well mixed.) Sprinkle the topping over the pumpkin mixture. Bake at 350°F until the topping begins to brown and the filling is beginning to set, about 35 to 45 minutes.

NUTRITIONAL INFORMATION PER SERVING:
Carbohydrates: 10 grams • Effective Carb Count: 6 grams
Protein: 9 grams • Fat: 11 grams • Calories: 165

REDUCED-FAT VARIATION:
Use fat-free half and half (or canned skim milk) in the filling
and use 1 ½ tablespoons of butter in the topping.
Carbohydrates: 13 grams • Effective Carb Count: 9 grams
Protein: 9 grams • Fat: 8 grams • Calories: 166

ZUCCHI-TATER PANCAKES

Serves 4

This really satisfies those potato cravings when they hit! You may use cooked spaghetti squash, or other Baked Winter Squash (page 216), instead of zucchini and reduce the soy protein to 3 tablespoons.

2 cups zucchini, grated
2 tablespoons onion, grated
2 small, or 1 large, cloves garlic, grated
1 egg, slightly beaten
6 tablespoons soy protein (not soy flour!)
½ tablespoon parsley flakes
½ teaspoon sea salt
⅛ teaspoon lemon pepper
5 drops hot chili oil (about ⅛ teaspoon, but not quite) or
a tiny pinch of cayenne
Bacon grease or lard
Butter, optional
Seasoning salt, optional

1. Using a food processor with a shredding/grating disk (or by hand), grate the zucchini, onion, and garlic.
2. Place the egg into a mixing bowl, add the zucchini, onion, and garlic and mix thoroughly. Add the soy protein, parsley, salt, lemon pepper, and chili oil. Mix well and allow the mixture to rest about 5 minutes.
3. Pour enough bacon grease into a large skillet to cover the bottom. Heat it over medium heat until it is hot. Using a ¼-cup measuring cup, scoop the zucchini mixture into the hot pan. Fry the patties on each side until they are golden brown, about 8 minutes total. Add additional cooking oil as needed. Serve warm with butter and a sprinkling of seasoning salt, if desired.

NUTRITIONAL INFORMATION PER SERVING:
Carbohydrates: 3 grams • Effective Carb Count: 2 grams
Protein: 11 grams • Fat: 8 grams • Calories: 131

Dressings and Sauces

ALMOND MILK

This recipe yields about 1 quart Almond Milk and about ⅓ cup almond meal

Almond Milk is a tasty way to get around using dairy, especially if you are on a candida restriction diet. While there are various nondairy "milks" available in health food and grocery stores, most of them contain some sort of sugar. Have no fear! You can make your own sugar-free Almond Milk at home. I've developed this low-carb version, which has fewer carbs than cream and can be useful for candida restrictions. For use in savory recipes, just omit the flavorings.

1 cup almonds, raw (or blanched, if available)
4 cups warm water
¼ teaspoon SteviaPlus or 1 packet sucralose
1 teaspoon vanilla
½ teaspoon almond extract

1. To blanch the almonds: Place the almonds in a microwave-safe bowl, and pour in enough water to cover them. Microwave on high power for 2 to 3 minutes. The skins on the almonds should become loose and peel easily. Remove and discard the skins. Place the blanched almonds into a blender container and discard the blanching water.
2. Pour the warm water into blender container, and begin to process the water and almonds on low speed, gradually turning the speed up to high. When I start blending on high speed, I end up with Almond Milk all over the kitchen! Blend the almonds and water on high speed until completely smooth, about 3 to 4 minutes. Turn the blender off.
3. Add the remaining ingredients through the hole in the blender's top; blend (beginning on low again) until well combined.
4. Place a clean towel, cheesecloth, or paper towel into a strainer placed over a large bowl. Pour the Almond Milk into the cloth-lined strainer. Allow it to completely drain, pressing out as much excess liquid as possible. Pour the milk into a pitcher and store it in the refrigerator for up to 2 weeks. Save the almond meal leftover from the milk-making process and allow it to air dry, stirring it at least daily. If the climate is very warm or humid, this may need to be done in the oven or food dehydrator to prevent the meal from becoming rancid.

NUTRITIONAL INFORMATION PER 1-CUP SERVING:
Carbohydrates: 4 grams • Effective Carb Count: 3 grams
Protein: 4 grams • Fat: 10 grams • Calories: 108

℘ The almond meal that remains after making Almond Milk adds a great fiber boost to baked goods. You can just mix it in with your other ground almonds and use as you would in any recipe that uses that ingredient.

BLENDER MAYONNAISE

Makes about 1 1/4 cups mayonnaise or 20 servings

This does require some effort, but this recipe, which I've adapted from *The Joy of Cooking*, is even better than the commercially prepared type. You can use as much as 3/4 cup olive oil and 1/4 cup each of the other oils, as olive oil has more beneficial fats, and still retain the flavor. *Warning:* Do not attempt to make mayonnaise if it is threatening to rain. It will not bind.

1 egg
1 teaspoon dry mustard
1 teaspoon sea salt
3 or 4 drops hot chili oil or a few grains of cayenne
1/4 teaspoon SteviaPlus or 1 packet sucralose
1/4 cup olive oil
1/2 cup sunflower or peanut oil (safflower or canola acceptable)
3 tablespoons lemon juice (fresh is always best!)
1/2 cup canola oil (sunflower or safflower acceptable)

1. Coddle egg: Fill a small saucepan with enough water to cover the egg. Bring the water to boiling; then gently place the whole egg into the boiling water for 20 seconds. Remove the egg from the boiling water and immerse it in a bowl of ice-cold water to stop it from cooking any further.
2. Place the coddled egg, mustard, salt, hot chili oil, and SteviaPlus into a blender container. Blend on high until the mixture is well combined. With the blender still running, remove the center piece of the blender's lid and VERY SLOWLY, in a small stream, pour the olive oil into the egg mixture.
3. Add the remaining ingredients in the order listed in the same manner. The mayonnaise will become very thick. The blender will need to be stopped periodically to stir the mayonnaise. Store it in a covered container in the refrigerator for up to 2 weeks.

NUTRITIONAL INFORMATION PER SERVING:
Carbohydrates: trace • Effective Carb Count: 0 grams
Protein: trace • Fat: 14 grams • Calories: 124

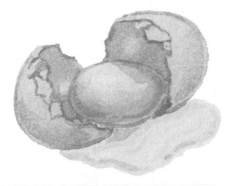

CINNAMON BUTTER

Serves 6

This butter is so rich and satisfying. It is great when something that tastes great is so simple! Excellent served with Pumpkin Waffles (page 80).

6 tablespoons butter, room temperature
1 teaspoon SteviaPlus
10 packets sucralose
1 ½ teaspoons cinnamon

Combine all ingredients in a small mixing bowl. With an electric mixer, whip butter on medium speed, about 2 minutes. Put into a serving dish and chill until ready to use.

NUTRITIONAL INFORMATION PER SERVING:
Carbohydrates: trace • Effective Carb Count: 0 grams
Protein: trace • Fat: 12 grams • Calories: 103

A NOTE ABOUT MILKS: For those following low-carb, low-fat plans, the choices for baking are different from those of individuals following low-carb, higher-fat plans. Generally, when cooking the low-fat way and/or restricting calories, one uses canned skim milk in baking and cooking. If you're looking for another option, try the Almond Milk (page 240) recipe in this book! Here's how it stacks up cup for cup against canned skim milk:

	ALMOND MILK	CANNED SKIM MILK
Carbohydrates	4 grams	29 grams
Effective Carb Count	3 grams	29 grams
Protein	4 grams	19 grams
Fat	10 grams	1 gram
Calories	108	199

As you can see, it has more fat grams, but they are healthy fats from almonds! Also the carb count is vastly different, as are the calories.

CREAMY FRESH BASIL SALAD DRESSING

Yields about 1 cup, approximately 16 servings

This recipe is a great use for fresh basil from the garden. This makes a great dip; just use 1½ tablespoons of water instead of 2 tablespoons.

1 egg
2 teaspoons lemon juice
6 1" basil leaves, fresh
2 tablespoons chives, fresh, chopped
⅛ teaspoon dry mustard powder
1 teaspoon seasoning salt
⅛ teaspoon black pepper
¾ cup olive oil (you may wish to use a mildly flavored one)
2 tablespoons water

1. Coddle egg: Fill a small saucepan with enough water to cover the egg. Bring the water to boiling; then place the whole egg into the boiling water for 20 seconds. Remove the egg from the boiling water and immerse it in ice-cold water to stop it from cooking any further.
2. Place the egg, lemon juice, and seasonings into a blender container. Blend on medium speed until well combined. Stop the blender and scrape down the seasonings from the sides of the container.
3. With the blender running, pour the olive oil in a very small stream through the hole in the top of the blender's cover. Continue to blend and add the water. Turn blender to high and blend for about 1 minute more. Store in a tightly covered container in the refrigerator for up to 2 weeks.

NUTRITIONAL INFORMATION PER SERVING:
Carbohydrates: trace • Effective Carb Count: 0 grams
Protein: trace • Fat: 10 grams • Calories: 94

CREAMY RANCH SALAD DRESSING

Yields about 1 cup, approximately 16 servings

This creamy buttermilk ranch–style salad dressing is completely dairy free–great for those with candida dietary restrictions. But you don't need to be off dairy to enjoy this tasty low-carb dressing! This makes a great dip; just use 1½ tablespoons of water instead of 3 tablespoons. Use fresh herbs for a terrific taste!

1 egg
2 teaspoons lemon juice
1 tablespoon minced onion, dried, or
2 tablespoons fresh sweet onion, minced
½ tablespoon parsley flakes
1 teaspoon chives
⅛ teaspoon thyme flakes
⅛ teaspoon celery seed
⅛ teaspoon dry mustard powder or hot chili oil
1 teaspoon seasoning salt
⅛ teaspoon black pepper
¾ cup olive oil (you may wish to use a mildly flavored one)
3 tablespoons water

1. Coddle egg: Fill a small saucepan with enough water to cover the egg. Bring the water to boiling; then gently place the whole egg into the boiling water for 20 seconds. Remove the egg from the boiling water and immerse it in ice-cold water to stop it from cooking any further.
2. Place the egg, lemon juice, and seasonings into a blender container. Blend on medium speed until well combined. Stop the blender and scrape down the seasonings from the sides of the container.
3. With the blender running, pour the olive oil in a very small stream through the hole in the top of the blender's cover. Continue to blend and add the water. Turn blender to high and blend for about 1 minute more. Store in a tightly covered container in the refrigerator for up to 2 weeks.

NUTRITIONAL INFORMATION PER SERVING:
Carbohydrates: trace • Effective Carb Count: 0 grams
Protein: trace • Fat: 10 grams • Calories: 95

CREAMY ROASTED GARLIC
SALAD DRESSING

Yields about 1 cup, approximately 16 servings

This has a very rich, creamy texture and flavor, like a homemade dressing at a very fancy restaurant! If you would like a Creamy Caesar Salad Dressing, use 3 or 4 cloves Roasted Garlic (page 230) and garnish your salad greens with freshly grated Parmesan cheese. Yum! This also makes a great dip!

1 egg
2 cloves Roasted Garlic
2 teaspoons lemon juice, fresh, if available
1/8 teaspoon dry mustard powder
1 teaspoon seasoning salt
1/8 teaspoon black pepper
3/4 cup olive oil (you may wish to use a mildly flavored one)
2 tablespoons water

1. Coddle egg: Fill a small saucepan with enough water to cover the egg. Bring the water to boiling; then place the whole egg into the boiling water for 20 seconds. Remove the egg from the boiling water and immerse it in ice-cold water to stop it from cooking any further.
2. Place the Roasted Garlic into a blender container. Add the lemon juice, mustard powder, egg, seasoning salt, and pepper. Blend on high until it is well combined.
3. While the blender is still running, slowly pour the oil in a very thin stream into the hole in the top of the blender's cover. Add the water and continue to blend about 1 minute. Store refrigerated in a container with a tightly fitting lid for up to 2 weeks.

NUTRITIONAL INFORMATION PER SERVING:
Carbohydrates: trace • Effective Carb Count: 0 grams
Protein: trace • Fat: 10 grams • Calories: 95

FIERY HOT MUSTARD

Serves 2

Use this as a dipping sauce for Egg Rolls (page 15) and Barbecue Pork (page 95). Serve it alongside sesame seeds for a really "authentic" feeling Asian meal.

2 tablespoons dry mustard powder
1 1/2 tablespoons water

Simply combine the ingredients in a small bowl and enjoy in small amounts as a condiment.

NUTRITIONAL INFORMATION PER SERVING:
Carbohydrates: 1 gram • Effective Carb Count: 0 grams
Protein: 1 gram • Fat: 1 gram • Calories: 20

As a homeschool science project, we studied the evaporation rates of different "salts." We used Epsom salts (magnesium), iodized table salt, and unrefined sea salt. We put 1/4 teaspoon of the salt into a cup filled with 1" of filtered water and had 1 glass of plain filtered water as a control. Then we set them on a windowsill and watched their evaporation rates. The results were actually quite surprising! We found that the sea salt evaporated the quickest, then the control, then the Epsom salts, then finally the table salt, which evaporated about ten days after the Epsom salts! Sea salt has been reported to act as a diuretic, while a great many folks complain about table salt causing bloating–the answer, at least in part, lies in their basic dissolution rates!

French Salad Dressing

Makes about 32 servings

Sometimes low-carbers need a change of pace from the basic ranch and Caesar salad dressings they usually consume. This allows a very different choice! This salad dressing also makes a wonderful marinade for chicken or pork.

½ cup tomato sauce
½ cup vinegar or bottled lemon juice
¼ cup lemon juice, fresh, if available
2 tablespoons minced onion, dried, or ¼ cup fresh
2 teaspoons paprika
2 teaspoons seasoning salt
1 teaspoon SteviaPlus
8 packets sucralose
1 cup olive oil (you may wish to choose a mildly flavored one)

In a blender container, place the tomato sauce, vinegar, lemon juice, onion, paprika, seasoning salt, SteviaPlus, and sucralose. Combine thoroughly. With the motor running on medium speed, slowly drizzle the oil through the hole in the lid of the blender. Mix thoroughly.

Nutritional information per serving:
Carbohydrates: 1 gram • Effective Carb Count: 0 grams
Protein: trace • Fat: 7 grams • Calories: 63

HAM GLAZE

Makes about ½ cup or 8 servings

Use this as a dipping sauce or yummy low-carb glaze for a baked ham.

1 tablespoon lemon juice, fresh
2 tablespoons water
1 teaspoon SteviaPlus
¾ teaspoon Sweet & Slender
½ teaspoon dry mustard powder
¼ teaspoon almond extract
¼ teaspoon orange zest
¼ cup defatted ham broth (from a sugar-free ham, if possible)
¼ teaspoon guar gum

Combine all of the ingredients in a small saucepan and simmer over medium-low heat until they are thickened.

NUTRITIONAL INFORMATION PER SERVING:
Carbohydrates: 1 gram • Effective Carb Count: 0 grams
Protein: trace • Fat: trace • Calories: 4

HOMEMADE YOGURT

Makes 8 servings plus starter

Making yogurt at home is actually quite simple. Once you've had your own homemade yogurt, you will probably never want storebought again!

1 8-ounce carton plain yogurt that specifies it is made from active cultures
1 quart milk, whole preferred

1. Allow the yogurt to stand out until it is completely at room temperature. This is the starter culture for the yogurt.
2. Do not try to rush this or any of the steps involved in this process or you will end up with failed yogurt.
3. Pour the milk into a clean, nonaluminum pot. On low temperature, bring the milk just to a boil. This will take nearly an hour. Do not rush this process. Remove the pot from the heat and cover it. Allow the milk to cool to 80°F.
4. Once the milk has cooled, add about ½ cup of the cooled milk into the starter. This helps it blend in better. Pour the starter into the cooled milk and stir it gently so that it is evenly dispersed throughout. Pour the milk into a clean quart jar and another pint jar. The quart jar is the yogurt to eat. The pint jar will be the starter for the next batch. Seal the jars with lids. Mark the starter with a big red *S* in permanent marker so that it won't accidentally get eaten.
5. Place the filled jars into a cool, dark place, like an empty cupboard, for 3 to 12 hours. If it is quite warm, it will take less time. If it is quite cool, it will take longer. You may place bath towels above and below your yogurt, then place a heating pad on top. Allowed to cure this way, it takes 4 hours. Also, do not disturb the yogurt while it is culturing. Otherwise you will end up with curds and whey!
6. After 3 to 12 hours, check the yogurt by gently tipping it to the side to see if it is thick. Once it has thickened, place it in the refrigerator until ready to use. It is yummy plain, all by itself, or it can be used as a basis for a great many recipes found in this book!

NUTRITIONAL INFORMATION PER SERVING:
Carbohydrates: 4 grams • Effective Carb Count: 4 grams
Protein: 9 grams • Fat: 8 grams • Calories: 150

REDUCED-FAT VARIATION:
Use skim milk.
Carbohydrates: 4 grams • Effective Carb Count: 4 grams
Protein: 14 grams • Fat: trace • Calories: 137

HOMEMADE YOGURT CHEESE
Makes 8 servings

Although the whey resulting from the cheese-making process isn't very nice to drink, it is great for other uses! It makes a wonderful "stripper" for the hair and a very nice facial. Simply pour warmed whey onto the hair and rub into the face before showering. Allow it to remain there for 5 to 10 minutes; then wash the hair and face as usual. The results will be clean, bouncy hair and glowing skin!

1 quart Homemade Yogurt (page 249) or kefir

1. Place a large colander over a large bowl. Line the colander with a nonterry tea towel. A very inexpensive, flat-surfaced towel will actually work better than most commercial cheesecloths. Carefully pour the yogurt into the cloth-lined colander. Cover the yogurt with a plate or lid so that nothing will inadvertently fall into it.
2. Place it into the refrigerator and allow the whey to drain off into the bowl. After several hours, check the consistency of the cheese. If it is strained just a couple of hours, it will be the consistency of sour cream. If it is strained longer, say overnight, then it will be the consistency of cream cheese. When the cheese is the consistency desired, remove it from the towel and place it into a covered container and refrigerate it.
3. Use it as desired in recipes calling for sour cream or cream cheese. If a sweeter, creamier cheese is desired, place the cheese into a mixing bowl and whip a little bit of sweetener into it with an electric mixer. A great many recipes in this book call for sour cream and cream cheese, many of which were developed with Homemade Yogurt Cheese!

NUTRITIONAL INFORMATION PER SERVING:
Carbohydrates: 4 grams • Effective Carb Count: 4 grams
Protein: 9 grams • Fat: 8 grams • Calories: 150

REDUCED-FAT VARIATION:
Use skim Homemade Yogurt (page 249).
Carbohydrates: 4 grams • Effective Carb Count: 4 grams
Protein: 14 grams • Fat: trace • Calories: 137

"Honey" Mustard Dipping Sauce

Serves 4

Some of the greatest recipes have been discovered by accident, and this "Honey" Mustard definitely fits the bill. I was trying to make a candida-friendly mustard/mayonnaise blend and ended up with this. Keep it on hand to serve with burgers, hot dogs, sausages, pork chops, Rutabaga Chips (page 33), Egg Rolls (page 15), Homemade Lunch Meat (page 116), etc.

¼ cup Blender Mayonnaise (page 241) or
commercially prepared mayonnaise
2 ½ teaspoons dry mustard powder
¼ teaspoon SteviaPlus or 1 packet sucralose
⅛ teaspoon garlic salt
1 ½ teaspoons lemon juice (fresh is always best!)

In a small dish, combine all of the ingredients, mixing well. Store this sauce refrigerated in a covered container for up to 2 weeks.

Nutritional information per serving:
Carbohydrates: trace • Effective Carb Count: 0 grams
Protein: trace • Fat: 12 grams • Calories: 103

Reduced-Fat Variation:
Use reduced-fat mayonnaise.
Carbohydrates: 3 grams • Effective Carb Count: 2 grams
Protein: trace • Fat: 3 grams • Calories: 39

There are so many obvious health benefits to low-carbing. People's blood pressure goes down, their blood sugar stabilizes, and they lose weight. The other, not-so-obvious benefits that are often seen are increased stamina, increased growth in the children, and increased resistance to common illnesses like the flu and colds. What a wonderful way of life!

LEMON BUTTER

Makes 8 servings

This simple sauce is great served with artichokes, asparagus, brussels sprouts, shellfish, etc.

¼ cup butter
1 ½ tablespoons lemon juice, fresh
Zest of 1 lemon (optional)

Place the butter and lemon juice into a microwave-safe dish. Microwave them on high for about 30 seconds, or until the butter is melted. Stir and enjoy!

NUTRITIONAL INFORMATION PER SERVING:
Carbohydrates: trace • Effective Carb Count: 0 grams
Protein: trace • Fat: 6 grams • Calories: 52

There is a lot of talk about "trigger foods" in low-carb circles. "Trigger foods" are foods that, basically, cause us to eat out of whack and fall off the plan! They can also be allergens, in my experience. How do you know what foods these are? You may become bloated or have cravings after eating a trigger food. They may also cause sleeplessness. Some common low-carb trigger foods are: sugar-free candies, meal replacement bars, sugar-free desserts, and diet sodas. Other high-carb foods are triggers as well, such as: French fries, burgers, ice cream, and regular sodas.

PUMPKIN KETCHUP

Makes about 32 servings

This is for the many of us who are allergic to the nightshade family of plants–including tomatoes! You don't have to be allergic to tomatoes to enjoy this yummy ketchup though!

1 medium onion, finely chopped
¼ cup water
1 29-ounce can pumpkin purée
¾ teaspoon SteviaPlus
10 packets sucralose
¾ teaspoon sea salt
¾ teaspoon cinnamon
¼ teaspoon dry mustard
½ teaspoon ground nutmeg
¼ teaspoon ground cloves
1 cup lemon juice, bottled
¾ cup water

1. Place the onion and water into a medium-sized pot with a lid. Cover the pot and cook the onion over medium heat for about 10 minutes, or until it is tender.
2. Combine the remaining ingredients in the pot and slowly bring the mixture to a simmer. Cook it for about 1½ hours, or until it is very thick. Pour the ketchup into a container with a lid and store it covered in the refrigerator up to 1 month, or part of it may be frozen.

NUTRITIONAL INFORMATION PER SERVING:
Carbohydrates: 3 grams • Effective Carb Count: 2 grams
Protein: trace • Fat: trace • Calories: 12

RICH STOCK

Yields about 2 gallons of stock

This recipe is a basic component of many soups and stews in this book. It is also essential for Sharron's Beef Jerky (page 34), which is a great snack to keep on hand all the time. You can make this after dinner with the leftover bones, fat, and skin from the meal. Just let it cook on low all night on a back burner. You can expect to wake to yummy smells and a growling tummy!

2 tablespoons lard, if doing beef or pork Rich Stock
5- to 9-quart stockpot with cover
Approximately ³/4 pound beef or pork fat/trimmings and bones (the bones are really important!) or 1 chicken or turkey carcass, meat removed, leaving only skin and bones

1 onion, peeled
2 carrots, peeled
2 large ribs celery
2 cloves garlic, peeled
2 bay leaves
Salt

1. For beef or pork Rich Stock: Place the lard into the stockpot and brown fat, trimmings, and bones over medium heat.
2. For chicken or turkey Rich Stock: Place the carcass into the stockpot.
3. For all: Cut the onion, carrots, and celery in half. Place the onion, carrots, celery, garlic, and bay leaves into the pot. Pour enough water in to fill the pot to within 3" of the rim. Cover the pot and bring it to a boil. Lower the heat until it is simmering very slowly, and allow it to cook for about 12 hours.
4. While this is simmering, a lot of foam and debris will come to the top. These are the impurities coming out of the stock. Remove them with a spoon and discard. The end result will be a wonderfully flavored, clear stock!
5. When the stock is a rich, golden color, it can be removed from the heat, salted to taste, and allowed to cool. Alternatively, if a reduced, more intensely flavored stock is desired, remove the lid, increase the heat, and bring the stock back to a slow boil. Continue to boil the stock until it has cooked down to ⅓ to ½ of its original volume. How much you reduce the stock will depend upon how intense you want the flavor of the stock to be. Add salt to taste.
6. Allow the stock to cool thoroughly; then strain it. Pour it into clean ice cube trays and freeze. After the stock has frozen, it can then be placed into freezer containers or zippered freezer bags and stored for several months.
7. To use: Remove as much stock as is needed and thaw for use in recipes requiring broth.

NUTRITIONAL INFORMATION PER SERVING:
Carbohydrates: trace • Effective Carb Count: 0 grams
Protein: trace • Fat: trace • Calories: 0

SEAFOOD COCKTAIL SAUCE

Serves 4

This makes a great dip for fish or chicken!

½ cup French Salad Dressing (page 247)
¾ teaspoon dill weed, dried
1 teaspoon horseradish
½ teaspoon garlic powder
½ teaspoon black pepper

Simply combine all of the ingredients and serve with your favorite seafood. This will keep refrigerated for about 10 days.

NUTRITIONAL INFORMATION PER SERVING:
Carbohydrates: 2 grams • Effective Carb Count: 1 gram
Protein: trace • Fat: 7 grams • Calories: 66

You may be wondering how to know if candida or allergies are an issue in your life. Here are a few questions to start you thinking: Are you often bothered by unexplainable symptoms like fatigue and moodiness? Do you get frequent infections like sinus, bladder, or yeast? Do you have frequent colds or flu symptoms? If you have any of these symptoms, you might consider seeing a qualified naturopathic physician. He or she would be able to provide the most comprehensive care.

Sugar-Free Pancake Syrup

Serves 4

We have to have syrup for our pancakes, don't we? Serve warm over Chubby Pancakes (page 59) or Wonderful Waffles (page 90).

½ teaspoon imitation maple flavoring
8 packets sucralose
½ tablespoon SteviaPlus
1 cup water
2 teaspoons arrowroot powder (or ¼ teaspoon guar gum)
mixed into 2 tablespoons water

Combine the maple flavoring, sucralose, SteviaPlus, and 1 cup water in a small saucepan. Heat until boiling. Pour the arrowroot/water mixture into the boiling syrup. Stir until thickened.

Nutritional information per serving:
Carbohydrates: 1 gram • Effective Carb Count: 0 grams
Protein: trace • Fat: trace • Calories: 6

℮ Arrowroot produces lovely sauces but does require some care. It is very delicate and doesn't like to be stirred too much. Be sure and mix the arrowroot into cold water, not right into the hot liquid. If you mix it into the hot liquid, you will end up with a little gelatin ball! Pour the arrowroot/water mixture into the boiling liquid and stir it until just combined. Remove it from the heat as soon as it thickens, otherwise it will begin to break down quickly.

SWEET AND SOUR SAUCE, LOW-CARBED

Yields about 6 servings

This is a traditional Philippine recipe, now low-carbed. Serve it as a dipping sauce for Egg Rolls (page 15), Barbecue Pork (page 95), or use it as a basting sauce for chicken or pork.

1 tablespoon cider vinegar
¼ teaspoon SteviaPlus
1 packet sucralose
½ teaspoon sea salt
1 tablespoon tomato sauce
¾ cup water
1 tablespoon arrowroot powder mixed into ¼ cup water

Combine the vinegar, SteviaPlus, sucralose, salt, tomato sauce, and water in a small saucepan. Bring to boil over medium heat. Stir in arrowroot/water mixture and boil briefly until thickened.

NUTRITIONAL INFORMATION PER SERVING:
Carbohydrates: 2 grams • Effective Carb Count: 1 gram
Protein: trace • Fat: trace • Calories: 6

Sweet and Zingy
Mustard Sauce

Makes 8 servings

This sauce is a great dip not only for Porcupines (page 132), but also for burgers, hot dogs, pork, chicken, or whatever! It even makes a nice addition to plain ol' chicken or tuna salad with mayo.

2 tablespoons dry mustard
½ teaspoon dried ginger, ground
¼ teaspoon lemon pepper
2 packets sucralose
*⅛ teaspoon chipotle pepper granules, roasted (or ¹⁄₁₆ teaspoon
cayenne if you can't find chipotle)*
1 tablespoon Bragg's Liquid Aminos, or soy sauce
2 tablespoons water

Combine all ingredients in a small dish. Serve as a dipping sauce. Cover and refrigerate any leftovers up to 1 week.

NUTRITIONAL INFORMATION PER SERVING:
Carbohydrates: trace • Effective Carb Count: 0 grams
Protein: trace • Fat: trace • Calories: 6

TARTAR SAUCE I

Makes 6 servings

Most tartar sauces are just a combination of pickles and mayonnaise. If you are treating a candida infection, those are off the list! The recipe came from a need to replace those items. Most folks like it better than the "old" way! Serve with Salmon Patties (page 177), fish, chicken, or pork.

¹⁄₃ cup Blender Mayonnaise (page 241) or
commercially prepared mayonnaise
1 ¹⁄₂ teaspoons minced onion, dried
1 teaspoon lemon juice, fresh
¹⁄₄ teaspoon dill weed
¹⁄₈ teaspoon lemon pepper

Combine all of the ingredients and mix well. Store in a covered container in the refrigerator for up to 2 weeks.

NUTRITIONAL INFORMATION PER SERVING:
Carbohydrates: trace • Effective Carb Count: 0 grams
Protein: trace • Fat: 10 grams • Calories: 89

REDUCED-FAT VARIATION:
Use reduced-fat mayonnaise.
Carbohydrates: 2 grams • Effective Carb Count: 1 gram
Protein: trace • Fat: 3 grams • Calories: 32

Tartar Sauce II

Makes 8 servings

If you don't have Blender Mayonnaise (page 241) and you want to make your own tartar sauce, try this tasty recipe instead.

1 cup sour cream
1 tablespoon minced onion, dried
³/₄ teaspoon dill weed
¹/₄ teaspoon orange zest
¹/₄ teaspoon seasoning salt
¹/₈ teaspoon lemon pepper
2 teaspoons lemon juice, fresh

Combine all of the ingredients in a small bowl and serve with your favorite fish. Store any leftovers covered in the refrigerator up to a week.

Nutritional information per serving:
Carbohydrates: 2 grams • Effective Carb Count: 1 gram
Protein: 1 gram • Fat: 6 grams • Calories: 64

Reduced-Fat Variation:
Use low-fat sour cream.
Carbohydrates: 2 grams • Effective Carb Count: 1 gram
Protein: 1 gram • Fat: 1 gram • Calories: 13

VANILLA SAUCE

Serves 6

This is a terrific simple sauce that is great served with Pumpkin Waffles (page 80) and Cinnamon Butter (page 242)!

1 cup water
¼ teaspoon SteviaPlus
3 packets sucralose
½ tablespoon arrowroot mixed into 2 tablespoons water
3 tablespoons butter
2 teaspoons vanilla

1. Bring the water to a boil in a small saucepan. Sprinkle the SteviaPlus and sucralose over the boiling water and stir until combined. Pour in the arrowroot/water mixture and stir until thickened and fairly clear.
2. Remove from heat and add the butter and vanilla, stirring until the butter melts. Serve warm.

NUTRITIONAL INFORMATION PER SERVING:
Carbohydrates: 1 gram • Effective Carb Count: 0 grams
Protein: trace • Fat: 6 grams • Calories: 57

REDUCED-FAT VARIATION:
Reduce the butter to ½ tablespoon.
Carbohydrates: 1 gram • Effective Carb Count: trace
Protein: trace • Fat: 1 gram • Calories: 15

VANILLA YOGURT

Serves 4

This makes a great sauce for pancakes, waffles, French toast, and the like (low-carb, of course!). It makes a nice dessert or addition to breakfast. You may also pour it over fruit for a fruit salad.

1 pint (2 cups) yogurt, whole milk
2 ½ teaspoons vanilla
¾ teaspoon Sweet & Slender
½ teaspoon SteviaPlus
Cinnamon, optional

In a small bowl, combine the yogurt, vanilla, Sweet & Slender, and SteviaPlus. Mix it well. Garnish the yogurt with cinnamon, if desired.

NUTRITIONAL INFORMATION PER SERVING:
Carbohydrates: 3 grams • Effective Carb Count: 2 grams
Protein: 4 grams • Fat: 4 grams • Calories: 86

REDUCED-FAT VARIATION:
Use nonfat yogurt.
Carbohydrates: 3 grams • Effective Carb Count: 2 grams
Protein: 7 grams • Fat: trace • Calories: 79

What are probiotic dairy products? The common candida treatment diet eliminates all dairy products (including cheese), vinegar, mushrooms, soy sauce, all forms of sugar (including fruit), peanuts, pistachios, and wheat. While it is common to eliminate all dairy on the candida restriction diet, probiotic dairy products could be very beneficial toward the healing process–foods like yogurt, kefir, and the various acidophilus-cultured cheeses, sour creams, and cream cheeses that are on the market.

VERY BERRY RHUBARB SAUCE

Serves 10

This is a terrific sauce served over Homemade Yogurt (page 249) or some low-carb ice cream. It can also be a very yummy side dish and can even be modified as a dessert. If you wish to use this as a stand-alone dessert served with cream or as a topping for cheesecake or pancakes, use 16 packets sucralose instead of 12.

2 pounds rhubarb, frozen or fresh, cut into ½" to 1" lengths
1 cup water
2 cups blueberries, frozen or fresh
1 apple, peeled and diced
1 pear, peeled and diced
1 teaspoon vanilla
1 teaspoon cinnamon
2 teaspoons SteviaPlus
12 packets sucralose

Combine all of the ingredients in a saucepan with a lid. Stir the fruit well and cover the pot. Cook over medium heat 15 to 20 minutes or until the fruit begins to become juicy. Remove the lid and continue cooking until the sauce reaches the thickness you desire.

NUTRITIONAL INFORMATION PER SERVING:
Carbohydrates: 12 grams • Effective Carb Count: 9 grams
Protein: 1 gram • Fat: trace • Calories: 50

Desserts

Aimee's Original French Silk Pie, Low-Carbed

Serves 8

This pie is just incredible! Once you try it, you won't believe it's sugar-free. For a quickie chocolate fix, just make the filling and pour it into muffin tins! The original recipe came from Aimee Nossum. Thank you, Aimee, for letting me use this really wonderful pie in my book!

Crust:

1 cup almonds, ground
½ cup soy protein (not soy flour!)
1 teaspoon SteviaPlus
4 packets sucralose
½ teaspoon cinnamon
6 tablespoons butter, room temperature

Filling:

3 ounces (squares) good-quality
baking chocolate, unsweetened
3 eggs
¾ cup butter, room temperature
1 teaspoon SteviaPlus
8 packets sucralose
1½ teaspoons vanilla

Topping:

1 cup whipping cream
¼ teaspoon SteviaPlus or 1½ packets sucralose
1 bar low-carb chocolate, optional

Recipe continues on page 267 ➤

Recipe continued from page 266

1. CRUST INSTRUCTIONS: Combine the crust ingredients with a pastry blender or food processor and press into a 9" pie pan. Bake it for 5 minutes at 450°F. Cool the crust completely before adding the filling.
2. FILLING INSTRUCTIONS: Break the chocolate into small pieces, and warm it in a small saucepan over the lowest possible heat. Stir it constantly until it is almost completely melted. Remove the pan from the heat and continue to stir the chocolate until it is thoroughly melted. Allow the chocolate to cool completely.
3. Since the eggs won't be cooked, coddle the eggs: Fill a small saucepan about half full with water. Bring the water to boiling; then place the whole eggs into the boiling water for 20 seconds. Remove the eggs from the boiling water, and immerse them in ice-cold water to stop them from cooking any further.
4. In a large mixing bowl with an electric mixer, cream the butter, SteviaPlus, and sucralose on medium speed for about 1 minute. Add the chocolate and vanilla, mixing until combined. Continue mixing, adding the eggs one at a time and beating for 5 minutes each. The total mixing time for the filling will be 15 minutes. Pour the filling into the pie shell. Chill the pie for at least 4 hours to set.
5. TOPPING INSTRUCTIONS: Whip the cream in a small mixing bowl with an electric mixer on medium-high speed until soft peaks form. Add the SteviaPlus to the cream and whip it until it is combined. Spread the topping onto the chilled pie. Sliver the low-carb chocolate bar with a vegetable peeler. Garnish the pie with the chocolate curls. Enjoy!

NUTRITIONAL INFORMATION PER SERVING:
Carbohydrates: 8 grams • Effective Carb Count: 5 grams
Protein: 14 grams • Fat: 49 grams • Calories: 507

If you are allergic to soy, vital wheat gluten may be substituted equally for the soy protein in most of the recipes in this book. Milk and egg protein and whey protein may not be substituted equally for soy protein.

ALMOND NEST COOKIES

Makes 24 cookies

These versatile little cookies can be filled not only with almonds, but also with low-carb jam, sugar-free candies, other nuts, or whatever strikes your fancy!

1³/4 cups almonds, ground
16 packets sucralose
2 teaspoons SteviaPlus
1 teaspoon baking soda
¹/2 cup soy protein (not soy flour!)
¹/2 cup coconut, unsweetened shredded
³/4 cup butter, room temperature
2 eggs
¹/2 tablespoon vanilla
1 teaspoon almond extract

Topping:

¹/2 cup almonds, ground
2 packets sucralose
¹/2 teaspoon SteviaPlus
2 tablespoons coconut, shredded unsweetened

Insert:

24 whole almonds, sugar-free gummi candies, sugar-free jelly beans, sugar-free jam, blueberries, other nuts, sugar-free chocolate chunks, etc.

1. Preheat the oven to 375°F. In a mixing bowl, combine the dry ingredients. Set them aside.
2. In a large mixing bowl with an electric mixer on medium speed, cream the butter, eggs, vanilla, and almond extract for about 1 minute, or until they are well combined. Gradually add the dry ingredients to the butter mixture by ¹/4 cupfuls, being sure the dough is well mixed after each addition.
3. Combine the topping ingredients. Form the dough into 1¹/2" balls and roll each in the topping. Place each rolled ball onto a parchment-lined baking sheet and press one of the inserts onto the top of each cookie. Bake the cookies for about 8 minutes at 375°F. They should still be soft when removed from the oven. Place the cookies on waxed paper or paper toweling to cool.

NUTRITIONAL INFORMATION PER SERVING (WITHOUT INSERTS):
Carbohydrates: 3 grams • Effective Carb Count: 2 grams
Protein: 6 grams • Fat: 14 grams • Calories: 152

Basic Low-Carb Icing

Frosts 3 dozen cookies

Use on cookies, cakes, crackers, and so forth. You can use just about any type of flavoring you desire for different effects. Experiment and have fun!

½ cup milk and egg protein
¼ teaspoon SteviaPlus
6 packets sucralose
¹/₁₆ teaspoon salt (that is ½ of ⅛ teaspoon)
½ teaspoon vanilla
½ cup half-and-half or water

Combine the dry ingredients in a small bowl. Add the vanilla and slowly add the half-and-half or water, depending upon the consistency desired. May be kept covered and refrigerated for up to 10 days.

Nutritional information per serving:
Carbohydrates: trace • Effective Carb Count: 0 grams
Protein: 3 grams • Fat: trace • Calories: 16

Reduced-Fat Variation:
Use canned skim milk (or water) instead of half-and-half.
Carbohydrates: 1 gram • Effective Carb Count: 1 gram
Protein: 3 grams • Fat: trace • Calories: 15

CARROT CAKE

Makes 8 servings

If you love carrot cake, then this low-carb recipe is for you. Try substituting squash if you don't like carrots, the ECC is the same! Frost with Cream Cheese Frosting (page 282), if desired.

1/4 cup soy protein (not soy flour!)
1 teaspoon baking soda
1 teaspoon baking powder
1 teaspoon cinnamon
1/2 teaspoon sea salt
3/4 cup almonds, ground
2 eggs, room temperature
2/3 cup butter, melted
1 teaspoon SteviaPlus
14 packets sucralose
1/2 cup pecans, broken
1 1/2 cups carrots, grated (about 3 whole carrots)
Cooking oil spray
Soy protein (as above)

1. Preheat the oven to 325°F. Sift together the first 5 ingredients in a small bowl. Add the ground almonds.
2. In a mixing bowl, combine the eggs, the melted butter, and the sweeteners and beat with an electric mixer for about 2 minutes on medium speed. Add the dry ingredients to the egg mixture and mix it for another 2 minutes. Add the pecans and carrots to the batter, stirring it well.
3. Spay an 8" round cake pan with cooking oil spray and dust it with soy protein. Pour the batter into the pan and bake it for about 35 to 45 minutes.

NUTRITIONAL INFORMATION PER SERVING:
Carbohydrates: 7 grams • Effective Carb Count: 5 grams
Protein: 9 grams • Fat: 27 grams • Calories: 294

REDUCED-FAT VARIATION:
Use unsweetened applesauce instead of the butter.
Carbohydrates: 9 grams • Effective Carb Count: 6 grams
Protein: 8 grams • Fat: 12 grams • Calories: 167

Do you use dark-colored baking pans? If so, then you will usually need to reduce your baking temperatures for most baked goods by 25°F. The darker color causes foods to brown more quickly. Neither dark nor clear pans are better than the other in terms of results.

Cast of Thousands on
Many Continents Chocolate Cake

Serves 6

Serve this with Chocolate Cream Cheese Frosting (page 275) for a yummy birthday treat! If you want chocolate brownies, instead of separating the egg and beating the whites, use 2 whole eggs and follow all of the remaining instructions.

½ cup almonds, ground
3 tablespoons soy flour
1 ½ tablespoons soy protein
(not soy flour!)
¼ teaspoon cream of tartar
¼ teaspoon baking soda
¼ teaspoon sea salt
¼ teaspoon baking powder

1 egg, separated
1 teaspoon SteviaPlus
4 packets sucralose
⅓ cup butter, room temperature
1 teaspoon vanilla
2 tablespoons cocoa powder
⅓ cup whipping cream

1. Line the bottom of a 9" cake pan with parchment paper, or spray the pan with cooking oil spray. Set it aside.
2. In a small bowl, combine the ground almonds, soy flour, soy protein, cream of tartar, baking soda, salt, and baking powder. Set this aside.
3. In a mixing bowl with an electric mixer on medium speed, beat the egg white until stiff but not dry. Set it aside.
4. In another bowl, with an electric mixer on medium speed, cream the SteviaPlus, sucralose, and butter until they are light and fluffy, about 2 minutes. Add the vanilla, egg yolk, and cocoa powder, beating well after each addition. Gradually add the dry ingredients alternately with the whipping cream, mixing until the batter is smooth after each addition. By hand, fold in the egg white. Pour the batter into the prepared pan.
5. Bake the cake at 350°F for 20 minutes or until a toothpick inserted in the center comes out clean. Allow it to rest for 5 minutes; then invert it onto a rack to cool. When completely cooled, frost with Chocolate Cream Cheese Frosting.

Nutritional information per serving:
Carbohydrates: 4 grams • Effective Carb Count: 3 grams
Protein: 5 grams • Fat: 16 grams • Calories: 167

Reduced-Fat Variation:
Use unsweetened applesauce instead of the butter
and canned skim milk instead of the cream.
Carbohydrates: 6 grams • Effective Carb Count: 5 grams
Protein: 6 grams • Fat: 5 grams • Calories: 88

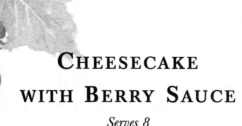

CHEESECAKE
WITH BERRY SAUCE

Serves 8

This is a wonderful treat to share with your sweet–no matter what the occasion! There will most likely be sauce leftover after the cheesecake is gone. It makes a yummy topping for low-carb pancakes or yogurt!

Crust:

1 cup almonds, ground
½ cup soy protein (not soy flour!)
1 teaspoon SteviaPlus
4 packets sucralose
½ teaspoon cinnamon
6 tablespoons butter

Filling:

2 cups (16 ounces) cream cheese, room temperature
1 cup (8 ounces) sour cream, room temperature
½ teaspoon vanilla
8 packets sucralose
1 teaspoon SteviaPlus
2 tablespoons milk and egg protein
¼ teaspoon sea salt
2 eggs plus 1 egg yolk, room temperature
¼ cup heavy cream, room temperature

Sauce:

⅓ cup water
4 cups berries (blueberries, blackberries, strawberries, etc.)
½ teaspoon SteviaPlus
3 packets sucralose
3 tablespoons milk and egg protein
¹⁄₁₆ teaspoon sea salt (that is ½ of ⅛ teaspoon)

Recipe continues on page 273 ➤

➤ Recipe continued from page 272

1. CRUST INSTRUCTIONS: Combine the crust ingredients well with a pastry blender or food processor and press into a 9" or 10" pie pan. Refrigerate the crust while preparing the filling.
2. FILLING AND BAKING INSTRUCTIONS: Preheat the oven to 375°F. In a large mixing bowl with an electric mixer, beat the cream cheese, sour cream, and vanilla on medium-low speed until fluffy, about 2 minutes. It is terribly important to have the filling ingredients at room temperature. A cheesecake is simply something that cannot be rushed!
3. In a small bowl, combine the sucralose, SteviaPlus, milk and egg protein, and salt. Gradually add these dry ingredients into the cheese mixture, beating only until combined.
4. Combine the eggs and the cream in another small bowl and mix them up well with a fork. Add the eggs and cream to the cheese mixture and beat it on low speed until it is just combined.
5. Pour the filling into the chilled pie crust and bake it at 375°F about 20 minutes. The sides should be puffy and the center still slightly jiggly. Leave the cheesecake in the oven and turn the oven off, leaving the door slightly ajar, for about 20 minutes. Remove the cheesecake from the oven and cool it thoroughly on a wire rack, then chill it in the refrigerator for at least 4 hours.
6. About 20 minutes before serving, remove the cheesecake from the refrigerator for easier slicing.
7. TOPPING INSTRUCTIONS: Combine all of the topping ingredients in a medium-sized saucepan over medium heat and cook them until they are thick and bubbling. Continue cooking for 2 minutes longer. Pour the topping into a heat-safe container, cover, and refrigerate it until it is completely cooled. Do not stir the sauce before serving over individual slices of the cheesecake.

NUTRITIONAL INFORMATION PER SERVING (CHEESECAKE):
Carbohydrates: 7 grams • Effective Carb Count: 5 grams
Protein: 21 grams • Fat: 47 grams • Calories: 514

NUTRITIONAL INFORMATION PER SERVING (BERRY SAUCE):
Carbohydrates: 3 grams • Effective Carb Count: 2 grams
Protein: 3 grams • Fat: trace • Calories: 21

CHILLY MINI MOUSSE TREATS

Makes about 15 treats

These are just way too good! As a variation you can use ¼ cup chocolate-flavored sugar-free syrup, plus ¼ cup pourable sucralose and either of the following: ¼ teaspoon coconut extract or ½ teaspoon instant coffee granules instead of the ½ cup sucralose specified.

1 square baking chocolate, unsweetened
(I prefer the brand made in Hershey, Pennsylvania!)
1 cup sour cream
½ tablespoon vanilla
¼ cup milk and egg protein
½ teaspoon SteviaPlus
½ cup pourable sucralose (or 12 packets sucralose)
⅛ teaspoon cinnamon
1/16 teaspoon sea salt (that is ½ of ⅛ teaspoon)

1. Melt the chocolate in a microwave-safe container, about 2 minutes.
2. Using a wire whisk, whip the remaining ingredients into the chocolate. Spoon this mixture into a mini-muffin tin and chill for ½ to 1 hour in the freezer.

NUTRITIONAL INFORMATION PER SERVING:
Carbohydrates: 1 gram • Effective Carb Count: 0 grams
Protein: 4 grams • Fat: 4 grams • Calories: 58

REDUCED-FAT VARIATION:
Use low-fat sour cream instead of regular.
Carbohydrates: 1 gram • Effective Carb Count: 0 grams
Protein: 4 grams • Fat: 1 gram • Calories: 31

℃ Milk and egg protein behaves differently in cooking than soy protein or other nut flours. It is tasteless in small quantities, but it does have a distinctive flavor when used in large quantities. It is not to be confused with other products such as whey protein and soy protein, and must be watched closely for added ingredients, especially sugar. As you cook with these proteins, you'll find that some brands differ greatly in their results. When beginning to use milk and egg protein, try some of the recipes requiring smaller amounts before making recipes that require larger amounts. This will help you determine the measurements of your brand.

CHOCOLATE CREAM CHEESE FROSTING

Serves 8

Both this recipe and the chocolate cake recipe came about at the request of a friend. She wanted something special to serve for her husband's birthday while keeping to a low-carb diet. Spread on Cast of Thousands on Many Continents Chocolate Cake (page 271) or Pleasing Almond Macadamia Dessert (page 298).

1 ½ tablespoons butter, room temperature
6 tablespoons cream cheese
2 ½ tablespoons cocoa powder
¾ teaspoon SteviaPlus
6 packets sucralose
2 ½ tablespoons cream
¾ teaspoon vanilla

In a mixing bowl with an electric mixer on medium speed, cream the butter and cream cheese until they are light and fluffy. Add the cocoa, SteviaPlus, sucralose, cream, and vanilla, mixing well after each addition.

NUTRITIONAL INFORMATION PER SERVING:
Carbohydrates: 1 gram • Effective Carb Count: 0 grams
Protein: 1 gram • Fat: 7 grams • Calories: 73

REDUCED-FAT VARIATION:
Use reduced-fat cream cheese and canned skim milk.
Carbohydrates: 2 grams • Effective Carb Count: 1 gram
Protein: 1 gram • Fat: 4 grams • Calories: 42

FOR PRETTY SERVING PLATES: If you've got a green thumb, edible flowers are a great addition to your garden . . . and your meals! Nasturtium blossoms have a peppery taste rather like radishes, and pansies taste like, well, pansies! Rose petals are also edible, and, of course, they taste like roses. Not only are these edible flowers much safer to have around with small children, but they also make lovely garnishes!

CHOCOLATE PEANUT BUTTER CANDY

Makes 12 candies

If you want candy peanut butter cups, but don't want the unpleasant side effects that malitol can bring, then you will definitely want to try this recipe! *Tip:* If you have excess chocolate leftover, pour it into a paper cup and drop nuts onto it. Chill it until it is firm, and enjoy a nutty chocolate treat! Thank you, Lori Rainey, for all your help with this recipe!

Chocolate coating:

2 squares good-quality baking
chocolate, unsweetened
1 tablespoon butter, unsalted
1 teaspoon SteviaPlus
7 packets sucralose
A few grains of sea salt
(way less than a pinch!)
⅛ teaspoon vanilla
½ tablespoon milk and egg protein

Filling:

½ cup peanut butter, creamy
(try to find one that is just
peanuts and salt)
½ cup milk and egg protein
½ tablespoon SteviaPlus
8 packets sucralose

1. Combine the chocolate and butter in a microwave-safe bowl and microwave on high power for about 1½ minutes, or until the chocolate melts, stirring partway through. Add the remaining coating ingredients and stir them until they are smooth.
2. Combine all of the filling ingredients, mixing well. This mixture will be very stiff. Form it into 12 equal balls.
3. One by one, roll the peanut butter balls in the chocolate with a spoon until they are fully coated. Using 2 forks, lift the candy out of the chocolate, holding it by the tips of the forks and allowing the excess chocolate to drip off. Place the candy onto a plate lined with waxed paper, and chill for 2 hours before serving. Be sure and give out lots of napkins!

NUTRITIONAL INFORMATION PER SERVING:
Carbohydrates: 4 grams • Effective Carb Count: 3 grams
Protein: 12 grams • Fat: 9 grams • Calories: 134

A FEW WORDS ABOUT BAKING CHOCOLATE: Please be careful which brand you purchase. Some brands are considerably inferior in quality, even though they may not be the least expensive. I prefer the brand made in Hershey, Pennsylvania, or you may be able to find the more expensive super-high quality foreign chocolates in your area. Be aware, using inferior quality chocolate will adversely affect the performance of your desserts!

CHOCOLATE PUDDING CAKE

Serves 8

This is a low-carb take on one of my childhood favorites. If you've never had pudding cake before, it is supposed to be a lot more like pudding and a lot less like cake!

Cake batter ingredients:

1 teaspoon SteviaPlus
6 packets sucralose
2/3 cup almonds, ground
1/3 cup soy protein (not soy flour!)
1/4 cup cocoa powder
2 teaspoons baking powder
1/4 teaspoon sea salt
1/2 teaspoon cinnamon
1/2 cup half-and-half
1/3 cup butter, melted
2 teaspoons vanilla

Additional ingredients:

1 1/4 teaspoons SteviaPlus
8 packets sucralose
1/4 cup cocoa powder
1 1/4 cups hot water

1. Preheat the oven to 350°F. Combine all of the dry cake batter ingredients in a mixing bowl. Stir the remaining batter ingredients into the dry ingredients. Beat the batter until it is smooth.
2. Pour the batter into a casserole dish with a rounded bottom, about 8" to 10" across. This is very important! In order for the cake to achieve a "pudding" effect, you must use a casserole dish with a rounded bottom so the pudding can form. Otherwise, you'll just end up with very moist cake!
3. Stir together the additional sweeteners and cocoa powder in a small dish. Sprinkle this evenly over the batter. Carefully pour the hot water over the batter. *Do not stir.*
4. Bake the cake at 350°F for about 35 to 40 minutes, until the center is almost set. Remove the cake from the oven and let it rest for about 15 minutes before serving. Spoon the sauce off the bottom of the pan over the cake when serving. Garnish with cream or whipped cream, if desired.

NUTRITIONAL INFORMATION PER SERVING:
Carbohydrates: 6 grams • Effective Carb Count: 3 grams
Protein: 8 grams • Fat: 16 grams • Calories: 186

REDUCED-FAT VARIATION:
Use canned skim milk instead of half-and-half and
unsweetened applesauce instead of butter.
Carbohydrates: 9 grams • Effective Carb Count: 6 grams
Protein: 9 grams • Fat: 7 grams • Calories: 115

Choco-Peanut Butter Cookies

Makes about 20 cookies

These are very, very yummy! You may be tempted to eat the dough without even baking it!

½ cup peanut butter (without sugar, of course!)
½ cup butter
1 teaspoon SteviaPlus
8 packets sucralose
1 teaspoon vanilla
2 eggs
1 teaspoon baking soda
¾ cup almonds, ground
⅓ cup soy protein (not soy flour!)
3 tablespoons cocoa powder

1. Preheat oven to 375°F. In a mixing bowl with an electric mixer on medium speed, mix peanut butter, butter, SteviaPlus, and sucralose until very creamy, about 2 minutes. Add vanilla and egg; continue to mix for another minute.
2. In a small bowl, combine remaining ingredients. With mixer running, add dry ingredients about ¼ cup at a time, combining thoroughly after each addition.
3. Place a sheet of parchment paper on a baking sheet. Roll dough into balls about the size of small walnuts. Gently press tops with the tines of a fork to flatten. Bake at 375°F for about 6 minutes. Don't overbake. They should still be soft.
4. Place cookies on a piece of waxed paper or cooling rack to cool. Store extras in a tightly covered container lined with a paper towel.

Nutritional information per serving:
Carbohydrates: 3 grams • Effective Carb Count: 2 grams
Protein: 4 grams • Fat: 11 grams • Calories: 117

℘ Should you measure almonds before or after grinding? It is simpler to grind up whole 1-pound bags of almonds at a time with a bit of soy protein powder (about ½ tablespoon for the pound of almonds) and then store them for future uses. There is no need for double measuring!

COCONUT MACAROONS

Makes 20 cookies

These low-carb, candida-friendly Coconut Macaroons sure taste like the real thing! Your family will never know the difference!

1 cup Almond Milk (page 240), unflavored
1 teaspoon SteviaPlus
8 packets sucralose
1 teaspoon vanilla
½ teaspoon almond extract
1/16 teaspoon sea salt (that is ½ of ⅛ teaspoon)
2 egg whites
1 ½ cups coconut, unsweetened shredded

1. Place the Almond Milk into a small saucepan. Cook and stir it over medium-low heat for approximately 40 minutes, until the mixture is very, very thick and reduced to ⅓ cup. Stir in the SteviaPlus, sucralose, vanilla, almond extract, and salt. Put the mixture into the refrigerator for approximately 15 minutes to cool it completely.
2. In a small mixing bowl with an electric mixer on high speed, whip the egg whites until stiff peaks form. Set it aside.
3. In a medium-sized mixing bowl, combine the cooled Almond Milk mixture and coconut, stirring well. Fold in the egg whites. Scoop by teaspoonfuls onto a parchment-lined baking sheet, about 1½" apart. Bake at 350°F for 8 to 10 minutes.

NUTRITIONAL INFORMATION PER SERVING:
Carbohydrates: 2 grams • Effective Carb Count: 1 gram
Protein: 1 gram • Fat: 4 grams • Calories: 42

Coconut Milk Glaze

Makes 8 servings

Serve as a glaze over low-carb muffins, brownies, desserts, crackers, etc. It is also a good dipping sauce for Coconut Chicken (page 197) and Coconut Shrimp (page 164).

3 tablespoons butter, melted
1/2 cup coconut milk (canned)
1/2 tablespoon soy protein
1/2 teaspoon SteviaPlus
2 packets sucralose

Combine all of the ingredients in a small saucepan. Cook the glaze over medium heat until it is quite thick, about 15 minutes.

NUTRITIONAL INFORMATION PER SERVING:
Carbohydrates: 1 gram • Effective Carb Count: 0 grams
Protein: 1 gram • Fat: 8 grams • Calories: 74

Coconut Silk Pie

Serves 8

Do you like coconut cream pie? This recipe is like a delicious cross between French silk and coconut cream. If you are a coconut lover, you are sure to enjoy this!

Filling:

3 eggs
¾ cup butter, room temperature
1 teaspoon SteviaPlus
8 packets sucralose
1½ teaspoons vanilla
½ teaspoon coconut extract (optional)
¾ cup coconut, unsweetened shredded

Crust:

1 cup almonds, ground
½ cup soy protein (not soy flour!)
1 teaspoon SteviaPlus
4 packets sucralose
½ teaspoon cinnamon
6 tablespoons butter, room temperature

Topping:

1 cup whipping cream
¼ teaspoon SteviaPlus or
1½ packets sucralose
1 tablespoon coconut, unsweetened
shredded, for garnish

1. Crust instructions: Combine all of the ingredients well with a pastry blender or food processor and press the crust into a 9" pie pan. Bake it for 5 minutes at 450°F. Cool the crust completely before adding filling.
2. Filling instructions: Since the eggs won't be cooked, coddle them. Fill a small saucepan about half full with water. Bring it to a full boil; then gently place the whole eggs into the boiling water for 20 seconds. Remove the eggs from the boiling water; then immerse them in ice-cold water to stop them from cooking any further.
3. In a large mixing bowl with an electric mixer, cream the butter, SteviaPlus, sucralose, and the extracts on medium speed for about 1 minute. Continue mixing and beat in the eggs one at a time for 5 minutes each. Total mixing time for the filling will be 15 minutes. At the end of the last 5 minutes of mixing, add the unsweetened shredded coconut, and mix until well combined. Pour the filling into the pie shell. Chill the pie for at least 4 hours to set.
4. Topping instructions: Whip the cream in a small mixing bowl with an electric mixer until soft peaks form. Add the SteviaPlus and whip until it is combined. Spread the cream onto the chilled pie. Sprinkle the top of the pie with the final shredded coconut for a pretty garnish. Enjoy!

Nutritional information per serving:
Carbohydrates: 7 grams • Effective Carb Count: 4 grams
Protein: 14 grams • Fat: 49 grams • Calories: 506

CREAM CHEESE FROSTING

Frosts 1 cake, 8 servings

This is great served with Zucchini Nut Bread (page 310) or Carrot Cake (page 270).

6 tablespoons butter
4 ounces cream cheese, softened (½ of an 8-ounce package or ½ cup)
1 teaspoon vanilla
1 ½ teaspoons SteviaPlus
16 packets sucralose
⅛ teaspoon salt
½ cup milk and egg protein
¼ cup water, or as needed

1. In a mixing bowl, cream the butter, cream cheese, vanilla, sweeteners, and salt with an electric mixer on medium speed for about a minute, until well combined.
2. Gradually add the milk and egg protein to the cheese mixture, incorporating completely before adding more. Add water as necessary to make the frosting spreadable, approximately ¼ cup, but it may need more or less. Spread the frosting on a cooled low-carb cake, sweet bread, crackers, or any of the other appropriate yummy desserts from this book!

NUTRITIONAL INFORMATION PER SERVING:
Carbohydrates: 1 gram • Effective Carb Count: 1 gram
Protein: 15 grams • Fat: 19 grams • Calories: 230

REDUCED-FAT VARIATION:
Omit the butter and use low-fat cream cheese.
Carbohydrates: 2 grams • Effective Carb Count: 2 grams
Protein: 15 grams • Fat: 7 grams • Calories: 128

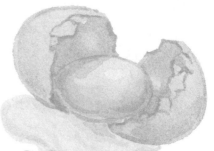

CREAMY DELICIOUS CHEESECAKE

Serves 8

Some occasions just cry for a special dessert. If you are a cheesecake lover, this is the one! This will be one of the best desserts—low- or high-carb—you'll ever have!

Crust:

1 cup almonds, ground
½ cup soy protein (not soy flour!)
1 teaspoon SteviaPlus
4 packets sucralose
½ teaspoon cinnamon
6 tablespoons butter, room temperature

Filling:

2 large eggs, room temperature
¾ pound cream cheese (not the kind of spreadable cream cheese
that comes in a tub), room temperature
½ teaspoon SteviaPlus
5 packets sucralose
½ teaspoon vanilla (not imitation vanilla flavoring)
½ teaspoon sea salt

Topping:

1 ½ cups sour cream
⅛ teaspoon SteviaPlus
3 packets sucralose
½ teaspoon vanilla
⅛ teaspoon sea salt

Recipe continues on page 284 ➤

➤ Recipe continued from page 283

1. Combine the crust ingredients well with a pastry blender or food processor and press into a 9" or 10" pie pan. Refrigerate the crust while preparing the filling.
2. Preheat the oven to 375°F. In a large mixing bowl with an electric mixer, beat the eggs. Add the remaining filling ingredients. Be careful not to overmix the filling! It should be well combined but not overbeaten. An overbeaten filling will create a cheesecake with a poor texture.
3. Mix the filling ingredients until well combined; then gently pour the filling into the chilled crust. Bake at 375°F about 20 minutes. The sides of the cheesecake should be puffed, but the center should still be slightly jiggly. Turn the oven off and open the door, leaving it slightly ajar. Allow the cheesecake to cool in the oven for about 20 minutes.
4. Remove the cheesecake from the oven, and place it on a wire cooling rack until it cools to room temperature. It is very important to allow the cheesecake to cool completely between steps. It is also very important to bring the ingredients to room temperature before beginning to make this wonderful dessert. The texture will be adversely affected if the steps aren't followed properly. I figure, if I am going to go to the trouble of doing this cheesecake, I might as well do it right!
5. When the cheesecake is cool, preheat the oven to 425°F. In a mixing bowl, combine the topping ingredients, and mix well. Pour the topping evenly over the cheesecake. Bake it for 5 minutes. Place it on a wire cooling rack and cool it completely to room temperature.
6. Chill it in the refrigerator 6 to 12 hours before serving. Allow it to stand at room temperature 20 to 30 minutes prior to serving. Store any leftovers covered in the refrigerator.

NUTRITIONAL INFORMATION PER SERVING:
Carbohydrates: 7 grams • Effective Carb Count: 5 grams
Protein: 16 grams • Fat: 42 grams • Calories: 458

FAKE FUDGE

Serves 1

This is the perfect quick and easy recipe when you feel like you need to satisfy that sweet tooth!

2 tablespoons cream cheese
½ tablespoon cream
1 packet sucralose
¼ teaspoon SteviaPlus
½ tablespoon cocoa powder

Place the cream cheese into a small microwave-safe dish and warm for about 20 seconds in the microwave. Add the cream, sucralose, SteviaPlus, and cocoa powder. Mix it well and eat it off of a spoon!

NUTRITIONAL INFORMATION PER SERVING:
Carbohydrates: 2 grams • Effective Carb Count: 1 gram
Protein: 3 grams • Fat: 12 grams • Calories: 126

REDUCED-FAT VARIATION:
Use canned skim milk and reduced-fat cream cheese.
Carbohydrates: 3 grams • Effective Carb Count: 2 grams
Protein: 3 grams • Fat: 4 grams • Calories: 49

Grandma Ruby's Buttermilk Sugar Cookies, a la Low-Carb

Makes 36 cookies

My best friend's mother, Ruby, makes amazing sugar cookies. While I was chatting with Ruby about these cookies, she told me that the original recipe was more than 100 years old when she received it nearly 50 years ago! This is my low-carb tribute to her and her cookies! You may sprinkle these with cinnamon and sucralose for snickerdoodles or with sugar-free candy bits for a fun touch!

3 cups almonds, ground
1 cup soy protein (not soy flour!)
1 teaspoon baking soda
1 teaspoon sea salt
1 teaspoon baking powder
1 cup lard

20 packets sucralose
2 1/4 teaspoons SteviaPlus
2 eggs
3/4 cup buttermilk, kefir, or yogurt
2 teaspoons vanilla

1. Place the ground almonds into a large mixing bowl. Sift together the soy protein with the baking soda, salt, and baking powder. Stir the almonds with the sifted ingredients to combine. Set them aside.
2. Cream the lard and the sweeteners with an electric mixer on medium speed until well combined, about 2 minutes. Add the eggs, buttermilk, and vanilla and continue to mix for about another minute. The mixture will be quite runny with lumps. Mix it until the lumps are all uniform in size.
3. Stir the dry ingredients into the wet ingredients a little bit at a time, combining them well. Cover the bowl with plastic wrap and refrigerate it for at least 2 hours. Roll the dough into 1½" balls and place them on baking sheets. Tap the tops of the cookies to help them flatten while baking.
4. The dough may also be rolled into 10" × 2" logs and wrapped with plastic wrap before chilling, if sliced and decorated cookies are desired. The dough may also be rolled into balls and frozen for up to 3 weeks and used as needed in small batches.
5. Bake the cookies at 350°F for about 8 to 12 minutes, or until slightly browned.

Nutritional information per serving:
Carbohydrates: 2 grams • Effective Carb Count: 1 gram
Protein: 6 grams • Fat: 12 grams • Calories: 135

❧ A NUT-GRINDING TIP: When putting the almonds into the food processor to grind, add a tablespoon or 2 of soy protein isolate before grinding. This allows the almonds to grind finer without turning to butter!

Holiday Caramels

Makes 20 servings

This recipe can be cooked for about half the time, until it is just becoming thick. Add broken pecans to it and you've got Caramel Pecan Sauce. If you like nutty caramels, cook it fully, and at the very last minute add ¼ to ½ cup broken pecans to the caramel.

> *2 cups cream, heavy whipping*
> *1 teaspoon SteviaPlus*
> *8 packets sucralose*
> *2 teaspoons vanilla*

1. Place all of the ingredients into a small saucepan. Cook and stir over medium heat until mixture becomes very thick and ultimately begins to break apart. This process will take approximately 1 hour. Keep cooking until the thick caramel mixture starts breaking up into clumps. If removed from heat before this time, the caramels won't set up.
2. Pour the caramel mixture into an 8" square dish and refrigerate until chilled, about 20 minutes. Cut into 20 squares.

NUTRITIONAL INFORMATION PER SERVING:
Carbohydrates: 1 gram • Effective Carb Count: 1 gram
Protein: 1 gram • Fat: 6 grams • Calories: 60

LEMON CHESS CUSTARD

Serves 8

This is such a simple and tasty dessert. You could try experimenting with different sugar-free syrups for different flavors like caramel or raspberry. Just be sure to reduce the other sweeteners in the recipe.

4 eggs
½ tablespoon SteviaPlus
4 packets sucralose
¾ cup Almond Milk (page 240) or
½ cup cream thinned to ¾ cup with water
¼ cup butter, melted
1 teaspoon lemon zest
2 tablespoons lemon juice, fresh
½ tablespoon arrowroot powder
1 tablespoon almonds, ground (optional)
1 ½ teaspoons vanilla

In a mixing bowl, beat eggs. Add remaining ingredients and mix well. Pour into a small (8" or 9") pie plate that has been sprayed with cooking spray. Place in an oven that has been preheated to 350°F. Bake about 25 minutes or until a knife inserted off center comes out clean. Place on a wire rack to cool.

NUTRITIONAL INFORMATION PER SERVING:
Carbohydrates: 1 gram • Effective Carb Count: 0 grams
Protein: 3 grams • Fat: 8 grams • Calories: 87

There are many different varieties of vanilla extract. They can cost from a few pennies to many dollars. If you're looking for a truly home-baked flavor, it may be worth your while to spend a little extra for *real* vanilla extract, rather than the imitation. You'll thank yourself when you take that first delicious bite!

LUSCIOUS BERRY FROZEN YOGURT

Makes about 8 ½-cup servings

Homemade frozen yogurt is such a wonderful treat! Just add your favorite berries and have a blast! Remember—you'll need an ice cream maker for this recipe.

1 quart whole milk yogurt
2 eggs
½ teaspoon SteviaPlus
6 packets sucralose
½ cup berries (blueberries, raspberries, blackberries, cranberries)
¼ teaspoon cinnamon
¼ teaspoon orange zest
¼ teaspoon almond extract

Combine all of the ingredients in a blender container and process on medium speed until they are well mixed. Pour into an ice cream freezer and follow the manufacturer's instructions.

NUTRITIONAL INFORMATION PER SERVING:
Carbohydrates: 3 grams • Effective Carb Count: 2 grams
Protein: 6 grams • Fat: 5 grams • Calories: 95

REDUCED-FAT VARIATION:
Use fat-free yogurt.
Carbohydrates: 3 grams • Effective Carb Count: 2 grams
Protein: 8 grams • Fat: 1 gram • Calories: 88

℃ A thought about "legal" sweets and treats while low-carbing: It is really best not to have them daily. Overindulgence is what caused many of us to gain the excess weight in the first place! Try to save "legal" desserts and sweets for a once- or twice-a-week treat.

LUSCIOUS LEMON BARS

Makes 9 servings

These Lemon Bars certainly live up to their name. If you like them served warm, use caution, as the crust may fall apart. The crust will set up nicely at room temperature.

Crust:

6 tablespoons butter, room temperature
1/4 teaspoon SteviaPlus
3 packets sucralose
1/4 teaspoon almond extract
1/2 teaspoon guar gum
2 tablespoons soy protein (not soy flour!)
1 tablespoon water
1 cup almonds, ground
Cooking oil spray

Topping:

3 eggs
1 1/2 teaspoons SteviaPlus
5 packets sucralose
3/4 teaspoon guar gum
1/2 teaspoon lemon zest
1/4 cup lemon juice, fresh
1/2 teaspoon baking powder

1. Preheat the oven to 350°F. In a small mixing bowl with an electric mixer, cream the butter, SteviaPlus, and sucralose on medium speed until the butter is light and fluffy, about 1 minute. Add the almond extract, guar gum, soy protein, water, and ground almonds, continuing to mix until it is thoroughly combined.
2. Spray an 8" or 9" baking dish with cooking oil spray. Using your fingers, press the crust into the dish. Bake it at 350°F for 15 minutes, until it is golden brown on top. Allow the crust to rest for 5 minutes. The resting of the crust is terribly important! Once, I skipped this step and the crust exploded when I poured on the topping! I stirred it together and we had "granola bars." They were yummy, but definitely not what I had planned!
3. While the crust is resting, crack the eggs into a clean mixing bowl. Mix well. Add the remaining topping ingredients one at a time by sprinkling each gently over the top of the egg mixture and mixing on low speed after each addition. It is really important to sprinkle the additions so that they are incorporated into the topping mixture individually. When I just dump it all in together, it makes little lumps. It is supposed to be smooth and creamy!
4. Gently pour the topping mixture over the crust and bake it at 350°F for 15 minutes. (*Optional:* You may sprinkle a packet of sucralose over the top of the bars when cooled, for a "sugar-sprinkled" appearance.) Cut into 9 pieces and serve warm from the oven or at room temperature.

NUTRITIONAL INFORMATION PER SERVING:
Carbohydrates: 4 grams • Effective Carb Count: 2 grams
Protein: 7 grams • Fat: 17 grams • Calories: 185

MACADAMIA NUT BUTTER COOKIES

Makes 18

The most fun part of this recipe is forming the balls of dough to make the cookies. Watch out for gooey hands!

½ cup macadamia nut butter
(approximately 5 ounces macadamia nuts, whole)
½ cup butter, room temperature
2 teaspoons SteviaPlus
8 packets sucralose
1 teaspoon vanilla
2 eggs
1 teaspoon baking soda
½ cup soy protein (not soy flour!)
1 cup almonds, ground

1. To make the nut butter: Place the nuts into a food processor with a chopping blade and process until they are creamy, about 2 to 4 minutes. At first, the nuts will form a meal; then the oil will begin to separate out of them. That is when the nut butter is formed.
2. In a small mixing bowl with an electric mixer on medium speed, cream the macadamia nut butter, butter, SteviaPlus, and sucralose for 2 minutes. Add the vanilla and egg, continuing to mix for 1 more minute.
3. In a small bowl, mix the baking soda, soy protein, and ground almonds. On low speed, gradually add the dry ingredients to the butter mixture, until thoroughly combined. The dough will be STICKY!
4. Dust your fingers with soy protein and form the dough into balls about the size of golf balls. Place them 2" apart on a baking sheet (lined with parchment paper, if desired, for easier cleanup), and bake at 375°F for 6 minutes. They should appear underdone. Allow the cookies to rest on the baking sheet for 1 to 2 minutes. Place cookies on a cooling rack to cool.

NUTRITIONAL INFORMATION PER SERVING:
Carbohydrates: 3 grams • Effective Carb Count: 2 grams
Protein: 6 grams • Fat: 15 grams • Calories: 163

MACADAMIA NUT BUTTER SNICKERDOODLES

Makes about 18 cookies

This is a fun, kid-friendly recipe. Be prepared to get messy, and don't be afraid to lick your fingers!

Ingredients:

5 ounces macadamia nuts,
ground to butter, or ½ cup
macadamia nut butter
⅓ cup butter, room temperature
1 teaspoon vanilla extract
2 eggs
3 tablespoons soy protein powder
1 ⅓ cups almonds, ground
1 teaspoon SteviaPlus
8 packets sucralose
1 teaspoon baking soda
⅛ teaspoon sea salt

Topping:

½ cup almonds, ground
2 packets sucralose
½ teaspoon SteviaPlus
½ teaspoon cinnamon

1. To make the macadamia nut butter, simply place the nuts into the hopper of a food processor. Process on high speed until the oil separates out of the ground nuts. It will become very sticky and usually will form into a ball.
2. In a mixing bowl with an electric mixer on medium speed, beat the macadamia nut butter and the butter for 2 minutes. Add the vanilla extract and the eggs and continue to beat the batter for 1 minute longer.
3. In a small bowl, combine the dry ingredients. Add this to the cookie batter by scant ¼ cups while mixing on low speed. Mix the dry ingredients thoroughly into the batter between each addition.
4. In another small bowl, combine the topping ingredients. Using a soup spoon scoop up the batter and drop it into the topping. Roll each cookie around in the topping so that it is thoroughly coated. Pick up the coated ball of dough, and roll it around in your hands until it forms a ball.
5. You may use parchment paper to line your baking pans for little or no cleanup after baking! Place the cookie on a cookie sheet, and tap the top of it so that it is slightly flattened. Repeat for remaining cookies. Place them approximately 2" apart and bake them for about 10 minutes at 350°F or until they are lightly browned.

NUTRITIONAL INFORMATION PER SERVING:
Carbohydrates: 4 grams • Effective Carb Count: 2 grams
Protein: 6 grams • Fat: 17 grams • Calories: 176

MELT IN YOUR MOUTH MOUSSE

2 servings

This is one simple recipe that should be a part of every low-carber's arsenal of "I'm dying for something sweet *right now!*" recipes. Quick to fix and extremely satisfying!

1 cup whipping cream
1 packet sucralose
¼ teaspoon SteviaPlus

Flavoring:

1 tablespoon cocoa powder, unsweetened, plus ½ teaspoon vanilla, or
1 tablespoon cocoa powder, unsweetened, plus ¼ teaspoon cinnamon, or
1 teaspoon imitation maple flavoring, or
1 tablespoon lemon juice (fresh is always best!), or
1½ teaspoons vanilla (garnish with cinnamon, optional)

Pour the cream into a mixing bowl and whip it with an electric mixer on high until soft peaks begin to form. Add the sucralose, SteviaPlus, and one of the flavorings. Mix until combined. Be sure that the mixing bowl and beaters are at least room temperature. If they are hot from washing, or it is a hot day, put them into the refrigerator for a few minutes to chill. The cream will turn out lighter and fluffier that way. Also, be careful not to overwhip. You don't want sweetened butter!

NUTRITIONAL INFORMATION PER SERVING:
Carbohydrates: 2 grams • Effective Carb Count: 2 grams
Protein: 1 gram • Fat: 15 grams • Calories: 146

If you don't have time to coddle your eggs or your burners are full, another way to be sure your eggs are bacteria-free is to immerse them into about 1 cup of water and ½ teaspoon vinegar. Just be sure to rinse the eggs before cracking them. You don't want vinegar water in your sauce!

MERINGUE KISSES

Makes about 30 Kisses

If you are doing a lower fat low-carb program, desserts can be a problem. With this delicious recipe, you will never even remember that you are watching your fat intake.

½ teaspoon SteviaPlus
4 packets sucralose
2 teaspoons cinnamon
¼ teaspoon nutmeg
3 egg whites
¼ teaspoon cream of tartar
¾ cup walnuts or pecans, broken into ½" pieces

1. Preheat the oven to 250°F. Place a piece of parchment paper onto a baking sheet, or spray the baking sheet with cooking oil spray. Set it aside.
2. In a small bowl, combine the SteviaPlus, sucralose, cinnamon, and nutmeg. Set aside. In a medium-sized bowl with an electric mixer on medium-high speed, beat the egg whites with the cream of tartar until soft peaks form. Gradually beat in the cinnamon mixture until stiff peaks form. Fold in the nuts by hand.
3. Drop by teaspoonfuls, about 1" apart, onto prepared baking sheets. Bake them for 35 to 40 minutes or until dry. Do *not* bake any longer than suggested. They will not look "done" because they are baked at such a low temperature. Remove from baking sheets and cool completely on a wire rack. Store covered.

NUTRITIONAL INFORMATION PER SERVING:
Carbohydrates: 1 gram • Effective Carb Count: 0 grams
Protein: 1 gram • Fat: 2 grams • Calories: 21

MMM COOKIES

Makes 9 cookies

This recipe is a low-carb twist on the standard Toll House cookie recipe. It is great with any sort of nuts or treats you would like to add to it!

1 ½ cups almonds, ground
⅔ cup soy protein (not soy flour!)
½ teaspoon baking soda
½ teaspoon baking powder
2 teaspoons SteviaPlus
12 packets sucralose
⅔ cup butter
2 eggs
2 teaspoons vanilla
1 cup total additions

Additions:

Sugar-free chocolate chips, broken walnut or
pecan pieces, macadamia halves, hazelnuts, etc.

1. In a small bowl, combine the ground almonds, soy protein, baking soda, baking powder, SteviaPlus, and sucralose. Set aside.
2. In a small bowl with an electric mixer, cream the butter on medium speed for 2 minutes. Add the egg and vanilla; turn the speed to low and cream for 1 minute.
3. Gradually add in dry ingredients by tablespoonfuls until combined. Stir in the additions by hand. Line a baking sheet with parchment paper. Form the dough into balls about the size of golf balls and place them approximately 2" apart onto the parchment. Tap the tops of the cookies so that they will spread out, otherwise they will end up looking like little mountains! Bake at 375°F for 7 minutes. They should look slightly underdone. Allow the cookies to rest on the baking sheet 1 minute; then put them on a cooling rack or paper towels to cool.

NUTRITIONAL INFORMATION PER SERVING (EXCLUDING ADDITIONS):
Carbohydrates: 2 grams • Effective Carb Count: 1 gram
Protein: 7 grams • Fat: 13 grams • Calories: 149

OOEY GOOEY KIDS' STUFF
(A LICK-THE-SPOON TREAT)

Serves 2 adults or 3 kids and 1 mommy!

This is one of those super-easy, super-yummy treats that your kids will come begging for all the time!

> 2 tablespoons almond butter
> 2 tablespoons cream cheese
> ½ teaspoon Sweet & Slender
> ¼ teaspoon SteviaPlus
> ½ teaspoon vanilla extract
> ¼ teaspoon cinnamon

Combine all of the ingredients in a small, microwave-safe dish. Place the dish into the microwave, and microwave on high power for about 20 seconds to soften. Mix well and eat off a spoon.

NUTRITIONAL INFORMATION PER SERVING:
Carbohydrates: 5 grams • Effective Carb Count: 4 grams
Protein: 3 grams • Fat: 14 grams • Calories: 157

REDUCED-FAT VARIATION:
Use low-fat cream cheese.
Carbohydrates: 5 grams • Effective Carb Count: 1 gram
Protein: 3 grams • Fat: 11 grams • Calories: 125

PEANUT BUTTER FINGERS

Makes 15 servings

This delightful recipe was developed by Lori Rainey. Thank you so much for sharing this yummy treat! *Note:* If you wish to avoid using products with malitol, then the coating from Chocolate Peanut Butter Candy (page 276) may be used instead of the sugar-free chocolate chips listed.

Base ingredients:

½ cup butter
12 packets sucralose
½ teaspoon SteviaPlus
½ cup peanut butter
2 eggs
½ teaspoon vanilla
¼ teaspoon baking soda
¼ teaspoon baking powder
¼ teaspoon salt
2 cups almonds, ground
2 tablespoons soy protein powder
Cooking oil spray

Filling:

¾ cup sugar-free chocolate chips
(or equivalent amount of chopped low-carb chocolate bars)

Topping ingredients:

⅓ cup peanut butter
6 packets sucralose
¼ teaspoon SteviaPlus
2 tablespoons cream
2 tablespoons water

1. In a mixing bowl with an electric mixer on medium speed, cream the first 4 ingredients for 2 minutes. Add the eggs and vanilla and mix them well.
2. Mix the dry ingredients in a separate bowl. Slowly add the dry ingredients to the butter mixture, until they are well blended.
3. Spread the base into a 9" × 13" pan that has been sprayed with cooking oil spray. Bake it at 350°F for 12 minutes or until light golden brown. Please do not overbake this! Underbaking is preferable to overbaking.
4. Immediately after removing the base from the oven, sprinkle it with the sugar-free chocolate chips. Cover the pan and allow the chocolate to soften. Carefully spread the softened chocolate over the surface with the back of a spoon. Allow it to cool to room temperature.
5. In a small mixing bowl, combine the topping ingredients until they are well mixed. Spread the cooled top with the topping. Cut into 15 bars.

NUTRITIONAL INFORMATION PER SERVING:
Carbohydrates: 7 grams • Effective Carb Count: 5 grams
Protein: 10 grams • Fat: 27 grams • Calories: 309

Pleasing
Almond Macadamia Dessert
Makes 9 servings

You can use any flavor sugar-free syrup you like for the cake. Raspberry, caramel, cinnamon . . . use your imagination! If you grind the macadamia nuts to nut butter, then the result will be like a brownie in texture. Add sugar-free chocolate syrup for the flavoring and you've got delicious, homemade, sugar-free chocolate brownies!

1 cup almonds, ground
1/2 cup macadamia nuts, ground
3/4 teaspoon SteviaPlus
1/3 cup sugar-free flavored specialty syrup
3/4 cup Almond Milk (page 240) or 1/2 cup heavy cream
thinned with water to make 3/4 cup
1/3 cup butter, room temperature
2 eggs
2 teaspoons baking powder
Cooking oil spray

1. Place all of the ingredients, except cooking oil spray, into a mixing bowl. On the lowest speed of a mixer, blend all ingredients until thoroughly combined. Turn the speed to medium, and beat the batter for 2 minutes, scraping the bowl often. It should become light and fluffy.
2. Spray a 9" square cake pan with cooking oil spray. Pour the batter into the pan. Bake at 375°F for 20 to 25 minutes, or until the dessert tests clean with a toothpick. Be careful not to open the oven too soon or it will fall! Place the dessert on a wire rack to cool. Serve it plain, sprinkled with a packet of sucralose, or spread with Chocolate Cream Cheese Frosting (page 275).

Nutritional information per serving:
Carbohydrates: 4 grams • Effective Carb Count: 2 grams
Protein: 6 grams • Fat: 21 grams • Calories: 213

Reduced-Fat Variation:
Use unsweetened applesauce instead of the butter.
Carbohydrates: 5 grams • Effective Carb Count: 3 grams
Protein: 6 grams • Fat: 14 grams • Calories: 156

Pumpkin Cheesecake

Serves 8

Pumpkin is a great low-carb veggie and makes a very special addition to this fine dessert. Great for the holidays!

Cooking oil spray

Filling:

2 8-ounce packages cream cheese,
softened
¼ teaspoon SteviaPlus
2 packets sucralose
3 eggs
1 15-ounce can pumpkin purée
1 teaspoon ginger
¼ teaspoon nutmeg (or use
1 ¼ teaspoons pumpkin pie spice
instead of using ginger and nutmeg)

Topping:

2 cups sour cream
¼ teaspoon SteviaPlus
2 packets sucralose
1 teaspoon vanilla

1. Preheat the oven to 350°F. Coat the bottom of a 10" pie plate with pan spray. Set it aside.
2. In a mixing bowl with an electric mixer, cream the cream cheese, SteviaPlus, and sucralose. Add the eggs and mix them lightly. Add the pumpkin, ginger, and nutmeg, mixing well. Be careful not to overmix! Spoon the filling into the pie plate.
3. Bake it for 50 minutes, or until a knife inserted off center comes out clean. Place the pan onto a cooling rack. Cool the cheesecake completely; then heat the oven to 400°F.
4. For the topping, thoroughly combine the sour cream, SteviaPlus, sucralose, and vanilla and spread over the top of the cheesecake. Bake it for 8 minutes longer. Cool to room temperature on a wire rack.
5. Chill the cheesecake, covered, for 4 hours or overnight. Allow it to stand at room temperature for 20 to 30 minutes before serving.

Nutritional information per serving:
Carbohydrates: 9 grams • Effective Carb Count: 7 grams
Protein: 9 grams • Fat: 34 grams • Calories: 366

Reduced-Fat Variation:
Use reduced-fat cream cheese and reduced-fat sour cream.
Carbohydrates: 9 grams • Effective Carb Count: 7 grams
Protein: 9 grams • Fat: 16 grams • Calories: 213

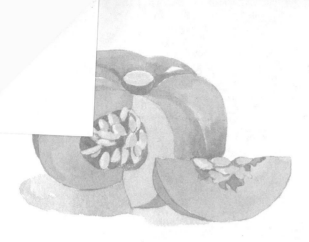

PUMPKIN PIE PUDDING

Makes 8 servings

This is a mildly flavored pumpkin dessert. Think of it like pumpkin pie without the crust!

1 29-ounce can pumpkin purée
³/₄ teaspoon SteviaPlus
6 packets sucralose
2 teaspoons pumpkin pie spice (or 1 teaspoon cinnamon,
¹/₂ teaspoon ginger, ¹/₂ teaspoon nutmeg)
¹/₂ teaspoon sea salt
3 eggs
1 cup Almond Milk (page 240), 1 cup cream, or
1 14-ounce can of coconut milk
Cooking oil spray

1. In a mixing bowl, combine the pumpkin, SteviaPlus, sucralose, pumpkin pie spice, and salt. Add the eggs and beat lightly. Add the Almond Milk, and mix well.
2. Pour the pumpkin mixture into a 9" pie plate that has been sprayed with cooking oil spray, and bake it for 45 minutes at 375°F, or until a knife inserted off center comes out clean. Serve the pudding warm with Almond Milk or cream poured over the top.

NUTRITIONAL INFORMATION PER SERVING:
Carbohydrates: 9 grams • Effective Carb Count: 6 grams
Protein: 3 grams • Fat: 2 grams • Calories: 61

PUMPKIN SWIRL CHEESECAKE

Serves 8

Do you like pumpkin pie? Do you like cheesecake? Do you ever have trouble deciding between the two? Now you don't have to decide! This is an absolutely wonderful treat for the holidays!

Crust:

1 cup raw almonds, ground
½ cup soy protein (not soy flour!)
1 teaspoon SteviaPlus
4 packets sucralose
½ teaspoon cinnamon
6 tablespoons butter, room temperature

Filling, part 1:

2 large eggs, room temperature
¾ pound cream cheese (not the kind of spreadable
cream cheese that comes in a tub!), room temperature
½ teaspoon SteviaPlus
5 packets sucralose
½ teaspoon vanilla
½ teaspoon sea salt

Filling, part 2:

1 15-ounce can pumpkin purée
½ teaspoon SteviaPlus
3 packets sucralose
½ teaspoon cinnamon
¼ teaspoon ginger
¼ teaspoon nutmeg
¼ teaspoon sea salt
2 eggs
1 cup half-and-half or cream

Recipe continues on page 302 ➤

➤ Recipe continued from page 301

1. CRUST INSTRUCTIONS: Combine the crust ingredients well with a pastry blender or food processor and press the crust into a 9" pie pan. Place it into the refrigerator to chill while mixing the filling ingredients.
2. FILLING, PART 1, MIXING INSTRUCTIONS: Preheat the oven to 375°F. In a large mixing bowl with an electric mixer on medium-low speed, beat the eggs.
3. Add the remaining filling ingredients. Be careful not to overmix the filling! It should be well combined but not overbeaten. An overbeaten filling will create a cheesecake with a poor texture. Mix the remaining filling ingredients, part 1, on medium speed until well combined. Set them aside.
4. FILLING, PART 2, MIXING INSTRUCTIONS: In a mixing bowl, combine the pumpkin, SteviaPlus, sucralose, spices, and salt. Add the eggs and beat lightly. Add the half-and-half, and mix well. Set it aside.
5. Gently pour half of the filling, part 1 (cheesecake), into the chilled crust. Carefully pour the filling, part 2 (pumpkin), onto the cheesecake layer. Finish with a layer of filling, part 1 (cheesecake), for a total of 3 layers. With a knife, carefully swirl the filling from the center going outward to the crust edge.
6. Bake at 375°F about 30 to 35 minutes. The sides of the cheesecake should be puffed, but the center should still be slightly jiggly. Turn off the oven and open the door, leaving it slightly ajar. Allow the cheesecake to cool in the oven for about 20 minutes.
7. Remove the cheesecake from the oven, and place it on a wire cooling rack until it cools to room temperature. It is very important to allow the cheesecake to cool completely. It is also very important to bring the ingredients to room temperature before beginning to make this wonderful dessert. The texture will be adversely affected if the steps aren't followed properly. I figure, if I am going to go to the trouble of doing this cheesecake, I might as well do it right!
8. Chill it in the refrigerator 6 to 12 hours before serving. Allow it to stand at room temperature 20 to 30 minutes prior to serving. Store any leftovers, covered, in the refrigerator.

NUTRITIONAL INFORMATION PER SERVING:
Carbohydrates: 11 grams • Effective Carb Count: 8 grams
Protein: 18 grams • Fat: 38 grams • Calories: 440

℃ Why haven't reduced-fat variations been provided for some of the more decadent desserts in this book? That is precisely the reason. They are decadent! When the fat is reduced in some of the more decadent recipes, they just aren't as satisfying. After all, if you are going to splurge and make a cheesecake, it needs to be a really amazing thing, not just some reduced-fat imitation! It is a splurge and should be thought of as such.

QUICK AND EASY RED PIE

Serves 8

Well, it doesn't have to be red! It could be red, green, blue, purple, or whatever color gelatin dessert you choose!

Crust ingredients:

3/4 cup almonds, ground
1/3 cup soy protein isolate
3/4 teaspoon SteviaPlus
3 packets sucralose
1/4 cup butter

Filling ingredients:

1 8-ounce package cream cheese, softened
1/4 cup sour cream
1/2 teaspoon SteviaPlus or 2 packets sucralose
0.3- to 0.44-ounce packet sugar-free gelatin dessert (4-serving size)
1/2 cup water, boiling

1. Combine the crust ingredients in a food processor, or by hand, and mix them until they are uniform. Press the crust into a small pie pan, approximately 7" across. Bake the crust at 400°F for about 8 minutes, or until it is beginning to brown. Remove it from the oven and place it on a cooling rack.
2. Meanwhile, in a small mixing bowl with an electric mixer on medium speed, combine the cream cheese, sour cream, and SteviaPlus until it is smooth. Dissolve the gelatin in the water and add it to the cream cheese mixture. Mix it on low speed until it is well mixed. Pour it at once into the pie crust. The crust does not need to be cooled before pouring the gelatin mixture into it.
3. Depending upon how soon you need the dessert, you may either put it into the freezer for about 30 minutes or refrigerate it for about 1 hour or so, until it is set and chilled. Remove the pie from the refrigerator or freezer about 5 minutes before serving, so that it is easier to dish up.

NUTRITIONAL INFORMATION PER SERVING:
Carbohydrates: 4 grams • Effective Carb Count: 3 grams
Protein: 10 grams • Fat: 24 grams • Calories: 258

REDUCED-FAT VARIATION:
Use reduced-fat cream cheese and low-fat sour cream.
Carbohydrates: 4 grams • Effective Carb Count: 3 grams
Protein: 11 grams • Fat: 19 grams • Calories: 220

Is soy protein different from soy flour? The difference is like night and day! Soy flour is whole ground soy beans–it has a gritty texture and a very strong flavor. Although folks keep assuring me that the taste cooks out of foods prepared with soy flour, that is not my experience! Soy protein, also referred to by some as "soy protein powder" or "soy protein isolate," is a pure protein powder. It is almost tasteless and is finely textured like wheat flour. It adds almost no carbs to recipes. Soy powder is yet another item. It is cooked dried soy beans. You will find *soy protein* used throughout this book.

RHUBARB CRUMBLE

Serves 6

Summer and rhubarb just go together! If you would like Strawberry Rhubarb Crumble: After pouring the rhubarb filling into the pan, add ¾ cup sliced fresh strawberries. Continue as directed.

Filling:

4 cups rhubarb
½ tablespoon Sweet & Slender
1 tablespoon SteviaPlus
¼ teaspoon orange zest
½ teaspoon cinnamon
2 tablespoons water
Cooking oil spray

Topping:

½ cup almonds, ground
3 tablespoons soy flour (not soy protein!)
1 tablespoon flax seeds (not ground)
⅓ cup soy protein powder (not soy flour!)
⅓ cup almonds, slivered
1 teaspoon SteviaPlus
1 teaspoon Sweet & Slender
¼ teaspoon sea salt
4 tablespoons butter, melted
½ teaspoon almond extract
1 teaspoon vanilla

1. Place all of the filling ingredients (except the cooking oil spray) into a medium-sized saucepan with a lid over medium heat. Cook covered, stirring occasionally, for about 10 minutes, or until the rhubarb is softened. Spray an 8" square baking pan with cooking oil spray, and pour the filling into the pan. Set it aside.
2. Place all of the topping ingredients into a small bowl and combine thoroughly. Sprinkle the topping over the fruit mixture in the baking pan. Bake the crumble at 350°F for about 25 minutes, or until the topping is golden. Serve warm or cold.

NUTRITIONAL INFORMATION PER SERVING:
Carbohydrates: 10 grams • Effective Carb Count: 6 grams
Protein: 12 grams • Fat: 19 grams • Calories: 250

SILKY CHOCO-PEANUT BUTTER PIE

Serves 8

Some things are just so yummy that it is hard to believe they are "diet" food!

Crust:

1 cup almonds, ground
1/2 cup soy protein (not soy flour!)
1 teaspoon SteviaPlus
4 packets sucralose
1/2 teaspoon cinnamon
6 tablespoons butter,
room temperature

Filling:

3 eggs
1/2 cup peanut butter, creamy
3/4 cup butter, room temperature
1 teaspoon SteviaPlus
8 packets sucralose
3 tablespoons cocoa powder, unsweetened
1 1/2 teaspoons vanilla

Topping:

1 cup whipping cream
1/4 teaspoon SteviaPlus or
1 1/2 packets sucralose
Cinnamon

1. Crust instructions: Combine all of the ingredients well with a pastry blender or food processor and press the crust into a 9" pie pan. Bake it for 5 minutes at 450°F. Cool the crust completely before adding filling.
2. Filling instructions: Since the eggs won't be cooked, coddle them. Fill a small saucepan about half full with water. Bring it to a full boil; then gently place the whole eggs into the boiling water for 20 seconds. Remove the eggs from the boiling water; then immerse them in ice-cold water to stop them from cooking any further.
3. In a large mixing bowl with an electric mixer, cream the peanut butter, butter, SteviaPlus, and sucralose on medium speed for about 1 minute. Add the cocoa powder and vanilla, mixing until combined. Continue mixing and beat in the eggs one at a time for 5 minutes each. Total mixing time for the filling will be 15 minutes. Pour the filling into the pie shell. Chill the pie for at least 4 hours to set.
4. Topping instructions: Whip the cream in a small mixing bowl with an electric mixer until soft peaks form. Add the SteviaPlus and whip until it is combined. Spread the cream onto the chilled pie. Sprinkle the top of the pie with a dusting of cinnamon. Enjoy!

NUTRITIONAL INFORMATION PER SERVING:

Carbohydrates: 9 grams • Effective Carb Count: 3 grams
Protein: 18 grams • Fat: 52 grams • Calories: 552

SOFT GINGER COOKIES

Makes about 38 cookies

Have you ever smelled fresh ginger cookies baking? Although these don't have the carbs and sugar of their high-carb cousins, they have that terrific aroma! And better yet, they taste as good as they smell! Be sure to freeze the extras so they don't go bad or get eaten all in one sitting!

1 ³/₄ cups almonds, ground
¹/₄ cup soy protein (not soy flour!)
¹/₄ cup milk and egg
protein (or soy protein)
1 teaspoon SteviaPlus
14 packets sucralose
1 tablespoon ground ginger
³/₄ teaspoon cinnamon
¹/₂ teaspoon ground cloves
¹/₂ teaspoon sea salt
1 teaspoon baking soda
1 teaspoon baking powder
¹/₂ cup butter, room temperature
2 tablespoons sour cream
¹/₄ cup pumpkin purée
2 eggs
2 teaspoons vanilla

Topping:

¹/₂ cup almonds, finely ground
¹/₄ teaspoon SteviaPlus
2 packets sucralose

1. In a large mixing bowl, combine all of the dry ingredients and set them aside.
2. In another large mixing bowl with an electric mixer on medium speed, cream the butter, sour cream, and pumpkin for about 2 minutes, until they are well combined. Add the eggs and vanilla, mixing for about another minute, until they are well combined. Gradually add the dry ingredients into the wet ingredients, mixing thoroughly after each addition.
3. Combine the topping ingredients in a small bowl and set aside.
4. Drop the dough by teaspoonfuls into the topping and roll. Place the coated balls of dough about 2" apart on parchment-lined cookie sheets. Lightly tap the tops of the cookies to flatten them.
5. Bake the cookies at 350°F about 8 minutes. The cookies will be quite soft. Allow them to rest on the baking sheet for about 1 minute before transferring them to waxed paper or paper toweling to cool.

NUTRITIONAL INFORMATION PER SERVING:
Carbohydrates: 2 grams • Effective Carb Count: 1 gram
Protein: 4 grams • Fat: 7 grams • Calories: 82

Strawberries, Peaches 'N' Cream

Serves 18

This is a truly decadent dessert. No one will even know it is sugar-free! You can use blueberries and create a festive Independence Day treat. Thank you, Lori Rainey, for sharing this superb recipe!

Crust:

2 cups raw almonds
1 cup soy protein (not soy flour!)
2 teaspoons SteviaPlus
8 packets sucralose
1 teaspoon cinnamon
³/₄ cup butter, room temperature

Filling:

2 eggs
³/₄ cup butter, room temperature
1 teaspoon SteviaPlus
8 packets sucralose
1 ½ teaspoons vanilla
1 ½ cups coconut, unsweetened shredded

Topping:

2 medium peaches
1 pound strawberries, fresh (1 pint)
2 cups whipping cream
¹/₄ teaspoon SteviaPlus
1 packet sucralose

1. Crust instructions: Finely chop the almonds in a food processor. Add the remaining crust ingredients and mix completely. Press the crust into a 9" × 13" × 2" pan, pressing the crust up the sides of the pan as you go. Bake it for about 7 minutes at 450°F. Cool the crust completely before filling it.
2. Filling instructions: Since the eggs won't be cooked, coddle them. Fill a small saucepan about half full with water. Bring the water to boiling; then place the whole eggs into the boiling water for 20 seconds. Remove the eggs from the boiling water, and immerse them in ice-cold water to stop them from cooking any further. Set them aside.
3. In a mixing bowl with an electric mixer on medium speed, cream the butter and sweeteners for about 1 minute. Add the vanilla and mix. Add the eggs one at a time, beating for 5 minutes each, for a total mixing time of 10 minutes. Turn the mixer to low speed and gradually add in the coconut. Spread the filling onto the cooled crust and chill for at least 30 minutes.
4. Just before serving time, slice the peaches. Place them onto the filling in a single layer, avoiding overlapping. Repeat with the strawberries.
5. Using a mixer on medium-high speed, whip the cream with the remaining sweeteners until soft peaks are formed. Spread the cream over the strawberries.

Nutritional information per serving:
Carbohydrates: 9 grams • Effective Carb Count: 6 grams
Protein: 11 grams • Fat: 34 grams • Calories: 374

ULTIMATE PUMPKIN PIE

Makes 2 8-serving pies

Serve this terrific pie at your next holiday meal. It is sure to be a hit! The recipe makes enough filling for 2 pies. You will need to make a second crust when ready to use the extra filling.

Crust:

1 cup almonds, ground
½ cup soy protein (not soy flour!)
1 teaspoon SteviaPlus
4 packets sucralose
6 tablespoons butter

Filling:

4 eggs
½ tablespoon SteviaPlus
6 packets sucralose
1 teaspoon sea salt
2 teaspoons cinnamon
1 teaspoon ginger
½ teaspoon ground cloves (or instead
of using cinnamon, ginger, and ground
cloves, use 3½ teaspoons pumpkin pie
spice—but using the individual spices
really makes a difference!)
1 29-ounce can pumpkin purée
3 cups Almond Milk (page 240) or
2 cups cream thinned
with water to 3 cups

1. Crust instructions: Combine the crust ingredients well with a pastry blender or food processor and press the crust into a 9" pie pan. Place it into the refrigerator to chill while mixing the filling ingredients.
2. Preheat the oven to 425°F. Put the filling ingredients into a mixing bowl, putting the eggs together on one side of the bowl. Using an electric mixer, mix the eggs first, then gradually incorporate them into the whole mixture. Mix until the filling is smooth.
3. Pour half of the filling into the pie shell, and reserve the remaining filling for later use. The extra filling may be kept refrigerated for up to 3 days or frozen in a freezer container. When ready to use, simply thaw and follow crust and baking instructions.
4. Bake the pie at 425°F for 15 minutes. Lower the heat to 350°F for about 25 minutes. A knife inserted off center should come out clean when the pie is done. Serve the pie warm with a dollop of whipped cream or Almond Milk poured over the top.

NUTRITIONAL INFORMATION PER SERVING:
Carbohydrates: 8 grams • Effective Carb Count: 5 grams
Protein: 12 grams • Fat: 18 grams • Calories: 235

YUMMY CHOCOLATE BALLS

Makes about 16 candies

This is another recipe that is great to get the kids involved in. These fun little candies are not only delicious, but they will keep for several days well covered in the refrigerator.

Candy:

1 8-ounce package cream cheese, softened
2 1/2 tablespoons cocoa powder, unsweetened
1/4 teaspoon cinnamon
1/16 teaspoon sea salt (that is 1/2 of 1/8 teaspoon!)
1 teaspoon vanilla
1 teaspoon SteviaPlus
4 packets sucralose
1 tablespoon milk and egg protein

Topping:

2/3 cup almonds, ground
1/2 teaspoon SteviaPlus
2 packets sucralose
1/4 teaspoon cinnamon

1. Combine all of the candy ingredients in a mixing bowl. Mix well on medium-low speed with an electric mixer until smooth. If you can get some kids to help you, this project is even more fun!
2. Combine the topping ingredients in a small dish. Distribute 1 sheet of waxed paper to each helper. Place approximately 1 tablespoon topping onto each piece of waxed paper. Drop the candy 1 teaspoonful at a time onto the paper. Using the palm of your hand, pat the candy into a ball while rolling it in the topping. Coat the candy evenly with the topping.
3. Prepare a serving platter by sprinkling about 1 tablespoon of topping onto it. As the candies are finished, place them onto the serving dish. Chill them until they are ready to be served.

NUTRITIONAL INFORMATION PER SERVING:
Carbohydrates: 2 grams • Effective Carb Count: 1 gram
Protein: 4 grams • Fat: 8 grams • Calories: 89

REDUCED-FAT VARIATION:
Use low-fat cream cheese instead of regular.
Carbohydrates: 2 grams • Effective Carb Count: 1 gram
Protein: 3 grams • Fat: 5 grams • Calories: 57

ZUCCHINI NUT BREAD

Makes 12 servings

When I was away at college, my mother used to bake her special Zucchini Nut Bread and send it to me in a care package. This is my low-carb tribute to my mother's kindness to me.

1 cup almonds, ground
½ cup soy protein
1 teaspoon cinnamon
½ teaspoon baking soda
¼ teaspoon baking powder
½ teaspoon sea salt
½ teaspoon nutmeg
1 tablespoon SteviaPlus
2 teaspoons Sweet & Slender
½ cup pecans, broken
1 cup zucchini, unpeeled, shredded
1 egg
¼ cup butter, melted
¼ teaspoon lemon or orange zest
Cooking oil spray or butter

1. Mix the dry ingredients together in a large mixing bowl. In another bowl, combine the wet ingredients. Pour the wet ingredients into the dry and stir until just combined. Pour into a sprayed or buttered 8" × 4" × 2" loaf pan.
2. Bake it at 350°F for about 40 to 50 minutes, or until a toothpick tests clean. Cool it lying on its side on a wire rack until it can be touched with bare hands, then invert it quickly onto a cooling rack. Using another rack, turn the bread so it is right side up. Slice and serve with butter or Cream Cheese Frosting (page 282).

NUTRITIONAL INFORMATION PER SERVING:
Carbohydrates: 4 grams • Effective Carb Count: 2 grams
Protein: 8 grams • Fat: 13 grams • Calories: 157

REDUCED-FAT VARIATION:
Use unsweetened applesauce instead of melted butter.
Carbohydrates: 4 grams • Effective Carb Count: 2 grams
Protein: 8 grams • Fat: 9 grams • Calories: 125

Appendix A
Sample Menus

This is just a sampling of the different meals you can create using the recipes in this book. Everything from plain and simple everyday fare all the way to holidays and special occasions! There are even things here for the kiddos!

Breakfasts

Zucchini Nut Muffins (page 91)
Skillet Squash Breakfast (page 86)

Farmer's Breakfast (page 68)
Low-carb tortillas (commercially
    prepared)

Broccoli, Steak, and Eggs (page 58)
Kefir Smoothie (page 23)

Chubby Pancakes (page 59) or
    Wonderful Waffles (page 90)
Sugar-Free Pancake Syrup (page 256)
Sharron's Pork Sausage (page 85)

Pumpkin Granola (page 76)
Almond Milk (page 240)

Spinach Quiche (page 89)
Breaded Zucchini (page 218)

Parsley Eggs with Walla Walla Sweet
    Sauce (page 72)
1946 Pork Sausage (page 54)

Breakfasts (continued)

Pumpkin Waffles (page 80)
Cinnamon Butter (page 242)
Vanilla Sauce (page 261)
Best Bacon (page 56)

Savory Omelettes with or Without
    Cheese (page 84)
Pumpkin Spice Muffins (page 78)

Quick and Easy Hot Cocoa (page 29)
Flax Cereal (page 69)
Half-and-half

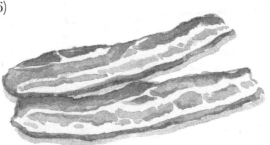

Lunches

Pork cutlet prepared using Kentucky-Style Seasoning (page 204)
"Honey" Mustard Dipping Sauce (page 251)
Fresh vegetables (cauliflower, broccoli, cucumber)

Rainbow Egg Salad (page 136)
Celery sticks
Zucchini slices
Pork rinds (commercially prepared)

Easy Cheesy Breakfast Pizza (page 66)
Tossed salad served with Creamy Ranch Salad Dressing (page 244) and Roasted Pumpkin Seeds (page 32)

Clam Cakes (page 8)
Tossed salad served with Creamy Roasted Garlic Salad Dressing (page 245)

Cream of Broccoli Soup (page 222)
Crackers (page 10)

Creamy Coconut Chicken Salad (page 198)
Peanut Butter Fingers (page 297)

Homemade Lunch Meat (page 116)
Celery sticks or cabbage chunks
Rutabaga Chips (page 33)

Peanut Butter Chicken Salad (page 208)
Luscious Berry Frozen Yogurt (page 289)

Dinners

Beef Gravy Supreme (page 96)
Rice-Aflower (page 227)
Macadamia Nut Butter Cookies (page 291)

Chunky Beef Soup (page 104)
Luscious Lemon Bars (page 290)
Josephine's Spicy Spaghetti Sauce (page 117)
Baked Winter Squash, spaghetti (page 216)
Mmm Cookies (page 295)

Wonderful Chicken Club Pizza (page 214)
Yummy Coleslaw (page 51)
Coconut Macaroons (page 279)

Seven Hills' Chili (page 142)
Meringue Kisses (page 294)

Beef Stew with Pumpkin (page 99)
Zucchini "Bread" Patties (page 38)

Salmon Chowder (page 174)
Clam Cakes (page 8)
Grandma Ruby's Buttermilk Sugar Cookies, a la Low-Carb (page 286)

Tuna Casserole (page 190)
Spinach with Onions and Garlic (page 234)
Carrot Cake (page 270)
Cream Cheese Frosting (page 282)

Special Occasions

Egg Rolls (page 15)
Barbecue Pork (page 95)
Roasted Garlic (page 230)
Sweet and Sour Sauce, Low-Carbed
(page 257)
Fiery Hot Mustard (page 246)
Sesame seeds
Lemon Chess Custard (page 288)

Lemony Beef and Asparagus Stir-Fry
(page 119)
Rice-Aflower (page 227)
Ultimate Pumpkin Pie (page 308)
Sole Amandine (page 186)
Spinach Salad with Lemon Dressing
(page 49)
Meringue Kisses (page 294) or Melt
in Your Mouth Mousse (page 293)

Elegant Chicken (page 202)
French-Style Green Beans (page 223)
Creamy Delicious Cheesecake (page 283)

Bonfire Barbecue Steak (page 100)
Roasted Veggies over a Bonfire
(page 231)
Mmm Cookies (page 295)

Steam Boat (page 144)
Aimee's Original French Silk Pie,
Low-Carbed (page 266)

Extra Special Egg Nog (page 17)
Roast Leg of Lamb (page 138)
Baked Winter Squash (page 216)
Coconut Silk Pie (page 281)

Salmon Patties (page 177)
Tartar Sauce I (page 259)
Slurp 'Em Up Cabbage Noodles
(page 233)
Cast of Thousands on Many Contin-
ents Chocolate Cake (page 271)
Chocolate Cream Cheese Frosting
(page 275)

Special Occasions (continued)

Crackers (page 10)
Smoked Salmon Dip (page 35)
Surf 'N' Turf (page 188)
Marinated Asparagus Salad with
Almonds (page 44)
Cheesecake with Berry Sauce
(page 272)

Kids' Stuff

Teeny Food (page 151)
Meringue Kisses (page 294)

Easy Cheesy Breakfast Pizza
(page 66)
Breaded Zucchini (page 218)
Almond Nest Cookies (page 268)

Cheese Crackers (page 4)
Beef Salami (page 2)
Kids' Guacamole (page 25)
Olives

Quick and Easy Hot Cocoa (page 29)
Rutabaga Chips (page 33)
Mini Corn Dogs, Low-Carbed
(page 126)
Pumpkin Ketchup (page 253)
Celery sticks

Lemonade (page 26)
Mock Potato Salad (page 46)
Shake It and Bake It! (page 210)
Ooey Gooey Kids' Stuff (page 296)

Mini Cheese Balls (page 27)
A variety of sliced fresh veggies
Yummy Chocolate Balls (page 309)

Croquettes (page 200)
Rice-Aflower Au Gratin (page 228)
Quick and Easy Red Pie (page 303)

Appendix B
Suggested Shopping List

Sweeteners

- SteviaPlus (the 4-ounce shaker bottle preferred, but the packets may be substituted)
- Sweet & Slender (the 4-ounce shaker bottle preferred, but the packets may be substituted)
- Sucralose packets

Meats

- Beef
- Chicken
- Eggs
- Fish
- Pork
- Shrimp
- Etc.

Note: Try to use the best quality fresh meat available.

Oils and Fats

- Bacon
- Butter
- Canola oil
- Canola oil cooking spray
- Lard
- Olive oil
- Sunflower oil

Dairy Products

- Cheeses–Parmesan, Colby, Monterey jack, etc.
- Cream, half-and-half
- Cream, heavy whipping
- Yogurt or kefir

Ethnic Cookery Items

- Bragg's Liquid Aminos or soy sauce
- Canned tomatoes (without sugar)
- Chili powder, chilies, or jalapeño peppers
- Chipotle pepper granules
- Cumin (ground)
- Fish sauce (found in the ethnic cookery section of most grocers)
- Hot chili oil
- Italian seasonings herb blend
- Low-carb tortillas (optional, and not if you have candida!)
- Sesame oil
- Sesame seeds
- Tomato sauce (without sugar)

Fruits and Vegetables

- Bottled lemon juice
- Broccoli
- Cabbage
- Cauliflower
- Celery
- Cucumber
- Green beans (canned, frozen, or fresh)
- Lemons
- Limes
- Olives (canned, black)
- Radishes
- Rhubarb
- Rutabagas
- Spinach (prewashed and bagged is nice!)
- Zucchini
- Berries—blueberries, strawberries, blackberries, cranberries, etc.

Nuts

- Blanched almonds (optional)
- Ground macadamia nuts (optional)
- Macadamia nuts
- Pecans
- Pumpkin seeds (hulled)
- Raw almonds
- Sunflower seeds (hulled)

Herbs, Seasonings, and Miscellany

- Almond extract
- Arrowroot powder
- Cinnamon
- Dried chives (or fresh if available)
- Dried onions
- Dried parsley
- Garlic
- Garlic granules
- Garlic salt
- Ground ginger
- Guar gum (if available)
- Lemon pepper (without sugar)
- Lemon thyme (or regular thyme)
- Milk and egg protein (one product—in the beverages section at most grocers)
- Mint (if no dried mint is available, use mint tea bags)
- Mustard powder
- Onions
- Pork rinds
- Rosemary
- Seasoning salt (without sugar)
- Soy protein (in the beverages section at most grocers)
- Vanilla (use real vanilla extract, not imitation!)

Appendix C
Carb Counts of Common Foods

Item	Carbs	Fiber	ECC
Almond, whole raw, 1 nut	.23	.14	.09
Almonds, blanched, 1 cup	28.91	15.08	13.83
Almonds, ground, 1 cup	18.75	11.21	7.54
Almonds, whole raw, 1 cup	28.03	16.7	11.28
Apple, 1 medium	21.04	3.72	17.32
Arrowroot powder, 1 tablespoon	7.05	.27	6.78
Asparagus, spear (6")	.72	.33	.39
Avocado, whole	14.85	10.05	4.80
Baking chocolate, 1 ounce	8.02	4.36	3.66
Baking powder, 1 teaspoon	1.27	trace	1.27
Baking soda, 1 teaspoon	0	0	0
Basil, 1 teaspoon	.85	.56	.29
Beans, green, 1 cup	7.85	3.74	4.11
Beans, green, 1 pound	32.42	15.44	16.97
Blueberries, 1 cup	20.48	3.91	16.57
Broccoli, chopped, 1 cup	4.61	2.64	1.97
Cabbage, chopped, 1 cup	4.83	2.04	2.79
Cabbage, shredded, 1 cup	3.80	1.61	2.19
Cabbage, whole, medium	49.30	20.88	28.42
Carrot, medium (5.5")	7.3	2.16	5.14
Cauliflower, whole, medium	29.9	14.37	15.53
Celery, large stalk (12")	2.33	1.08	1.25
Celery seed, 1 teaspoon	.82	.23	.59
Cheese, Cheddar, grated, 1 cup	1.44	n/a	1.44
Cheese, cream, 1 ounce	.75	n/a	.75
Cheese, cream, 1 tablespoon	.38	n/a	.38
Cheese, Monterey jack, grated, 1 cup	.76	n/a	.76
Cheese, mozzarella, grated, 1 cup	3.54	n/a	3.54
Cheese, mozzarella, 1 ounce	.89	n/a	.89
Cheese, Parmesan, 1 tablespoon	.18	n/a	.18
Cheese, Swiss, grated, 1 cup	3.65	n/a	3.65
Chili powder, 1 teaspoon	1.42	.88	.54

Item	Carbs	Fiber	ECC
Chives, 1 teaspoon	.04	.02	.02
Cinnamon, 1 teaspoon	1.83	1.24	.59
Cloves, ground, 1 teaspoon	1.28	.71	.57
Cocoa powder, 1 tablespoon	2.93	1.79	1.14
Coconut, unsweetened, ½ cup	10	7	3
Cornstarch, 1 tablespoon	7.3	.07	7.23
Cream, half-and-half, 1 cup	10.4	n/a	10.4
Cream, whipping, 1 cup	6.64	n/a	6.64
Cream of tartar, 1 teaspoon	1.84	trace	1.84
Cumin, 1 teaspoon	.92	.22	.7
Dill weed, 1 teaspoon	.55	.13	.42
Egg, whole, large	.61	n/a	.61
Egg white, large	.34	n/a	.34
Fennel seeds, 1 teaspoon	1.04	.79	.25
Garlic, 1 clove	.99	.06	.93
Garlic powder, 1 teaspoon	2.03	.27	1.76
Ginger, ground, 1 teaspoon	1.27	.22	1.05
Guar gum, 1 teaspoon (from package)	2.5	2.5	0
Lemon juice, bottled, 1 cup	15.81	.97	14.84
Lemon juice, bottled, 1 tablespoon	.98	.06	.92
Lemon juice, fresh, 1 cup	21.05	.97	20.08
Lemon juice, fresh, 2 tablespoons	2.63	.12	2.51
Lemon zest, 1 teaspoon	.32	.21	.11
Lemon thyme, 1 teaspoon	.19	.11	.08
Lime juice, 2 tablespoons	2.77	.12	2.65
Macadamia nuts, 1 cup	18.51	11.52	6.99
Macadamia nuts, 1 ounce	3.79	2.26	1.53
Marjoram, 1 teaspoon	.36	.24	.12
Milk and egg protein, 28 grams (figures taken from package)	1	0	1
Mint leaves, 2 tablespoons	.47	.25	.22
Mushroom, medium	.73	.21	.52
Mustard seed, 1 teaspoon	1.15	.48	.67
Nutmeg, 1 teaspoon	1.08	.45	.63
Oats, dry, 1 cup	54.27	8.58	45.69
Okra, 1 cup	7.63	3.2	4.43
Olive, 1 large	.27	.14	.13
Onion, fresh, chopped, 1 cup	13.8	2.88	10.92
Onion, fresh, medium	9.49	1.98	7.51
Onion, green, medium (4.5")	1.10	.39	.71
Onion flakes, dried, 1 tablespoon	4.16	.46	3.7
Orange zest, 1 teaspoon	.50	.21	.29
Oregano, ground, 1 teaspoon	.96	.64	.32

Item	Carbs	Fiber	ECC
Paprika, 1 teaspoon	1.17	.43	.74
Parsley, dried, 1 tablespoon	.67	.39	.28
Peaches, 1 cup	18.87	3.4	15.47
Peanut butter, 2 tablespoons	6.17	1.88	4.29
Pear, 1 medium	25.08	3.98	21.1
Peas, frozen, 1 cup	9.86	3.38	6.48
Pecan halves, 1 cup	14.96	10.36	4.6
Pepper, bell, medium	7.65	2.14	5.51
Pepper, black, 1 teaspoon	1.36	.55	.81
Pepper, cayenne, 1 teaspoon	1.01	.49	.52
Pepper, chili, dried	.37	.1	.22
Pepper, jalapeño	.82	.39	.43
Pumpkin, canned, 1 cup	19.79	7.1	12.69
Pumpkin seeds, 1 cup	24.57	5.38	19.19
Radish, 1 medium	.16	.07	.09
Rhubarb, frozen, 1 cup	6.98	2.46	4.52
Rosemary, 1 teaspoon	.14	.09	.05
Rutabaga, small	15.61	4.8	10.81
Sage, 1 teaspoon	.42	.28	.14
Sesame seeds, 1 tablespoon	2.11	1.06	1.05
Sour cream, 1 cup	9.82	n/a	9.82
Soy flour, 1 tablespoon	1.83	.49	1.34
Soy protein, 1 ounce (¼ cup)	2.08	1.58	.5
Spinach, 1 cup	1.05	.81	.24
Squash, spaghetti, 1 cup	10.01	2.17	7.84
Squash, winter, 1 cup	17.93	5.74	12.19
Strawberries, sliced, 1 cup	11.65	3.81	7.84
Sunflower seeds, 1 tablespoon	1.72	.96	.75
Thyme, fresh, 1 teaspoon	.19	.11	.08
Tomato, medium	5.7	1.35	4.35
Tomatoes, canned, 1 cup	10.48	2.4	8.08
Tomato sauce, 1 cup	17.59	3.43	14.16
Turnip, small	3.8	1.09	2.71
Vanilla, 1 teaspoon	.53	n/a	.53
Walnuts, chopped, 1 cup	15.12	6.25	8.87
Water chestnuts, sliced, ½ cup	8.7	1.75	6.95
Zucchini, chopped, 1 cup	3.59	1.48	2.11
Zucchini, medium	5.68	2.35	3.33

Please note: All information presented was taken from the USDA Agricultural Research Service Nutrient Data Laboratory.

Appendix D
Conversion Charts for Sugar Substitutes

Sucralose

I use the Splenda No Calorie Sweetener brand of sucralose product. Each packet weighs 1 gram. *Note:* The pourable Splenda is made to be used in the same way as regular sugar. It contains much more filler, thus, more carbs, so I don't prefer it.

Stevia

I use the brand SteviaPlus by Wisdom Herbs (*www.wisdomherbs.com*). It is a stevia extract that is a fine white powder combined with a healthy dietary fiber called FOS. It is my understanding that FOS helps stabilize blood sugar levels. The FOS also makes this product milder and easier to cook with than other stevia products. *Note:* Other brands of stevia may not have the same conversion values.

Sweet & Slender

Sweet & Slender is a great new product on the market. It is made by the same manufacturer as SteviaPlus, Wisdom Herbs. It is made from an intensely sweet fruit called Luo Han Guo. While it is a terrific sweetener on its own or in combination with SteviaPlus, I prefer its use as a flavor enhancer. It just seems to bring out the best in foods!

Sucralose conversion chart:
1 packet = 2 teaspoons sugar
3 packets = 2 tablespoons sugar
6 packets = ¼ cup sugar
8 packets = ⅓ cup sugar
12 packets = ½ cup sugar
24 packets = 1 cup sugar

eviaPlus conversion chart for use with sucralose:
⅛ teaspoon SteviaPlus = 1 tablespoon plus ½ teaspoon sugar
¼ teaspoon SteviaPlus = 2½ tablespoons sugar
½ teaspoon SteviaPlus = ⅓ cup sugar
¾ teaspoon SteviaPlus = ½ cup sugar
1 teaspoon SteviaPlus = ⅔ cup sugar
½ tablespoon SteviaPlus = 1 cup sugar
1 tablespoon SteviaPlus = 2 cups sugar

Sweet & Slender conversion chart:
⅛ teaspoon Sweet & Slender = 1½ teaspoons sugar
¼ teaspoon Sweet & Slender = 1 tablespoon sugar
½ teaspoon Sweet & Slender = 2 tablespoons sugar
1 teaspoon Sweet & Slender = ¼ cup sugar
½ tablespoon Sweet & Slender = ⅓ cup sugar
2 teaspoons Sweet & Slender = ½ cup sugar
1 tablespoon Sweet & Slender = ⅔ cup sugar
1½ tablespoons Sweet & Slender = 1 cup sugar

SteviaPlus conversion chart:
¼ teaspoon SteviaPlus = 2 teaspoons sugar
½ teaspoon SteviaPlus = 1 tablespoon + 1 teaspoon sugar
1 teaspoon SteviaPlus = 2⅔ tablespoons sugar
1½ teaspoons SteviaPlus = ¼ cup sugar
1 tablespoon SteviaPlus = ½ cup sugar
1½ tablespoons SteviaPlus = ¾ cup sugar
2 tablespoons SteviaPlus = 1 cup sugar

Bibliography

Atkins, Robert C., MD. *Dr. Atkins's New Diet Revolution*. New York: Avon Books, 1992, 1999.

Better Homes and Gardens New Cook Book. Des Moines, IA: Meredith Corporation, 1981, 1987.

Chili Peppers, 13 March 2003, Mexican Food to Go. *www.texmextogo.com/chilipeppers facts.htm.*

Crook, William G. *Chronic Fatigue and the Yeast Connection*. Jackson, TN: Professional Books, 1992.

Enig, Mary, PhD, and Sally Fallon. *The Skinny on Fats,* 26 February 2003, The Weston A. Price Foundation. *www.westonaprice.org/know_your_fats/skinny.html.*

Ortman, Mark. *A Simple Guide to Self-Publishing*. Kirkland, WA: Wise Owl Books, 1994.

Rombauer, Irma S., and Marion Rombauer-Becker. *Joy of Cooking*. Indianapolis, IN: Bobbs-Merrill Company, 1931, 1975.

Wolfe, J. Kevin. *You Can Write a Cookbook*. Cincinnati, OH: Writer's Digest Books, 2000.

The Yogurt Exception, 26 February 2003, Low-Carb Luxury. *www.lowcarbluxury.com/yogurt.html.*

Index